DATE DUE

11/20/06	
12/06/06	
12/14/06	

DEMCO, INC. 38-2931

DATE DUE

The Reciprocating Self

HUMAN DEVELOPMENT IN THEOLOGICAL PERSPECTIVE

Jack O. Balswick, Pamela Ebstyne King

and Kevin S. Reimer

InterVarsity Press

Downers Grove, Illinois

InterVarsity Press
P.O. Box 1400, Downers Grove, IL 60515-1426
World Wide Web: www.ivpress.com
E-mail: mail@ivpress.com

InterVarsity Press® is the book-publishing division of InterVarsity Christian Fellowship/USA®, a student movement active on campus at hundreds of universities, colleges and schools of nursing in the United States of America, and a member movement of the International Fellowship of Evangelical Students. For information about local and regional activities, write Public Relations Dept., InterVarsity Christian Fellowship/USA, 6400 Schroeder Rd., P.O. Box 7895, Madison, WI 53707-7895, or visit the IVCF website at <www.intervarsity.org>.

Scripture quotations, unless otherwise noted, are from the New Revised Standard Version of the Bible, *copyright 1989 by the Division of Christian Education of the National Council of the Churches of Christ in the USA. Used by permission. All rights reserved.*

A Sunday Afternoon on the Island of la Grand Jatte *by George Seurat used by permission of the Art Institute of Chicago, IL/Bridgeman Art Library.*

The Kiss *by Gustav Klimt used by permission of Erich Lessing/Art Resource, NY.*

Farnsworth House *by Ludwig Mies Van Der Rohe used by permission of the Landmarks Preservation Council of Illinois.*

Baby's First Caress *by Mary Cassatt used by permission of New Britain Museum of American Art.*

Design: Cindy Kiple
Images: old man: Photodisc Collection/Getty Images
   man: Ryan McVay/Getty Images
   child: Mike Powell/Getty Images
   baby: Rubberball Productions/Getty Images

ISBN 0-8308-2793-5

Printed in the United States of America ∞

Library of Congress Cataloging-in-Publication Data

Balswick, Jack O.
 The reciprocating self; human development in theological
 perspective / Jack O. Balswick, Pamela Ebstyne King, Kevin S.
 Reimer.
 p. cm.
 Includes bibliographical references and index.
 ISBN 0-8308-2793-5 (pbk.: alk paper)
 1. Life cycle, Human—Religious aspects—Christianity. 2.
 Developmental psychology—Religious aspects—Christianity. 3.
 Maturation (Psychology)—Religious aspects—Christianity. 4.
 Christianity—Psychology. I. King, Pamela Ebstyne, 1968- II.
Reimer,
 Kevin S., 1968- III. Title.
 BV4597.555B25 2005
 261.5'15—dc22

                 2004029846

P	18	17	16	15	14	13	12	11	10	9	8	7	6	5	4	3	2	1
Y	18	17	16	15	14	13	12	11	10	09	08	07	06	05				

To my students past, present and future. J.O.B.

To Bradford and Aidan. P.E.K.

To Naomi and Danielle. K.S.R.

Contents

Preface

THE PURPOSE OF *The Reciprocating Self: Human Development in Theological Perspective* is to present an integrated view of human development that is based on social science research and biblical truths. We do this by drawing on a biblical model of relationality, where the created goal or purpose of human development is to become a *reciprocating self*—fully and securely related to others and to God. The ideas for this book came to us as we struggled together to teach human development in a holistic manner.

A parallel purpose to providing an understanding of human development within a theological perspective is to provide a context for the reader to understand his or her own developmental issues. As we trace the reciprocating self through developmental life span stages we will be able to address stage-specific *developmental issues*. A developmental issue is a concern, tension, worry or crisis encountered by the self in the context of change. The source of change can be personal and internal—bodily, mentally, emotionally, socially—or external—relational, familial, communal, societal. Since internal and external change is continual and interactive, life is a process of facing one developmental issue after another.

Awareness of development issues are most salient at developmental transitional points—learning to talk and walk, beginning to eat unassisted, going to school, developing secondary sexual physical features, leaving home, obtaining full-time employment, becoming engaged and then married, having a child for the first time, parenting an adolescent, watching your children move away from home, retiring, experiencing a decline in physical and mental health, and finally, facing imminent death. God has created human beings for relationship, and it is our contention that to be a self in reciprocating relationships is of major importance in negotiating the developmental issues.

Since this book is an attempt by three different persons to address a common topic, it is fitting that we introduce ourselves by sharing our own developmental issues. We do this by introducing ourselves in the same way we ask students in our developmental classes to introduce themselves on the first day of class:

Jack

Hi, I'm Jack and I have developmental issues. As I put the finishing touches on this book I have just celebrated my sixty-fifth birthday. At an age when many choose to retire, I find myself still enjoying the life of teaching at a seminary. Herein lies the crux of my developmental issue: am I still capable of teaching at the high level expected at this school, or have I started on an accelerating state of decline? I began teaching some forty years ago when students were satisfied with a dynamic lecture that was coherent enough for them to take understandable notes. Along the way, I supplemented my lectures with overheads outlining what I was saying. Several years ago, as part of the computer revolution, the younger professors began developing multimedia PowerPoint presentations. I am now struggling to transfer my lectures into PowerPoint presentations with all the bells and whistles. It does not help that I team-teach several classes with Pam, who keeps students in rapt attention with her own PowerPoint presentations. Am I too old to continue teaching? Should I "move over" and let a younger person take my place? This questioning of my continued academic abilities is a core developmental issue.

My developmental issues are not only academic in nature. Three times a week I play volleyball with a group of men at the local YMCA. I use to consider myself a pretty good spiker, and I continue to play this position. As my knees have weakened, I have undergone several arthroscopic surgeries, and I now wear knee braces for support when I play. I have started to seriously wonder if it is not time that I become a setter instead. Needless to say, spiking is a more macho contribution that setting, and I pride myself that at my age I can still do it. But as my spiking becomes weaker and weaker, I hear the taunts of the other players—"Was that a spike or a dink?"—and I encounter another developmental issue.

I'm a grandfather and have been so for the last eighteen years. During that time I have actively engaged in a variety of activities such as acrobatic wrestling, surfing, snowboarding, mountain biking and backpacking with my two oldest grandsons, Curtis and Jacob (ages eighteen and seventeen). My two youngest grandsons, Liam and Taylor, are pushing four and five, and I have started engaging in acrobatic wrestling with them. As I struggle to lift them in the air for a flip, I find that my strength and skills are greatly diminished from what they were when I was a fifty-year-old grandfather. My desire to be an active grandfather to Liam and Taylor brings with it a development issue. (Similar developmental issues can be found in the chapters eleven and twelve on middle and elderly adulthood.) However, I'm not the only one with developmental issues, as you will quickly learn from Pam and Kevin's comments.

Pam

Hi, I'm Pam, and boy, do I have developmental issues. At the completion of this manuscript I am thirty-five years old and have just given birth to my first child, a son named Aidan, ten weeks ago. This is a huge transition for me. As my friends, family and colleagues will attest, I have been very motivated and intentional about my work. I have always understood my work as a calling from God and I take very seriously being a steward of my training, gifts and resources to build God's kingdom. For me, work is not only a job but a vocation in which I find great meaning and satisfaction. Upon the birth of my son, my world has been turned upside down as I am completely taken and captivated by this little gift of life. I am now feeling the pull (tension?) between continuing my ministry as a professor in a seminary and a Presbyterian minister and being a mother. Embedded in this struggle are several developmental issues. I am learning what it means to be a parent and how this affects my identity and sense of meaning. My husband and I are learning to adjust our marriage to accommodate a third member of our family. On a professional level, my identity as a minister, seminary professor and researcher is still in flux.

I have decided to initially return to work part time. Although this seems like the right decision for now, I cannot help but question, is this enough time at home with Aidan? Can I be a "good enough mother" and still work? Will this hamper my career development as an aspiring researcher and professor? How will I adjust to people perceiving me as "mom" as opposed to "Rev. Dr. King"? How will my emotional investment in my son affect the energy I put into mentoring my students? Will I continue to be able to serve simultaneously as minister and professor while working part time? How will these multiple demands affect my relationship with my husband, Brad? How will his work as a filmmaker and entrepreneur be affected by our son? With only ten weeks under my belt as a mother and not yet having returned to work from maternity leave, I do not have answers to these questions.

In addition to these issues, my professional identity is in formation. Although I am thirty-five, I feel I am still trying to reconcile my vocational identity—as minister, teacher and researcher. Although my work has always focused on youth, I originally worked with youth through church-based ministry whereas now I study youth through research. At this point in my life, I am trying to integrate the many "hats" that I wear both professionally and personally. I continue to look for opportunities where I can teach, pastor, reflect theologically, generate empirical psychological understanding and bring about social change. Projects like this book delight me because they allow me to draw on biblical truth and theological understanding as well as psychological theory and research. Consequently, much of my research and writing at this time focus on issues of spiritual and religious development in young people.

How my professional goals will fit with my life as a parent, I am not sure. I have reconciled myself to the fact that life comes in seasons and that not everything has to happen in each season. At the printing of this book, I am not sure what this season will look like, other than that it will be filled with the smiles, gurgles and shrieks of my son as well as some progress with various research projects and manuscripts. But I will continue to recite Proverbs 3:5-6 as a personal mantra:

> Trust in the LORD with all your heart
>   and lean on your own understanding;
> in all your ways acknowledge him,
>   and he will make your path straight.

Kevin

Hi, I'm Kevin, and I have developmental issues. I'm thirty-six years old, married, and the father of two girls ages twelve and nine. I have taught in graduate schools since I was thirty. Unlike Jack, I'm in the process of becoming established in a particular career. To an extent, this is spillover from the identity resolution phase of my twenties. During that time of my life I was involved in pastoral work with families and children in several large congregations. While I enjoyed these experiences, it was clear that they would not permit me the opportunity to regularly teach and conduct research. This realization led me back to graduate school to pursue a doctorate in psychology. I now have somewhat schizophrenic "multiple identities" as an ordained Presbyterian minister and as a university professor in a doctoral psychology program. I also have a grant-funded research program in cognitive developmental psychology and psychology of religion. While the prolonged identity resolution phase is increasingly common in our culture, it is not easy. Recently I spoke with Dr. Parker Palmer, noted author and educator. I felt better about my own identity process when Parker told me that he was planning a year-long sabbatical, auspiciously to "figure out what I want to be when I grow up."

I envy Parker for the quantity of time he has available to consider issues of identity. At sixty-six, Parker has much time to think. By contrast, my wife and I typically feel as though we are moving at a half-sprint, working and busily parenting our two daughters. The so-called productive years of early middle age place significant challenges before individuals and couples, particularly given the complexities of child-rearing in an accelerated culture. During this period of our lives, I am particularly thankful for my wonderful partnership with Lynn, and the mutuality that enables us to successfully navigate the restoration of a home of character, birthday parties and adolescent hormones.

My entire work history has revolved around children. But it is through my own children, Naomi and Danielle, that I have significantly wrestled with developmental issues. At each stage of their development I have been challenged to consider the utility of my own psychological training and the limitations of my faith in God. Parents quickly discover that they need God, as our children tend to mirror back to us the less attractive features of our brokenness. Children are both a great blessing and a struggle, making this period of my life richer for its impact on my understanding of relationships, human experience and the grace of a merciful God. For me, developmental encounter with my own children is a present reminder of our fundamental identity as God's beloved sons and daughters.

Acknowledgments

We could not have written this book without the help of numerous people. We would like to acknowledge the many students at Fuller Theological Seminary, Mennonite Brethren Biblical Seminary and Azusa Pacific University who endured our attempts through lecture and written drafts to communicate the material that has become the content of this book. A number of students, by drawing on their own personal developmental issues and theological and psychological insights, have given valuable suggestions. We also thank Kathy Daw, who has spent many hours typing and checking references and other details for us.

Personal acknowledgment must go to the persons who have contributed most to our own development and developmental stability and well-being. For Jack, this includes Mom and Dad Balswick, who went to be with the Lord several years ago; my wife, Judy, whose retirement this year I'm hoping will pay dividends in the form of more home-cooked meals; my two married children: Jacque, her husband Dana, and my four grandsons Curt, Jacob, Taylor and Liam, and my son Joel and his wife Uyen.

For Pam, this includes those who have taught me about reciprocity—my parents, Doug and Bonnie Ebstyne, who carefully and adoringly provided me with scaffolding and love; my brothers Bryan and Michael who have wrestled with me and cheered me on; my in-laws, Robert and Dorothy King, who have always treated me with mutuality and respect; my sibs-in-law Jennifer, Timothy, Cynthia and Alan, who have supported me and buoyed me up; my colleagues and mentors who have challenged me to think ecologically and teleologically about the nature of thriving individuals: Peter Benson, William Damon, James Furrow, Richard Lerner and Linda Wagener; the one who has taught me more about reciprocity than anyone, my partner in life, Bradford, who has afforded me the time to work on this project; and our new son, Aidan, who has brought new meaning to relationships and love.

For Kevin this includes my two daughters Naomi and Danielle, who were a remarkable inspiration to study developmental psychology in the first place. It is in their growth and beauty that I am continually reminded of God's divine initiative in human development. I'm deeply indebted to my wife, Lynn, who quietly made space for me to pursue and complete the many hours of travel, writing and research that went into the project. Finally, during work on the book, I have profited enormously from conversations in matters theological and anthropological with F. LeRon Shults, a friend who is just plain fun.

Finally, we would like to acknowledge and thank Gary Deddo, who has been more than an editor as he has guided us through the process of writing this book. He is a theologian in his own right, whose own writing and thoughts on a biblical view of relationality have greatly assisted us in completing this project. We also thank an anonymous reviewer and our teacher, colleague, and friend Ray Anderson, whose imprint on this book can be seen from beginning to end.

PART ONE

Toward an Integrated Model
of Human Development

The Developmental Dilemma

OUR PURPOSE IN WRITING THIS BOOK is to address what we call the *developmental dilemma*—the fact that existing developmental theory lacks a guiding teleology. Developmental teleology refers to developmental completeness or a theologically informed understanding of the *goal* of development. Our goal in this book is to define and develop a working teleology and discuss it in regards to developmental stages. The developmental dilemma is important to acknowledge because it rears its nasty head in the face of the student of psychology who is looking for a coherent Christian perspective of development or who hopes for an integration between theology and psychology.

Development theories, whether they bend toward a biological, sociocultural or psychodynamics emphasis, all share a common commitment to a naturalistic worldview. The methodology of developmental psychology is to compare and contrast within cultural differences and crosscultural ethnographic evidence in order to determine what is normative or possible in terms of human development.

At one level it might be argued that all developmental theories inherently possess either an explicit or implicit teleology. Thus for example *adaptation* might be proposed as the key teleological concept for Piaget's cognitive development theory, *pleasure seeking* and *ego integrity* in Freud and Erikson's developmental theories respectively, and *complexity* in neurological models of human development. Note however that in each case the teleology is limited by the possibilities provided by naturalistic assumptions. The question raised in the song made popular by the singer Peggy Lee was *Is That All There Is?* Are we to be content with a teleology of human development that is limited to the bounds of a naturalistic worldview? In understanding the purpose or goal of human development, is that all there is?

Before answering this question we suggest that three additional factors have also contributed to the current developmental dilemma. The *first* is the limited nature and fragmented scope of existing developmental theories. The enormous scope of material on human development can serve as a barrier to the emergence of a metatheory explaining development in its entirety. Consequently, existing theories describe aspects and portions of the developmental process—whether cognition in infants, identity development in adolescents or generativity in adulthood. As a result developmental theory lacks an organizing principle through which to understand and evaluate these theories. Psychological and sociological contributions may offer insights into developmental processes, but they do not provide a framework for understanding the goals or ends of development.

A second barrier to the emergence of a more comprehensive theory of development is the presence of cultural and psychological therapies promoting the existence of an *empty self*. In *Constructing the Self, Constructing America,* Philip Cushman (1995) identifies the empty self as a result of the lack of a developmental teleology that would offer a solution other than self-focused therapies. He articulates how the development of modern psychotherapy is intertwined with the evolution of American consumerism and how both affect the way we perceive and experience the self. He describes how current theories and therapeutic practices promote a sense of self with an insatiable need to consume in the interminable human quest for self-fulfillment and for self-realization. The American values of independence and self-fulfillment have led the American psychotherapeutic culture to nurture individuals who are focused on self-care and personal fulfillment. He critiques the American therapeutic community for promoting individuals who are preoccupied and in perpetual need of filling and fulfilling themselves. Despite Cushman's harangue, he gives no alternative, no teleology to cure this empty self.

In addition to the veritable smorgasbord of developmental theories and the perpetuating empty self, modern philosophies' view of the human condition is the *third* factor contributing to the developmental dilemma. This empty self is a product of the modern project—the pursuit of truth, univer-

sals, freedom and control. The modern project has become the modern predicament, resulting in an era of fragmented, lonely, isolated people. One of
the main moves of modernity has been to displace God from the transcendent to the immanent sphere, shifting the locus of the divine from a God
who is Other to impersonal forces within the human mind and will—into
human subjectivity. Playing a major role in this shift, Kant posits that the will
is absolutely self-determining and finite. By doing so he displaces the infinite divine will from the universe and makes the will a matter of a subjective,
self-reflective process. The Creator is replaced by the created. Theologian-
philosopher Colin Gunton describes the loss of sense of self as the result of
self-reflection. He writes, "When individual self-contemplation becomes the
basis of self, rather than the relation to the divine and human others on
which our reality actually depends, the self *begins to disappear*" (Gunton,
1993, p. 118, italics added).

Perpetuating the image of humans as empty selves in need of filling is
neither helpful nor healthful. And we contend it is not theologically accurate
either.

It would be easy to address the teleological question strictly in theological
terms. Thus the Westminster Shorter Catechism states that the goal of humanity is to know God and enjoy him forever. A more relevant answer for
understanding the purpose or goal of development might be found in Gunton's quote above: the goal is found in a person's "relation to the divine and
human other." Christian theology and social science theory converge to suggest that the self does not need to be viewed from the perspective of being
empty but rather as a reciprocating self. In this book we turn to theological
anthropology as a source for understanding both the process and goals of
human development. We propose that a theological understanding of development will provide a lens through which to view and understand existing
theories. This book seeks to provide a Christian response to the empty self
by drawing on theological anthropology and psychological theory in order
to provide an alternative view of selfhood—the *reciprocating self.*

The Turn to Relationality

In his recent book *Reforming Theological Anthropology: After the Philosophical Turn to Relationality*, F. LeRon Shults documents a paradigm shift in
how social scientists, philosophers and theologians alike think about human
nature. From Aristotle to Kant the *substance* of particular things—like an in-

dividual person—was of primary importance. Since Kant *relationality* has become the key focus. Shults states:

> The philosophical turn to relationality has shaped not only the way we think about knowing and being, but also our understandings of human acting. In the early modern period human (free) agency had been dualistically separated from (mechanistically determined) nature, and this split registered its effect on anthropological theories. In contemporary psychology . . . humans and communities are more often described in ways that recognize that their *relations* are constitutive. A person is no longer defined as an "individual substance of a rational nature" (Boethius) or as a "punctual self" (Locke). Instead of autonomous subjects that stand over against the natural world and other subjects, today human self-consciousness is understood as always and already embedded in relations between self, other, and world. (2003, p. 31)

Another recent example of the move to relationality within theological anthropology can be seen in Stanley Grenz's book *The Social God and the Relational Self: A Trinitarian Theology of the Imago Dei* (2001). Like Shults, Grenz develops his theological anthropology by focusing on relationality as the key aspect of being human. As the subtitle to his book suggests, Grenz anchors his understanding of the human self in trinitarian theology. Grenz states, "Theological insights regarding the manner in which the three Trinitarian persons are persons-in-relation and gain their personal identity by means of their interrelationality hold promise for understanding what it means to be human persons in the wake of the demise of the centered self and the advent of the Global Soul" (2001, p. 9).

As Grenz points out, the call to extend trinitarian theology to the understanding of the self is not new. It can be seem in Karl Barth's *Epistle to the Romans* (1918/1963) and in the writings of such eminent theologians as Emil Brunner, Dietrich Bonhoeffer, Martin Buber, John Macmurry and James Torrance. Torrance argues, "What we need today is a better understanding of the person not just as an individual but as someone who finds his or her true being-in-communion with God and with others, the counterpart of a Trinitarian doctrine of God" (1989, p. 15). The call to extend a trinitarian understanding of the self continues in the current writings of such theologians as Jürgen Moltmann (1996), Colin Gunton (1993), Miroslav Volf (1998), Ray Anderson (1982) and Gary Deddo (1999).

Following the turn to relationality that began in philosophical thought, there has been a near parallel focus on relationality in the thought of social scientists as well as theologians. Shults observes, "In psychology proper, the turn is most obvious in 'object relations' theory where the agential relation of a person to objects is essential to his or her development identity" (2003, p. 31). The view of the self that was seen in terms of its *substance* has been replaced in developmental theories by a new view of the self that is seen in terms of a person's embeddedness in *relationships*.

Like the theologians cited above we believe a correspondence exists between relationality in the holy Trinity and relationality in human beings. The specific purpose of this book is to draw on the biblical view of relationality within the holy Trinity as a basis for understanding the human self. This biblical model allows us to assess the human self as an interactive being. This we identify as the *reciprocating self*—the self that, in all its uniqueness and fullness of being, *engages fully in relationship with another* in all its particularity.

There has been at least one previous attempt to accomplish what we seek to do in this book. Until his recent death James Loder (1989, 1998) has sought to utilize a theological model in understanding the purpose of human development. Loder uses the concept of the *human spirit* in his discussion of human development. While he neither directly bases his analysis on trinitarian theology nor specifically defines what he means by *human spirit,* it is quite clear that he is using the term in a way similar to how we intend to use the term *reciprocating self.* Loder writes of the correspondence between the *human spirit* and the *divine spirit:* "Although distinctly different in origin, destiny, and magnitude, the human spirit and the Divine Spirit are made for each other, according to a relationality ultimately designed to replicate the relationality of the divine and the human in the person of Jesus" (p. 16). Note the common emphasis on the importance of relationality. Loder accepts what he calls a *differentiated relationality* of human spirit to Holy Spirit. He suggests that "the human spirit is to humanity what the Holy Spirit is to God (I Cor. 2:10), so these two are interrelated according to the bipolar relationality" (p. 35). A reciprocating self makes a differentiated relationality possible. A reciprocating self is the internal self-structure that makes differentiated relationality possible.

Loder's discussion poses an interesting challenge to Christian psychologists who take seriously the substantial body of literature that demonstrates a connection between neurological activity in the brain with the mind, self and behavior. "Human spirit" in Loder's understanding might be easily transposed into an interpretation of "soul," yet we are reluctant to define the reciprocating self as a soul. Certainly a reciprocating self engaged in a vital relationship with God retains "soulish" characteristics. However, the reciprocating self in our understanding exists as an emerging aspect of personal identity understood in the context of relationship, both with God and with others. This is a complex idea that requires additional consideration with regard to traditional notions of human nature.

Body, Soul and the Reciprocating Self

In Christian theology the concept of *soul* has been used to argue for the special uniqueness of human beings among all of God's creation. A body-soul dualism (or even a tripartite body-soul-spirit model) is a common way for Christians to understand human beings as unique and distinct created human spirits. In *radical dualism* the soul "is separable from the body, and the person is identified with the former" (Brown, Murphy and Malony, 1998, p. 24). In this view humans are seen as physical beings who also have a nonmaterial soul. Human beings experience God through the soul. Classic body-soul dualism had its origins in the philosopher Plato, but it can be traced through Augustine to Descartes. In a slightly modified view, *holistic dualism* holds that "the person is a composite of separable 'parts' but is to be identified with the whole, whose normal functioning is as a unity" (Brown, Murphy and Malony, 1998, p. 24). It is probably fair to say that most traditional Christian theologies have presented a version of one of these dualistic models.

Of these two dualistic positions we see holistic dualism as most viable. The major problem with these positions, however, is in explaining the nature of the interaction between the material body and the nonmaterial soul (Brown, Murphy and Malony, 1998). Dualism also creates the problem of multiple agencies, of decision making "by committee." An added problem is that with the advancement of knowledge on biological contributions to human behavior, there is a decreasing residue of leftover higher human functions that have not yet been explained by body elements. In dualistic models the soul comes to be less and less important in explaining human agency and behavior.

A third way to solve the body-soul issue can be seen in the *eliminative/reductive materialism* model. In this model "the person is a physical organism, whose emotional, moral, and religious experiences will ultimately be explained by the physical sciences" (Brown, Murphy and Malony, 1998, p. 25). Donald MacKay calls this position "nothingbuttery," for within naturalistic assumptions, which this model is based on, human beings are nothing but material beings. This is the most common model within the natural and social sciences today.

In their book *Whatever Happened to the Soul?* Brown, Murphy and Malony propose the rather radical-sounding suggestion that there is no such thing as *the* soul, but rather human beings are distinguished by their capacity to have *soulishness* (1998, pp. 24-25). In this model of *nonreductive physicalism* "the person is a physical organism whose complex functioning, both in society and in relation to God, gives rise to 'higher' human capacities such as morality and spirituality." In this model it is not necessary to postulate a second or third ontological entity (soul and mind) to account for brain capacities and distinctiveness. Soul and mind are understood as *physiologically embodied*. This model is nonreductive in the sense that human behavior cannot be exhaustively explained by analysis at the lowest level (bottom-up explanations). Rather, higher level (top-down) explanations supervene statements about the physiological. In this monist model nature, body, soul, mind, spirit or any other description all refer to the same entity.

An important element in the nonreductive physicalism model is the concept of *emergent function,* where new functions emerge out of the complexities of lower levels. A formal definition of an emergent function is *a mode of operation in a complex system that cannot be explained by scrutiny of lower levels, although it is dependent on the lower-level operation.* The interactive operation of lower systems result in the emergence of higher functioning. However, once a higher-level system emerges, it exerts top-down determinative influences on the operations of lower system levels.

In nonreductive physicalism there is no soul, but rather human beings have soulishness. Soulishness is in the depth and sophistication needed to relate to God, others and self. A person does not have a soul but rather is a soul. Soul, for human beings, is a physically embodied property of human nature and thus not an entity with distinctive existence, awareness and agency. Soul is defined as *the net sum of those encounters in which embodied humans relate to and commune with God (who is spirit) or with one another in a manner that reaches deeply into the essence of our creaturely, historical and communal selves.* The human soul is a physically embodied property of human nature, and thus not an entity with distinctive existence, awareness and agency.

In *Whatever Happened to the Soul?* the authors conceptualize soul as an emergent property of *personal relatedness.* Thus in his chapter " 'Bodies— That Is, Human Lives': A Re-Examination of Human Nature in the Bible," the New Testament scholar Joel Green points out that the concept of the soul in Scripture is primarily used to point to the capacity and experience of deep personal relatedness. Human uniqueness in God's creation is primarily due to the capacity for covenantal relationships. Green states that

> the Old Testament does not locate human uniqueness in a doctrine of a (poten-
> tially disembodied) soul, but emphasizes instead the character of humanity as
> God's covenant partner, his counterpart in relationship. The *imago Dei* tradition
> highlights the location of human beings within the larger human family, empha-
> sizing the human's covenantal relationships with other humans, and situates the
> human family in meaningful relationship with the whole cosmos. (p. 172)

In chapter three we will elaborate on Green's suggestion that covenantal relationship is an important foundation for the reciprocating self's develop-ment. Perhaps more important than deciding how soul is defined—in terms of a person *having* a soul or *being* a soul—is to understand that soul needs to be referred to not as a substance but in terms of relationality. In "On Be-ing Human: The Spiritual Saga of a Creaturely Soul" Ray Anderson defined the soul "as that which represents the whole person as a physical, personal, and spiritual being, especially the inner core of an individual's life as created and upheld by God" (*Whatever Happened to the Soul?* 1998, p.193). Humans are unique from nonhuman creatures because they have been created to be in *relationship* with God. This intrinsic relationality is at the core of every individual human being, the basis for a reciprocating self.

The Plan of This Book

To accomplish our task we have divided this book into three parts. In the second chapter of part one we provide the theological rationale behind the use of the concept of the reciprocating self. A trinitarian analogy of being and becoming will serve as our model for understanding the goal of human development as the capacity of being a reciprocating self.

Developmental theories give an understanding of how development takes place, but as we indicated previously, they tend to be limited in pro-viding a teleological focus capable of pointing to the type of *relational con-*

text in which human development ideally takes place. Chapter three seeks to provide a biblical basis for such an ideal relational context.

The biblical depiction of God's relationship to human beings is used as a model for how God desires human beings to be in relationship with each other. We argue that a reciprocating self can develop best in a relational context that is characterized by *unconditional love commitment, gracing, empowering* and *intimacy*. The developing person is not only affected by but also affects the social context in which development takes place. Thus our model of human development is also one of reciprocal influence—of mutual influence between the person and the external social structure or the environment.

Whereas no human developmental theory spells out the desired relational context as specifically as Scripture, there are significant aspects within each developmental theory that correspond to the biblical model we present. Thus chapters four and five provide a selected overview of developmental theories in light of their correspondence with our model. Chapter four focuses on the major developmental theories that give a perspective on infant and child development—psychoanalytic, object relations, social learning, symbolic interaction and cognitive-development theories. Chapter four concludes by giving a comparative overview of the capacity of developmental theories to handle such human phenomena as choice and agency, sin and internal conflict, and communal aspects of personhood. In chapter five we give an overview of developmental theories that focus on the sociocultural context human development takes place in. These include Vygotsky's social-context theory, Lerner's developmental-systems theory and Bronfenbrenner's ecological theory.

In part two we trace the development of the self from birth to death, noting the relational context in which the self develops and changes. Daniel Levinson (1996) notes that development is continual and can be at the same time up *(adolescing)* or down *(senescing)*. Here we encounter the *developmental dilemma,* namely, what criteria can be used to distinguish *adolescing* from *senescing*. The developmental teleology and the concept of the reciprocating self as presented in part one will serve as the underlining principles to follow human developmental throughout life.

Part two is divided into six sequential chapters, each devoted to a major human developmental life-span stage. Each of the life-span development chapters is organized according to the following outline. First, we give a brief overview of the developmental tasks of the present stage of development. A description of the type of scaffolding typically needed during this developmental stage follows. This helps us to examine the nested contexts development takes place in. Specifically, we begin by describing the microsystem, that level where dyadic relationships are the core focus of attention. Next, our attention moves to the mesosystem: the important group contexts where development takes place. Then we take up the influence of the exosystem, those systems that impact an individual even though they are not a participant in the system. Finally, we examine the macrosystem as a cultural context for understanding human development. The last section of each chapter gives an overview of the potential strengths, limitations and developmental issues of the person as a reciprocating self.

In emphasizing a dimension of human development that is generally neglected—the theological—we obviously do not give proportional attention to the breadth of physiological or socio-psycho-cultural factors that contribute to human development. Our bias can be seen in our attempt to move beyond the boundaries imposed by naturalistic assumptions and to consider the moral, spiritual and religious dimensions of human development. In part three we attempt to fill out these often-neglected developmental dimensions. In chapter twelve we utilize such concepts as moral identity and moral transformation in attempting to move the understanding of moral development beyond a traditional cognitive stage-development model. In chapter thirteen we try to move beyond a traditional cognitive model of faith development by focusing separately on spiritual and religious development. We utilize the concept of a differentiated faith in attempting to describe the reciprocal self as reflective of a biblically anchored understanding of faith. A truly differentiated faith will find residence in a faith community. Chapter fourteen in turn focuses on the nature of the reciprocating religious community. Based on the theological insights of such theologians as Jürgen Moltmann and Miroslav Volf we find the trinitarian model of relationality to be appropriately applicable to the lived-out body of Christ. Given the obvious focus in this book on development throughout human life, this chapter includes discussions of *intergenerational reciprocity* and *congregational differentiation.*

The source of the model we propose for the church—the body of Christ—is thus the same as for individual human development, which is not found in human wisdom but in the very relationality of our triune God, and the relationship God seeks to establish with us.

2

The Reciprocating Self

A TRINITARIAN ANALOGY OF BEING AND BECOMING

GIVEN THE COMPLEXITY AND DEPTH OF THIS theological subject and the limitations of a book addressing human development, this chapter summarizes main points of a trinitarian anthropology in order to propose a developmental teleology. Specifically, we address the significance of the two relational polarities of the Trinity—particularity and relationality. Additionally, we explore reciprocity as the form of relationality exhibited among the three persons who exist as one being.

Within the social sciences there is a renewed interest in the realm of spirituality and religion. This provides for a dialogue between theologians and psychologists that has not occurred since the early 1900s. For most of the twentieth century psychologists' commitment to modern science has precluded interest in spiritual, religious or theological issues related to human development (Roehlkepartain et al., 2005; Kerestes and Youniss, 2002). This has resulted in both a relative lack of research and theory on spiritual and religious development and a lack of theologically informed understanding of human development. Consequently, when teaching within a faith-based context, there are few sources to draw on for elucidating two crucial issues related to development: (1) a biblical or theological perspective of good or optimal development, and (2) the psychological processes that are involved in spiritual or religious development. The former is of central concern to this book and will be addressed throughout. The latter is of specific interest to us (the authors) and will be addressed directly in chapter thirteen.

The field of systematic theology is also in transition—especially as it relates to theological anthropology. In the current theological zeitgeist the

imago Dei, the doctrine of the image of God, is often understood more from
a relational perspective and less from a structural or impersonal ontological
perspective. This trend started to emerge with Karl Barth in the early 1900s
and gained great momentum in the latter decades of the twentieth century,
with growing consensus among theologians that the uniqueness of the
imago Dei is best understood through categories of relationality rather than
inert structure (see Anderson, Gunton, Grenz, Shults, Volf and Zizioulas).
Such a theological climate opens doors for dialogue between psychology
and theology in regard to human development.

These two trends create an optimal climate for exploring the potential
contributions psychology and theology have for understanding human development. Our primary intention is to provide an integrated perspective of
human development. By *integrated* we mean to draw on theology and the
social sciences as resources for understanding the processes and goals involved in human development. We hope to offer the reader a means of understanding what good or optimal development might be through presenting a *developmental teleology,* or a theological understanding of the goal of
development.

Defining good or optimal development has not been a traditional task of
the psychological sciences. Psychology has not focused on teleological issues. In general, developmental theories describe processes of psychological development (e.g., cognitive development, identity development) and
normative development. For example, Erik Erikson's psychosocial stages
suggest normal developmental benchmarks for the eight stages of the life
cycle. In addition developmental theories also describe pathological development, or that which deviates from the norm. In fact, the field of psychology has predominantly focused on pathology and healing mental illness. Although different theorists have explored positive aspects of psychology
(Antonovosky, 1987; Jahoda, 1958; Erikson, 1959), a disproportionate
amount of scientific psychology has focused on pathology and repair (Aspinwall and Staudinger, 2003), rather than positive or optimal development.

This emphasis on disease and treatment is more natural for the field of
psychology. Given the limited "tools" of psychology as a scientific field of
inquiry based on the modern values of reductionism and universals, making
claims about *ideal* development is a challenge. It is easier to restore normal
functioning and bring persons back to an original state than to determine
what is good or optimal. The healing approach in psychology has been fa-

cilitated by the fact that it is easier to define the desired or adaptive direction of change if the goal is to restore an earlier or "normal" state. It is much more difficult to define optimal development.

Psychology does not have the epistemological tools to address issues of teleology. Aspinwall and Staudinger (2003) point out that if psychologists intend to define good or optimal development, they must address several difficult questions. For example, do they determine optimal development based on adaptiveness or human functioning? If so, how do psychologists operationalize adaptiveness or functioning? Do they use subjective indicators and ask people for their subjective opinion if they are doing well or are mature? Or do they use objective measures and examine factors like longevity and define optimal development by those who live the longest? Do psychologists consult value or ethical systems? Do they consider democratic ideals as a lens for viewing good development? Do they consider the virtues of Aristotelian ethics? These are questions traditionally asked by theologians and philosophers, not psychologists.

Furthermore, psychologists tend to follow a consensus criterion of truth, not absolute truth. As scientists, psychologists turn to empirical research to determine what people generally agree on. Consequently, truth is not deemed absolute but is determined by consensus opinion. For example, research on wisdom has reliably demonstrated high levels of consensus or agreement about whether or not a judgment satisfies the definition of wisdom. In this case the research identifies the consensus understanding of wisdom and does not have to define wisdom based on one philosophical tradition or another.

The *Imago Dei* and Human Development

However, as Christian psychologists we have an advantage. We are not only scientists but also believers in a creation that reflects something of its Creator and Redeemer. We are not limited to the resources of psychology, but can tap into the resources of our theology. Although both these traditions of thought address issues pertaining to maturity and growth as humans, they are not parallel lines of inquiry and do not address questions of human nature on the same level. A Christian theological anthropology provides a worldview in which psychological theory can be critically engaged and shaped. The Bible offers a symbolic world that creates perceptual categories through which we can interpret reality (Hays, 1996). Our aim is to propose a developmental teleology—a theological understanding of becoming a complete human being. We propose an understanding of the structures of ideal personhood in light of the interrelations of the triune God. In doing so we draw upon a theological analogy, warranted by the doctrine of the *imago Dei,* that makes a comparison from the unique trinitarian persons in relationship to human persons being and becoming in relationship (Gunton, 1993). This theologically grounded analogy, then, provides us a worldview or lens through which we can examine various developmental theories to see how they may contribute to our understanding of the human being as reciprocating self.

The theological inquiry of the likeness of God found in human nature is referred to as theological anthropology. Theological anthropology is the pursuit of a biblical understanding of being human and is a core facet of systematic theology. Theological anthropology may take as its starting point the affirmation that humans are made according to *imago Dei* (Latin for "image of God"), found in the book of Genesis 1:26-27:

> Then God said, "Let us make humankind in our image,
>> according to our likeness." . . .
> So God created humankind in his image,
> in the image of God he created them;
> male and female he created them. (Gen 1:26-27)

Much ink has been spilled on interpreting what that "image," or "likeness," means. What does it mean to bear the image of God? Does being human mean being a part of a family? Does it have to do with being male and female? Being a certain ethnicity? Walking on water? Does it include things such as playing or having a sense of humor?

Within the field of systematic theology debates continue regarding accepted interpretations of the *imago Dei* (see, for example, Brown, 1991; Plantinga, 1989). Traditionally, the *imago Dei* was viewed from a structural perspective and thought to refer to certain characteristics or capacities inherent in the structure of human nature. From this perspective humans reflect the image of God because they possess within the substantive form of human nature some of the qualities God possesses. Theologians have not always agreed on the specific feature(s) found in the human nature that marks the divine image and thus makes humans similar to God. Culture and context have often played a part in determining what specific characteristic(s) comprise the image of God. However, since the time of the early church fathers, reason and will have been most often identified as what comprise the divine image within humans.

However, this structural view of the *imago Dei* is no longer unquestionably accepted as the correct view of theological anthropology. As the Christian tradition developed in dialogue with Western philosophical trends, the *imago Dei* passages were directed towards application to the *individual* self. During the last century, however, this emphasis on the individual self has been challenged. With the resurgence in the study of the Trinity—the threeness of the one God—an anthropology of the *relational* self has emerged. The perspective of the *imago Dei* presented in this volume draws on the relational social understanding of the Trinity. With the teaching and authority of Scripture as our basis, we utilize the works of theologians such as Ray Anderson, Colin Gunton, Miroslav Volf, Stanley Grenz, Karl Barth, F. LeRon Shults and others who share this relational understanding of the *imago Dei*.

Being created according to the image of God is very important to a Christian view of human development. Grenz (2001) contends, "Throughout much of Christian history, the link made in scripture between humans and the divine image has served as the foundation for the task of constructing a Christian conception of the human person or the self" (p. 183). Interpretation of the *imago Dei* strongly influences our understanding of what it means to be human. Consequently it has a significant bearing on our understanding of the processes and goals of human development.

The doctrine of the Trinity reveals that God exists as Father, Son and Holy Spirit. The three divine persons of the Godhead live in unity as one, yet remain three distinct persons. The communion of the Godhead does not compromise the distinctiveness of the three. In this way, *particularity* and *relatedness* co-occur because their relatedness is characterized by perfect *reciprocity* where the three live with and for each other. In the following paragraphs we conclude that to live as beings made in the image of God is to exist as reciprocating selves, as unique individuals living in relationship with others. We then assert that developmental teleology, the goal of human development as God intends, is the reciprocating self. To live according to God's design is to glorify God as a distinct human being in communion with God and others in mutually giving and receiving relationships.

Parenthetically, it can be noted that in *The Evolving Self, Problem and Process in Human Development* (1982), Robert Kegan suggests a similar tension existing in human development. Kegan sees human development as taking place through a set of stages that are merely temporary solutions "to the lifelong tension between the yearning for inclusion and distinctness" (p. 108). It is noteworthy that Kegan arrives at this insight from the accumulative psychological research on human development independent of reference to theological anthropology.

Within the Trinity there is unity and uniqueness (or diversity). In trinitarian theology relatedness comes hand in hand with particularity. The theological concept of *perichoresis* refers to the mutual indwelling within the Godhead, meaning that the three persons of the Trinity dwell with and within each other. Thus it describes God's own mode of being in communion that does not sacrifice difference or diversity. "God is what he is only as a communion of persons, the particularity of whom remains at the center of all he is, for each has his own distinctive way of being" (Gunton, 1993, p. 191). John Zizioulas writes that the being of God is not some blank unity but a being in communion. The particularity of Father, Son and Spirit is as vital as their unity as one. In addition, there is an ontological interdependence and reciprocity of three persons of the Trinity.

The Gospel of John emphasizes this conception of relatedness without absorption (Gunton, 1993). In the Fourth Gospel, Jesus the Son talks more about his relationship with the Father than he does in the Synoptic Gospels (Smith, 1995). Jesus claims simultaneous communion with and distinction from the Father. He paradoxically claims a degree of equality with the Father and that "the Father is greater than I" (Jn 14:28). Jesus testifies how he has no independent status apart from the Father. The Son does nothing by himself but only follows the actions of the Father (Jn 5:19). He has no independent will or judgment. "There is complete unity of action between Father and Son, and complete dependence of the Son on the Father" (Barrett, 1978, p. 257). The Son reflects the character of the Father to the extent that to see Jesus is to see the Father (Jn 14:9). John's depiction of Jesus clearly provides one of the main meanings of sonship: essential identity with the Father. Jesus later attests to the unity of Father and Son when he prays, "You, Father, are in me and I am in you" (Jn 17:21). Not only does Jesus testify to the unity of the Father and Son but also to the distinction between the two. The Gospel clarifies that the Father has committed the power to give life and the responsibility of judgment to the Son. Making the case that the Father and the Son share unity within diversity, he tells the disciples, "For just as the Father has life in himself, so he has granted the Son to have life in himself" (Jn 5:26).

Theology of Particularity

These passages suggest that the divine Being includes particularity and relationality. We will first develop a theology of particularity. Inherent in the *imago Dei* is the value of uniqueness. God exists as three distinct persons—the Father, Son and Holy Spirit. One is never compromised by another. The Father remains the Father, the Son remains the Son, and the Spirit remains the Spirit, each contributing uniquely to salvation history. Yet at the same time the three remain one. However, the unity of the Trinity does not jeopardize the uniqueness of the Father, Son and Spirit (Torrance, 1989; Torrance, 1992). Through the Nicene Creed we affirm the unique relations among the members of the Trinity:

> We believe in one God,
> the Father, the Almighty,
> maker of heaven and earth . . .
>
> We believe in one Lord, Jesus Christ,
> the only Son of God, . . .
> For us and for our salvation . . .
>
> We believe in the Holy Spirit, the Lord, the giver of life,
> who proceeds from the Father and the Son

At the heart of orthodox theology is the recognition of the coherence of the different activities attributed to the Father, Son and Holy Spirit. For example, it is the Holy Spirit who enables us to participate in the Son's ongoing life of worship of the Father. Our salvation and our glorification of God are not possible without each member of the Trinity.

The significance of uniqueness is further demonstrated through the work of the Spirit. Our Christian tradition often emphasizes the unifying work of the Spirit. The Spirit draws persons through Christ to the Father, and it is the Spirit that unifies the communion of saints. It is important to recognize that although the Spirit is the reconciling and unifying agent at work in human-divine relationships and among humans, such work does not abolish but rather maintains or even strengthens particularity. We are unified not for assimilation or homogenization but for relationship with others—relationship that does not subvert but establishes and affirms the other whether God or humans (Gunton, 1993). Through the same Spirit individuals are given different gifts—healing, wisdom, prophecy, preaching, discernment, speaking in tongues . . . and these gifts are given "for the common good" (1 Cor 12:7).

These unique gifts contribute to our unity. The body of believers finds completeness in our diversity. Paul pointedly asks, "If the whole body were an eye, where would the hearing be? If the whole body were hearing, where would the sense of smell be?" (1 Cor 12:17). The particularities enable a unified whole.

As the analogy of the body and its many parts illustrates, relatedness comes hand in hand with particularity. For there is no distinction without unity. The personal identities of the members of the Trinity emerge out of their relationships. By definition there is no father without a child. An individual recognizes his or her uniqueness in relationship with another. In a sense the other provides an orientation for the self to be made known. I (Pam) have always told my classes that after I got married I began to know myself more fully and see my "particularities" more clearly. The closer and more intimately I have grown with my husband, the more I have learned about myself. It is in relationship with another that we more fully encounter not only the other but ourselves. Spouses are excellent for helping us see our particularities! My experience of marriage has been like looking into a mirror. The closer I draw near to the mirror (in this instance, my husband), the more I notice not only all the personality blemishes but also my strengths, unique aspects of my personality and my identity.

Theology of Relationality

Although Christians affirm the distinct members of the Trinity, Christianity is a monotheistic faith. We believe in one God. One of the greatest mysteries of the Christian faith is our understanding of the triune nature of God—that God can be simultaneously one being and three persons. Karl Barth wrote, "The divine modes of being mutually condition and permeate one another so completely that one is always in the other two" (*Church Dogmatics* 1/1, 1975, p. 370). Although the three are distinct, they are not separate; they exist with and for each other. John commences his Gospel with this astounding reality: "In the beginning was the Word, and the Word was with God, and the Word was God" (Jn 1:1). John testifies to the *distinction between* and *unity of* the Father and Son. Not only was the Father with the Word (the Son), but the Word was God. We have already seen that Jesus witnesses to the unity of the Father and the Son by recounting not only his utter dependence on the Father but also by declaring that those who see the Son, see the Father.

Thus we understand that relationality is at the heart of the Trinity. Human beings reflect this relationality. Just as God exists in relationship, humans are to exist in relationship. "To be human is to be created in and for relationship with divine and human others" (Gunton, 1993, p. 222). This concept is broadly represented in the New Testament. All believers are called by God to be a part of a relational community, placed in the body of Christ by the Spirit (1 Cor 12:13). In reminding us that community is what God intends, Bonhoeffer suggests that "Christian brotherhood is not an ideal we must realize; it is rather a reality created by God in Christ in which we may participate" (1954, p. 30). For theologian Stan Grenz (2001), the image of God does not lie in the individual, but in the relationality of the persons in community.

The Importance of Reciprocity

Reciprocity is the glue that holds the relational polarities of uniqueness and unity together. Unity and uniqueness—in reciprocity—is at the heart of the triune God. The three persons remain unique through their mutual interrelatedness. The theological term *perichoresis* (co-inherence, mutual indwelling) was applied to the Trinity to capture the unique nature of these reciprocal interrelations. Each person of the Trinity finds being in each other without coalescence. Reflections of the reciprocity between the Father and the Son can be found, for example, in the Gospel of John. The Father and the Son are one and the Son was also sent by the Father. The Father has committed both the bestowal of life and the responsibility of judgment to the Son. Yet the Son judges and wills only as the Father does. The Father gives power and authority to the Son, and the Son reciprocates by following the Father's example.

The reciprocal dynamic is further seen in the high-priestly prayer of John 17. Jesus prays, "Father, I desire that those also, whom you have given me, may be with me where I am, to see my glory, which you have given me because you loved me before the foundation of the world" (Jn 17:24). The Father lavishes divine love on the Son and thus glorifies him. In turn the Son reciprocates the love received from the Father and in this manner glorifies the Father eternally (Gunton, 1993, p. 327). This is not an example of codependent back scratching—I'll give you glory if you give me glory. Rather, in love the Father gives life to the Son, and the Son chooses of his own will to glorify the Father.

Moltmann nicely summarizes: "According to the Christian doctrine of the Trinity the three divine Persons exist with one another, for one another and in one another. They exist in one another because they mutually give each other space for full unfolding. By existing mutually in each other, they form their unique Trinitarian fellowship" (1996, p. 298). The mutual reciprocity between the Father, Son and Spirit allows them to experience diversity within union—to experience simultaneous unity and uniqueness. Within the Trinity there is no impinging on one another. They each contribute uniquely to their united working. The particularity of Father, Son and Spirit is as vital as their relatedness. Through the Spirit we participate in the Son's life of communion with the Father (Torrance, 1989, 1992).

Theological anthropology would suggest that bearing the image of God means living as unique individuals in reciprocating relationships with others. To be human is to be a particular being in relationships, distinct and unique, yet inseparably bound up with the other. "All particulars are formed by their relationship to God and the creator and redeemer and to each other" (Gunton, 1993, p. 207). Particularity is discovered in relationship with our Creator, our Redeemer, our Sustainer and with each other. If humankind is to realize its created intention, humankind must then be understood as socialkind (Gunton, 1993). For it is the self's encounter with divine and human other that enables it to realize its uniqueness. To be human is to be in relationship with another. Humans experience their unique selves most fully when in a healthy relationship with God or another. Macmurray states, "Persons constitute each other, make each other what they are" (1961, p. 17). In Luke 17:20-21, Jesus proclaims, "The kingdom of God is among you," suggesting to some commentators that God's reign is initially evident in the relationships between believers and only a sign of what is to become—or to develop.

This relational understanding of the *imago Dei* suggests that being human involves living in reciprocating, authentic relationships with others. Following the pattern of the trinitarian relationships, such relationships are characterized by mutuality, give and take, and they enable the self to be known most fully in the process of knowing another. In such relationships there is space to simultaneously be oneself and to be in relationship with each other. There is room to encounter the other and to encounter the self through the other. The self is never lost in face of the other. The other does not impinge on the self, but the other promotes the presence of the self. In the reciprocating relationship there is give and take, and take and give. A high view of both the self and other is required to value the giving and the receiving. In mathematics the definition of *reciprocal* reflects this simultaneous distinction within unity. According to Webster's Dictionary, a reciprocal is "a pair of quantities whose product is unity." We could say that to be human is to live as unique quantities whose product is unity.

Who cannot help but pause and say, "Yes, that's it!" As humans we all long to be known, to have the deepest and darkest parts of our soul and psyche uncovered, affirmed and loved. We all long to be loved and to know we are special—or even just OK. The deepest parts of ourselves rejoice when we read Psalm 139, poetically describing our uniquely created self as a wonderful work of the living God:

> For it was you who formed my inward parts;
>   you knit me together in my mother's womb.
> I praise you, for I am fearfully and wonderfully made.
>   Wonderful are your works;
> that I know very well.
>   My frame was not hidden from you,
> when I was being made in secret,
>   intricately woven in the depths of the earth. (vv.13-15)

Everything is created by God to be and become what it is, and not another. We are distinct and particular beings.

This concept of the reciprocating self can be graphically illustrated in a common tradition in Christian wedding ceremonies—the lighting of the unity candle. In this ritual the families of the bride and groom each light a candle symbolizing the life of the bride and groom respectively. During the ceremony the bride and groom take their respective candles and simultaneously light another candle as a symbol of their lives coming together as one. One of my (Pam) most profound pastoral pet peeves is when, after lighting the unity candle, the bride and groom then blow out their individual candles. I want to scream at the top of my lungs, "No! Stop! Don't blow yourself out. You keep on continuing!" Marriage is not about the abolition of the uniqueness of the two coming together as one. It is the unity of two distinct lives. Marriage at its best brings two individuals together through the Spirit in Christ to glorify God through a new life together and simultaneously enables each individual to become the person that God created them to be. By lighting the unity candle and allowing the individual flames to burn, this ritual (thus enacted correctly) beautifully illustrates our understanding of the reciprocating self.

It is important to step back and clarify a point that could be misconstrued regarding the *imago Dei*. Human nature is endowed with the image of God, but human beings are not constituted by the triune nature. We recognize that God is triune and human beings are not (Anderson, 1982). Humans are not identical with the *imago* but bear the *imago*. Nor are we trying to build the case that individual humans are composed of three entities, aspects or functions—whether they are Father, Son and Spirit; id, ego and superego; or body, mind and spirit. This is not our intention. We are suggesting that to bear the *imago Dei* is to reflect the Trinity's unity and uniqueness within our own relations with the divine and the human other. The relational life of the triune God is not represented *within* ourselves but *among* ourselves.

The Self and the Divine Other

We are created to be in relationship with God. This relationship is to be characterized by uniqueness, unity and reciprocity. Similar to the interrelationships within the Trinity, humans are to experience simultaneous communion with God that does not jeopardize our particularity.

Throughout the Bible, God continually affirms human uniqueness. Jesus' interaction with the woman at the well in Samaria (Jn 4:1-42) illustrates this point. He interacts with her as a unique individual with specific needs. He recognizes and accepts her as a woman and a Samaritan. He not only addresses the felt need of her thirst, but he speaks to her specific emotional and relational problems. Jesus also gradually reveals his own unique identity. The woman recognizes him first as a Jew, then as a rabbi and finally as a prophet. Jesus responds by declaring his distinction as the Messiah and the means by which to worship God. In this interaction, both the particularities of the woman and of Christ remain intact. The encounter between Jesus and the woman at the well also illustrates reciprocal giving—Christ recognizes the woman's needs and offers to quench her spiritual thirst. She in turn goes out and proclaims the truth given by Jesus and draws others to believe and worship Jesus.

A person's relationship with God is characterized by the uniqueness of both the created and the Creator, and the unity between the two. This is evident when Jesus prays, "As you, Father, are in me and I am in you, may they also be in us" (Jn 17:21). Throughout the Bible life is found in Christ, not on our own: "I have come that you might have life, and have it abundantly" (Jn 10:10). Full life is found in relationship with Christ. The Spirit's role in this is to "realize the true being of each created thing by bringing it, through Christ, into saving relation with God the Father" (Gunton, 1993, p. 189). We are most human when we are jointly united to Christ through the Holy Spirit, enabling us to participate in the Son's union with and glorification of the Father. Grenz declares that this is the telos for which we were created. "Glorifying the Father in the Son together with all creation is the ultimate expression of the *imago Dei* and therefore marks the *telos* for which humans were created in the beginning" (2001, p. 327).

The goal of our lives—the point of human life—is to glorify the Father in the Son and through the Spirit. Being drawn into the worship life of the Trinity not only involves the glorification of God but also includes the glorification of all creation. "By being drawn into the dynamic of the triune life, the new humanity participates in this eternal reciprocal glorification" (Grenz, 2001, p. 327). In the end the Spirit will bring together all believers with all of creation, gathering them into the Son, the one in whom all things "hold together" or find interconnectedness (Col 1:17). Thus while the Spirit leads those who are found "in Christ" to glorify the Father through the Son, the Father glorifies them in the Son by the Spirit (Grenz, 2001). Because Christ and his people are unified as one, his people will also share in his glorification (Hoekema, 1986).

It is a marvel that in this union and reciprocity with the life of the Trinity, human particularity is not lost. In our relationship with God we not only encounter the living God, but we become most fully ourselves. Just as within the Godhead the three persons, Father, Son and Holy Spirit, exist with, for and in one another, so God does this with creation, giving us the space we need to be ourselves while remaining in relation to him. "God's indwelling presence gives to created being forever the 'broad space in which there is no more cramping' " (Moltmann, 1996, p. 308). God acts not as a dominating Other but the One in whom we live and move and have our being. Moltmann explains that relatedness to God does not threaten the distinctiveness of creation. "It is neither necessary for the world to dissolve into God, as pantheism says, nor for God to be dissolved in the world, as atheism maintains. God remains God, and the world remains creation" (1996, p. 307). Our relationship with God does not sacrifice our particularity; rather it allows us to become more fully who God created us to be. Trinitarian theology reminds us that we are most human when Jesus Christ brings us into the presence of the Father, drawing us to him by the Holy Spirit.

A graphic counterexample is the early desert fathers known as the pillar saints. These monastic saints permanently perched upon tall pillars, raising and lowering food and supplies to live. In this way their quest for holiness and closeness to God was minimally disturbed. But according to our relational understanding of the *imago Dei*—to live in the likeness of God is to live as distinct individuals in relationship with God and fellow believers— these pillar saints only got it half right. Yes, they nobly dedicated their lives to communion with God, but they neglected fellowship and Christian community. They missed out on part of their God-designed nature.

Perhaps a better image than a pillar for the Christian life is the cross. For when we look at the cross, our eyes are directed heavenward toward God, and we are reminded that our humanity is found in our relationship with God. Simultaneously, just as Christ stretched out his arms on the cross, our eyes are directed horizontally, reaching to our fellow sisters and brothers. To be human is not to live in exclusive relationship with God but to live in relationship with God *and* humans. For it is in and through these relationships that we not only grow to become the unique persons that God created us to be, but we will enable others to become who God created them to be, all the while participating in the life of the Son, through the Spirit, bringing glory to the Father.

The Self and the Human Other

To bear the image of God is to live in reciprocating relationships with God and our fellow human beings. Martin Buber, a Jewish theologian, referred to this type of relationship as an "I-Thou" relationship. Buber's (1970) theological anthropology was that human beings are to be in relationships where a whole self, the "I," is in mutual relationship with a whole other, the "Thou." This supposes an authentic personal encounter of both the I and the Thou. One is not dominant; the other is not inferior. The relationship is characterized especially by the reciprocity of communication. Buber starkly contrasted I-Thou with I-it ways of relating; the former being appropriate to the way a person should relate to humans and God, the latter, the way to relate properly to the impersonal natural world. Buber regarded relating to persons as if they were things as a violation of humanity and God. Engaging in such I-it relationships among persons, the "I" could only experience him- or herself as superior, while also failing to see the other as a whole self, experiencing the other only as an impersonal "it." Both persons were thereby dehumanized.

In an I-Thou relationship a person would acknowledge and respect the difference between themselves and others while maintaining a communicative relationship with them. They would experience unity in their mutual recognition of being Thou to each other but each remain personally distinct as I. Only in the context of encountering the other as Thou does the self truly encounter itself. In such a relationship both "persons encounter their own being in the other" (Anderson, 1982, p. 46). Buber writes, "I require a Thou to become; becoming I, I say Thou" (Buber, 1970, p. 62).

Using Buber's theory of relatedness, a circumplex model is presented (figure 2.1) in order to illustrate the reciprocating self and its valuations. The names of the four models of relatedness are derived from Buber's writing on the I-Thou relationship and are to be interpreted according to the theological anthropology we have been presenting. We also offer a number of artistic expressions which capture much of the contrasting qualities of relationality we are considering.

These four models of relatedness are presented in a circumplex model which is organized on two axes. The two axes represent the view of the self and the view of the other. The *x* axis represents a continuum of the perception of self. The high end indicates having a strong and secure sense of self,

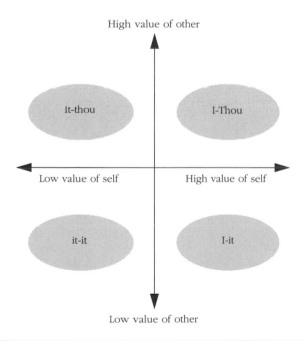

Figure 2.1. Circumplex model

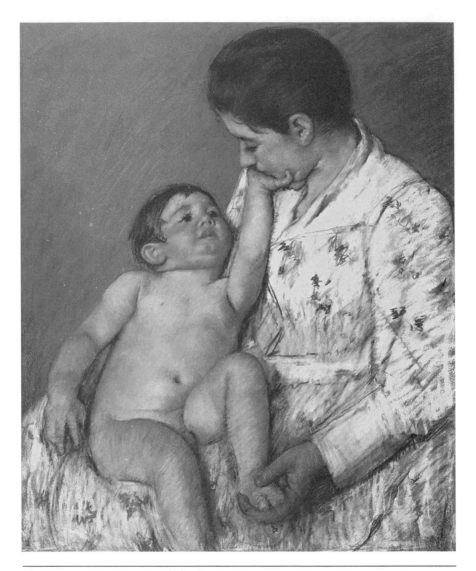

Figure 2.2. Mary Cassatt's *Baby's First Caress*

and the low end indicates an unclear and insecure sense of self. The y axis
represents the view of the other. The high end suggests a recognition of a
unique other that is both recognized and respected. The upper right quadrant, indicated by a high sense of self and other represents the I-Thou relationship. The lower-right quadrant measured by a higher view of self than

other, represents the I-it relationship; the lower-left quadrant indicates a low sense of self and other represents the dissociated it-it relationship; and finally the upper-left quadrant represents the it-Thou relationship, suggesting a lower view of self than other.

I-Thou relationship. The first quadrant represents the I-Thou relationship, which is characterized by a high view of the self and a high view of the other. As explained by Buber the I-Thou relationship simultaneously facilitates uniqueness and unity. The self and other both experience the presence of the other in such a way that enables both to develop. Ideally neither impingement nor domination occur in the context of the relationship. Rather, both the self and other are recognized and appreciated as unique, differentiated selves. Such a relationship enables the self and other to become more fully what God created them to be and to experience their particularity more fully in their unity.

Mary Cassatt's *Baby's First Caress* literally paints a picture of the I-Thou relationship (fig. 2.2). The mutual touch and expression of the mother and child portray a simultaneous encountering of the self and other. As the baby caresses the mother's chin, the mother not only encounters her child but becomes aware of her own feelings as her face tingles at the finger tips of her child's fingers. As the mother touches the baby's foot, the baby's own caress is validated by the mirroring action of the mother, and the child becomes aware of his or her own feet through the touch of the mother's hand.

In addition to the convergence of the gazes of mother and child, even the technique and style of the artist give a sense of unity and connection between them. The lines of the baby's arms follow the neckline and upper-arm line of the mother. The baby's thighs are almost perfectly parallel with the mother's forearm, neck line and the line connecting the baby's and mother's eyes. Cassatt's brush strokes create a harmonious melody that intertwines the two and that at no time distracts the viewer from the uniqueness of the beautiful babe and the tender, adoring mother. This painting vividly illustrates the following remark by Hans Urs von Balthazar: "And yet the child is aware, in the first opening of its mind's eyes. Its 'I' awakens in the experience of a 'Thou': in its mother's smile through which it learns that is contained, affirmed, and loved in a relationship which is incomprehensibly encompassing, already actual, sheltering and nourishing" (cited in Neuhaus, 2000, p. 98).

I-it relationship. The I-it relationship is in sharp contrast to the I-Thou.

The I-it relationship is characterized by a high view of the self and a low view of the other. The other is not experienced as a whole being, is not appreciated in its entirety. In the I-it relationship the other serves as an object, in a functional or utilitarian role for the self, regardless of the created uniqueness of the object. The self in the I-it relationship merely interacts with human others as objects. The other is instrumental, not integral, to the I's being. Individuals who related to the other as an it are often dismissing. They have a positive view of themselves and a negative view of others. Such individuals avoid closeness with others because of negative expectations. However, they maintain a sense of self-worth through defensively denying the value of intimate relationships. Such individuals experience superficial relationships with others. Thus the interconnectedness of the I-Thou represents to them a struggle.

The neo-impressionist George Seurat's *A Sunday Afternoon on the Island of la Grande Jatte* (fig. 2.3) exemplifies the I-it relationship. The artist, who is known to be the ultimate example of the artist as scientist, used the technique of pointillism, or divisionism, on a massive canvas in order to depict a number of people enjoying a sunny afternoon in a park. Looking closely, we notice that the individuals in the picture are just that—individuals. Although people are walking or sitting side by side, with the exception of one couple, there is no engagement between individuals. There appears to be no true encounter of the other. Except for geographic proximity there is no evidence of relationality. Additionally, on closer examination we realize that these people are made of dots. Consistent with the thought and science of the modern era that sought universal laws, systems of natural order, and reduction of matter into parts, people in Seurat's painting are reducible to mere particles. The painting does not portray humans as interconnected beings but rather as entities composed of individual parts.

Fusion: The it-Thou relationship. Another distortion of the I-Thou relationship is the fused relationship in which the individual holds a low view of self and a high view of the other. Although the other is more highly regarded than the self, this is not done in a healthy, differentiated manner. Rather the other is seen as a source of security or identity for the self. The other is not recognized as a unique, respected individual but rather as one who exists in order to conform to the needs of the self. Such individuals seek close relationships with another in order to gain a sense of acceptance or validation. They seem to believe that if others will act properly toward

Figure 2.3. George Seurat's *A Sunday Afternoon on the Island of la Grande Jatte*

them, they will attain a secure self. This can lead to a fused personality. Individual uniqueness and distintictiveness are lost. No space for individual self-expression exists in this model of relatedness. Nor is there room for reciprocity. Neither the self nor the other have any space for personal development. Consequently, the other's unique self is not validated and is lost as it conforms to the thoughts, feelings and needs of the wounded self. In "Buberian" terms this form of relatedness could be called it-thou. In this formulation the self is referred to as an it rather than as an I in order to emphasize the low view of the self. Because the self sees the other as having something to contribute, the word *thou* rather than *it* is used to convey that the other is perceived as necessary to the self's being. The word *thou* is not capitalized in order to denote that the other is not mutually related to as in the I-Thou relationship.

The Viennese Art Deco painter Gustav Klimt reflects this tendency in his work. Time and again one body is conformed to another in a way that insinuates a fusion, a loss of uniqueness, especially by the other. For example in *The Kiss* the most evident distinction in the painting is the boundary surrounding the joined bodies, separating them from the background (fig. 2.4). In contrast the boundary between the two selves is hardly visible. The woman's body, as the other, is being conformed to fit to the man's form, as the self. The self and other lose their distinction as they become one. The conformity of the other to the self and the lack of a distinct boundary between the two illustrate a neurotic fusion. This painting illustrates how the "other"—in this case the woman—has no space for developing. Rather she is forced to conform to the man's needs. This is a vivid illustration of a person seeking out another to complete the self. This might represent an attempt to reduce anxiety because the person does not have an internalized sense of self. In popular culture this painting has been romanticized and can be found on Valentine's Day cards, mugs and calendars. At first glance the union between the lovers appears romantic, but on viewing the image through the lens of the reciprocating self, the sacrifice of individuality becomes more apparent, and the painting must be regarded as more neurotic than romantic.

Dissociation: The it-it relationship. The opposite of fusion is dissociation, where the self attempts to exist on its own, not in relationship with another. In the final quadrant the it-it relationship is characterized by a low view of self and a low view of other. Unlike the previous model, where not enough space between self and other exists for self-expression, there is too much space in this dynamic. The self does not perceive itself worthy of

Figure 2.4. Gustav Klimt's *The Kiss*

closeness with another, nor does it expect the other to offer closeness. Such individuals have often been hurt in close relationships. The negative expectations they form cause them to avoid interpersonal closeness to avoid the pain of loss and rejection. Defensively, they remain in isolation.

The modern architect Ludwig Mies Van Der Rohe graphically illustrates this detachment in his *Farnsworth House* (fig. 2.5). The architect designed his buildings to be perfectly self-contained systems that reflect what he understood to be the natural order. They exist on their own, irrespective of their environment. Such is the case with the *Farnsworth House,* which suggests no continuity with its surroundings. The house stands on its own as a self-contained system. There is no relationship between the severe, modern building and the rural landscape. This building reflects the dissociation experienced by the fearful individual. Just like the modern building, the fearful self looks out on the world from its isolated existence in ontological aloneness, not experiencing intimacy.

The Reciprocating Self

Exploring the above stances of relatedness provides a basis by which the reciprocating self may be understood. The reciprocating self is the self that in

Figure 2.5. *Farnsworth House* by Ludwig Mies Van Der Rohe

all its uniqueness and fullness of being engages fully in relationship with another in all its particularity. The reciprocating self is the I or Thou in the I-Thou relationship. Buber writes, "Relation is reciprocity" (1970, p. 62). It is the self that enters into mutual relationships with another, where distinction and unity are experienced simultaneously. The I-Thou selves reciprocate, having the capacity to give and to take. The reciprocating self does not treat the other as a mere utilitarian object from which it only takes. It does not seek fusion, where it takes to the extent that it demands the loss and sacrifice of the other. It is not dissociated—where there is no give or take. Rather the reciprocating self lives in a mutual relationship of sharing and receiving with another.

Conclusion

The purpose of this book is to provide a theological perspective on human development. As such, the notion of the reciprocating self serves as our developmental teleology. In other words our understanding of God's intention for human development is for us to become particular beings in relationship with the divine and the human other. In mutually reciprocating relationships we encounter the other and ourselves most fully. Although this is an eschatological goal, meaning that reciprocating selves will only come to completion in the eschaton, the goal of all history, we affirm the significance of enabling others now, as far as possible, to become reciprocating selves.

As we turn toward the discussion of life-span development we will be examining theories, developmental processes and life-span issues with the lens of the reciprocating self. In this way our developmental teleology will help us focus on the aspects of human development that help or hinder the formation of the reciprocating self.

It is our belief that God's intention for individual development is inextricably intertwined with our relations with God and one another. We use this understanding of being human to provide insight into existing developmental theories and to discuss how they might help or hinder our understanding of being human.

3

Reciprocating Relationships

IN THE LAST CHAPTER WE USED A TRINITARIAN MODEL to suggest that the goal of human development is for individual humans to become reciprocating selves in the same manner as persons of the holy Trinity are with each other. They are one yet maintain their distinct personhood. In this chapter we seek to complete our theological model of human development by introducing a second biblical model—the depiction of *God's relationship to human beings*. A precedent for this was set in the writings of Ray Anderson (1982, 1985) and Gary Deddo (1999), who utilized the biblical concept of God's *covenant love* as an example of what God desires in human relationships. We argue that human relationships are meant to be reciprocal *unconditional commitments* characterized by reciprocal *gracing, empowering* and *intimacy*. We propose that human relationships are *authentic*—the way there are meant to be—to the extent that they are modeled after the way God enters into relationships with humans. This way of relating is necessary to foster both the development of the reciprocating self and to sustain it's authentic quality.

Stephen Post (1994) has suggested that a theology of family relationships might be developed by means of an *analogical-familial* theological approach. This approach has been used in three books, one dealing with family relationships (Balswick and Balswick, 1999a), another with sexual relationships (Balswick and Balswick, 1999b) and the third with parent-child relationships (Balswick et al. 2003). In each case a theology of human relationships is built on the biblical model of God in relationship with humankind. In the Old Testament, for example, God is described as relating to Israel as a parent (father), as a spouse and as a faithful lover. In the New Testament God is frequently described as a groom in relationship to his bride, the church. We will examine the whole of Scripture through the lenses of these analogies to help understand God's relationship to human beings.

Our beginning point in developing a theology of personal relationships is found in God's covenantal relationship with the nation of Israel. Ray Anderson notes that in Scripture "humanity is determined as existence in covenant relation with God" (1982, p. 37). In describing the relational components of covenant, Stuart McLean makes the following observations: (1) people are social and live in community; (2) the basic unit of family and of covenant is the dyad; (3) persons living in community will experience struggle and conflict as well as harmony; (4) persons living in covenant must be willing to forgive and be forgiven; (5) persons living in covenant must accept their bondedness to each other; (6) persons living in covenant will accept law in the form of patterns and order in relationships; and (7) persons living in covenant will have a temporal awareness as they carry a memory of the past, live in the present and anticipate the future (1984, pp. 4-32).

Relationships That Form a Reciprocating Self

We propose an analogical-personal relational theology based on scriptural teachings on God in relationship. We believe that the reciprocating self can be nurtured best when (1) personal relationships are characterized by a *covenant* (unconditional love) commitment rather than a conditional commitment; (2) when the response to failure in relationship is characterized by *gracing* rather than shaming; (3) when persons in relationship use their power, giftedness and resources to *empower* rather than to control the other; and (4) when the relationship is characterized by an openness that can lead to *intimacy* rather than isolation. Although the core biblical analogy of God in relationship is supremely applicable to marriage and parent-child relationships, it is also generalizable to what God desires in relationships in general, which is our focus in this chapter.

The maturing of a reciprocating self can best be thought of as a developmental process nurtured by ever-deepening levels of *covenant, grace, empowering* and *intimacy.* This sequential change is represented in figure 3.1, an inward spiral depicting the potential for personal relationships to grow into ever-deeper levels of reciprocal commitment, grace, empowering and intimacy.

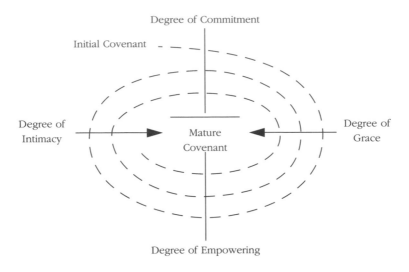

Figure 3.1. A theology of reciprocating relationships

Concomitantly, an *undifferentiated self* develops into a *reciprocating self* in mature relationships. As an infant develops language and the capacity to communicate, a self is formed. This beginning self, however, is an undifferentiated self, a self that is almost indistinguishable from the primary caretaker(s). The infant has the *capacity* to become a reciprocating self, but for this to happen the child needs to be in relationships with mature or reciprocating selves. Using the parent-child relationship as an example, the relationship between a parent and infant child begins as a unilateral (one-way) love commitment; as the parent lives out that commitment the relationship may grow into a bilateral (reciprocal) love commitment. In order for growth to take place in a relationship there must be involvement by both persons. Initially a child has no self and cannot enter into a reciprocating relationship. But through socialization the self develops increasing capacities for relatedness (see chaps. 6-7). The more mature the reciprocating self of the caretakers, the greater the likelihood that a child will develop into a reciprocating self. The less the caretakers' capacity to relate as reciprocating selves, the more retarded a child's development into a reciprocating self.

Even at the adult level, when one person in the relationship is unable or unwilling to reciprocate covenant love, grace, empowering or intimacy, growth in interpersonal relationships can be blocked or retarded. Thus growth in a relationship can come to a standstill at any point in this cycle. Since relationships are dynamic and ever-changing, if a relationship does not spiral into deeper levels of commitment, grace, empowering, and intimacy, then it will stagnate and fixate on *contract* rather than covenant, *law* rather than grace, *possessive power* rather than empowering, and *distance* rather than intimacy.

Parenthetically, we should note that we are not proposing a tightening of dyadic relationships that would exclude or ignore less primary relationships. On the contrary, the depth of bonding in primary relationships nurtures the reciprocating self and equips it to enter into empowering relationships with persons in the wider human community. While our early chapters on human development (chaps. 6-8) point to a child needing a certain degree of exclusivity in interpersonal relationships, our chapters on adult development (chaps. 9-11) will point out that the maturity that comes out of exclusive relationships are meant to become *inclusive.* Thus in our last chapter we will utilize the trinitarian relational model to suggest that the reciprocal self needs to be embedded in the *reciprocal community.* The true church—as the body of Christ—is to be *unbounded* in showing care and love.

Although the relational dimensions of covenant, grace, empowering and intimacy will be described separately, in reality they often overlap and should not be pressed into a logical, sequential linear model of interpersonal relationships. It could be argued that in any attempt to base a human model of relating on a divine example is a set-up for failure. While human beings are created in the image of God, we are fallen creatures who fail in all aspects of our relationship. It is true that no human being can ever make a covenant commitment in the way that God covenants with us. It is equally true that no mere human will be able to respond with grace and forgiveness to the same degree that God offers grace. Human empowering attempts likewise fall short of the empowering model set by Jesus Christ. Finally, human attempts at intimacy will pale into insignificance when compared to the knowing and caring shown by God. Nevertheless, through God's active relating to humans and God's incarnate presence in Jesus Christ a perfect model of relationship is revealed in Scripture. As we live out our lives and relationships according to God's purpose, we have God as an active relational model.

Covenant

The central point of covenant is an *unconditional commitment,* which is demonstrated supremely by God. Genesis 6:18 is the first biblical mention of a covenant. God says to Noah, "I will establish my covenant with you; and you shall come into the ark." Noah is told by God what he must do: "[Take] your sons, your wife, and your sons' wives with you. And of every living thing, of all flesh, you shall bring two of every king into the ark, to keep them alive with you; they shall be male and female" (Gen 6:18-19). In Genesis 6:22 we read: "Noah did this; he did all that God commanded him." In Genesis 9:9-10 God repeats this promise of covenant: "I am establishing my covenant with you and your descendants after you, and with every living creature that is with you." Notice that the passage also indicates that this covenant is extended to include nonhuman creatures.

In Genesis 15:18 the covenant is extended to Abraham. Genesis 17 amplifies on the covenant God made with Abraham:

> The LORD appeared to Abram and said to him, "I am God Almighty; walk before me and be blameless. And I will make my covenant between me and you, and make you exceedingly numerous." Then Abram fell on his face; and God said to him, "As for me, this is my covenant with you: You shall be the ancestor of a multitude of nations. . . . I will establish my covenant between me and you, and your offspring after you throughout their generations, for an everlasting covenant, to be God to you and your offspring after you." (vv. 1-4, 7)

Genesis 17:9 focuses on Abraham's role in the covenant: "God said to Abraham, 'As for you, you shall keep my covenant, you and your offspring after you throughout their generations.' "

These two accounts reveal several important characteristics of God as the covenant-maker. First, we see that neither Noah nor Abraham was offered any choice in the matter. God's covenant offer was not "Now I am going to commit myself to you *if* this is your desire." It is clear that the establishment of the covenant was based entirely on God's action. God's offer was not contractual; it was not based on Noah's or Abraham's keeping their end of the bargain. Whether Noah or Abraham accepted the covenant or not, God's commitment was firm. The second thing we learn about God as covenant-maker is that he strongly desired (some might say commanded) a response from both Noah and Abraham. The strength of God's desire did not, however, make his covenantal offer conditional. God was not free to retract the offer if Noah or Abraham did not reciprocate. God's offer was "an everlasting covenant."

A third aspect of God's covenant was that the potential benefits or blessings it provided were conditional. Noah and Abraham were given an option by God *within* the covenant. If they were to benefit from the covenant, Noah and Abraham had to agree to fulfill their end of the bargain. While receiving any of the blessings was conditional, the continuation of God's love was not conditioned on the nature of Noah's or Abraham's response. A fourth observation is that God extended the covenant to more than just these two individuals. Noah's and Abraham's families were included in the covenant as well. In the case of Abraham God extended "an everlasting covenant" to "generations." Even more extensive, God's covenant with Noah was extended to include "every living creature." Further evidence of the unconditional nature of the covenant is the fact that Noah could not respond on behalf of the animals, nor could Abraham anticipate the obedience of his descendants.

The relationship between God and the children of Israel is best understood through the analogy of an unconditional parental commitment to a child. Scripture reveals a cycle of (1) Israel's turning away from God and getting into difficulty; (2) God's reaching out and forgiving them; (3) Israel's being reconciled into the intended parent-child relationship; and (4) Israel's blessing and renewal in their relationship to God. Similarly, the central message of the book of Hosea is that God pursued unfaithful Israel as a jilted lover.

The supreme expression of unconditional love is modeled in the life and death of Jesus. When the Pharisees and scribes criticized him for welcoming and sitting with sinners, Jesus responded with the story of the prodigal son (Lk 15). Just as the father in the story welcomed his wayward son home with open arms, Jesus responded with unconditional love to a people who had rejected his Father. The unconditional nature of God's love is most clearly expressed in 1 John 4:19: "We love because he first loved us." Likewise this unconditional love is expressed in 1 John 4:10: "In this is love, not that we loved God, but that he loved us." God's love is unconditional!

The issue of reciprocity needs to be discussed in light of the unconditional quality of God's covenant commitment. Although there is no question regarding the unconditional nature of covenant love, in a relational context covenant can be used of unilateral or bilateral relationships. Figure 3.2 depicts the alternative types of commitment found in relationships.

Covenantal relationships are based on unconditional commitments, but they can be either unilateral (one-way) or reciprocal (two-way). In order for

	Conditional	Unconditional
Unilateral	Modern Open	Initial Covenant
Bilateral	Contract	Mature Covenant

Figure 3.2. Types of commitment

a true relationship to exist between two persons, there must be some degree of reciprocity involved. Thus some might question if an exclusive one-way commitment should even be called a relationship. On a continuum representing degrees of reciprocity in commitment, the concepts unilateral and bilateral should be understood as polar opposites.

In figure 3.2 a unilateral unconditional relationship is labeled "Initial Covenant," while a bilateral unconditional relationship is labeled "Mature Covenant." All biblical references to covenants are examples of initial covenants since God initiates them. It would be erroneous to think of an unconditional unilateral relationship as partial, dependent or even immature, because from the individual's perspective a personal covenant without restrictions is being offered. Unilateral unconditional commitment entails the attractive possibility of someday becoming bilateral. That initial covenants become reciprocal and mutual (bilateral unconditional commitments) is God's desire.

Caring parents make an unconditional commitment of love to a child when it is born. At the beginning of life the infants are unable to reciprocate their parent's unconditional commitment. A relationship that began as an initial (unilateral) covenant can develop into a mature (bilateral) relationship as the child matures. When parents themselves age and become more dependent on their adult children, true reciprocity occurs because unconditional love has come full cycle. Here, in a mature bilateral commitment, reciprocal and unconditional love is especially rewarding.

Perhaps as a corrective to those who interpret the meaning of covenant exclusively in a bilateral context, James Torrance (1975) has described a covenant as unilateral and a contract as bilateral. We must remember, however, that Torrance is speaking of the establishment of the covenant between God and humans. Our covenant relation with God is not established equally by us and God; God is the initiator. Once established, the human is graciously given room to reciprocate in an asymmetrical yet bilateral way. The covenant relationship between God and humans cannot be directly applied in exactly the same way to human relationships. Although both God-human and human-human relationships are reciprocal, it may be more appropriate to speak of human-human relationships in terms of *mutuality*. Torrance's primary concern is the contrast between a gracious covenant and the conditional nature of a contractual relationship. Covenant relations between God and humans and between human and humans are of the gracious sort, not the contractual sort, whether established unilaterally or bilaterally. The lack of conditions is the primary and shared aspect in both types of covenantal relationships.

Two types of conditional interpersonal relationships are represented in the first column of figure 3.2. The cell at the bottom left represents a quid pro quo arrangement, where a relationship is based on both partners fulfilling their agreed-on end of the bargain. When two people adopt this conditional stance, a relationship, even a friendship, amounts to a *contract*. Both participants in the relationship consider it satisfactory if they get about as much as they give. In reality, much of the daily routine in life is carried out according to informal contractual agreements. Advocates of covenant-based relationships recognize the importance of the mutual satisfaction and fairness. Although there may be contractual agreements within a covenant, a true covenant relationship will not be based on contract alone.

An emerging type of relationship, which we call the *modern open* arrangement, is symptomatic of a society in which persons are hesitant to make commitments in relationships. The 100 percent increase in premarital cohabitation in the last twenty years is characteristic of persons not even willing to enter a contractual relationship. The understanding, often unspoken, is that either party can terminate the relationship if it is felt that personal needs are not being met or that someone else might better meet one's needs.

Grace

From a human perspective the unconditional love of God makes no sense except as an offer of grace. It is difficult to distinguish between covenant and grace because covenant *is* grace by its very nature. We are called to share in a gracious relationship with God. *Grace* is truly a relational word and a natural extension of covenant love. Rogerson suggests that God desires the establishment of *structures of grace,* defined as "a social arrangement designed to mitigate hardship and misfortune, and grounded in God's mercy," to strengthen relationships (1996, p. 41). Rogerson finds support for this in such Old Testament texts as Exodus 22:25-27: "If you lend money to my people, to the poor among you, you shall not deal with them as a creditor; you shall not exact interest from them. If you take your neighbor's cloak in pawn, you shall restore before the sun goes down." In his analysis of Old Testament writing on the family, Rogerson concludes, "What is really important is that theologically-driven efforts were made to counteract the forces that undermined the family" (1996, p. 41).

Whereas relationships based on contract lead to an atmosphere of law, relationships based on covenant lead to grace and forgiveness. As designed by God, personal relationships are meant to be lived out in an atmosphere of grace and not law. In order for community to be a context for right relationships there must be a willingness to forgive (Borrowdale, 1996). The meaning and joy of being a Christian would be deadened if our relationship with God were conceived in terms of law and not grace. The same is true for relationships in the Christian community. Law leads to legalism, whereas grace provides a freedom from legalism, whether it is at the individual or community level. When community members act responsibly out of love and consideration for one another, they are acting as a community of grace.

The incarnation, in which Christ came in human form to reconcile the world to God, is the supreme act of God's grace to humankind. The basis for human love and forgiveness is God's act of divine love and forgiveness. As we have been forgiven, we can likewise forgive others. The love of God within makes it possible for us to love others in God's unconditional way.

This does not mean that there is no place for law, rules, guidelines or regulations in personal relationships. We need to be informed by the apostle Paul's writings, "Christ ends the law and brings righteousness for everyone who has faith" (Rom 10:4 NEB). Laws, rules or regulations are not in themselves bad; they might serve to point the way to how God relates. Being imperfect, human beings can never fulfill the law. They must recognize that Christ is the end of the law in the sense that he is its perfect fulfillment. Due to Christ's perfection and righteousness, we can be counted as righteous. Righteousness and salvation are dependent on faith in Christ and not on keeping the law. However, something of God's ideal (the law) can be known when grace is applied to relationships even though no one can measure up to that ideal. In a community of grace, forgiveness will be offered when persons disappoint and fail each other.

The opposite of gracing is *shaming*. In a community of law where perfection is demanded, the person who disappoints and fails to live up to the standard will be *shamed*. In shame-based communities rules and regulations are rigidly set up to govern relationships. This kind of pressure for flawlessness adds guilt to the failure that is inevitable in such a situation. It is noteworthy that the less a relationship is based on trust and commitment, the more it needs legal definitions of what is expected in the relationship. Sociologically we would refer to such relationships as *formal,* as opposed to *informal* relationships that are more often based on personal commitment.

Although the covenant of grace rules out law as a basis for relationships, community members living in grace will accept law as patterns, order and responsibilities in relationships. In reality, much of our daily living has agreed-on rules for regularity and order. McLean's insights are helpful here:

> In the covenantal root metaphor, law and covenant belong together. The dyadic relationship necessarily involves creating specific forms, rules, and laws to guide community and personal relationships. The need for law, pattern, and form is mandatory, but the particular shape of law needs to be understood as relative to the actualization of dialogical-dialectical relationships, the creation of whole persons-in-community. The issue becomes which forms, which laws, which patterns are appropriate to the maintenance of humanity? (1984, p. 24)

The application of the concept of grace in relationships is a special challenge in societal structures based on impersonal but legally defined ways of relating. Grace means that order and regularity are present for the sake of the needs and enhancement of each person in the relationship, and not as a means of repressing and limiting the other.

At the personal level it is helpful to distinguish between shame and guilt. Guilt is the feeling that one has when one *does a wrong;* shame is the feeling that one *is a wrong.* Breaking the law results in the feeling of guilt, and if the law is just, this is as it should be. Shame, on the other hand, is based on the feeling that one is *not good enough,* that one is deficient at the core. Theologically there is a place for shame. It can be seen in the Genesis account of Adam and Eve, who felt shame—that they were not good enough—before God after they sought wisdom apart from God.

However, the type of shame that emerges in nongracing personal relationships is neurotic or toxic shame. Such shame can be seen in churches, families and parent-child relationships. While visiting friends my wife and I (Jack) were met at the door by five-year-old Jenny. Jenny led us to her bedroom where she excitedly showed us that she had learned to make her bed by herself. Upon viewing Jenny's bed her mother exclaimed, "But Jenny, there are some wrinkles in the cover." In spite of the age-appropriate task Jenny had accomplished in making her bed, Jenny's posture changed from one of self-confidence and self-esteem to one of shame. Following her mother's message she felt she was not good enough. Children who grow up in shame-based families can come to have shame-based personalities, lacking the ability to feel good about themselves, even when objective criteria would seem to demand it.

Empowering

Power in personal relationships is the ability to influence another person. Note the emphasis on the ability or potential to influence, and not the actual exercising of the ability. Power is based on the *resources* each person brings to the relationship, where a resource is something that the other values. Thus a resource can be a material possession such as money or valuable objects, or it can be a personal quality such as nurture, intelligence or humor. If these qualities are valued by the other then they can be "converted" into power—the ability to influence.

Perhaps due to the tendency for humans to act in self-centered ways, the social-science literature has focused on the use of power to control the other. In this regard, *least interest theory* (Waller, 1938) proposed that the person who shows the least interest in the relationship automatically assumed a "one up" position, or a position of power, because they are indicating that they do not value or need what the other has to give in the relationship. Inversely, the person who is desperate to keep the relationship going assumes the least powerful position. This is the line taken by much social-science research on how power is used in relationships—it is assumed that people will attempt to use their power to influence or control the behavior of the other. The person without power will try to gain it, while the one with power will try to maintain the more powerful position.

Empowerment is the opposite and far less common in relationships. In an empowering relationship one person uses his or her power *for* the other. This contrasts with *controlling*, which is the process of using power *over* the other. Erich Fromm pointed to parenting as an empowering process when he observed that the socialization of children is the process of getting them to want to do what they have to do. Here empowerment is the process whereby external control (the wishes of the more powerful) is transferred into internal control (the child actually wanting to do what the parent desires). We could charge that such a view of empowerment is selfishly motivation, but it is probably true that even in our most altruistic acts we fail to act selflessly.

In *Love and Will* (1969) Rollo May distinguished between five ways of using power in relationship. *Exploitation* influences by brute force, *manipulation* influences by devious sociopsychological means, *competition* influences through the possession and use of personal resources, *nutritive* power influences by providing socioemotional comfort and security (like parents with young children), and finally *integrative* power is the use of personal power for another's sake. While nutritive power is done with the right motive, integrative power is clearly what we refer to as empowering. Jesus and Gandhi are examples Rollo May points to as persons who used integrative power.

The supreme biblical model for empowering can be see in the humanity of Jesus Christ, who was totally human as well as totally God. Empowerment is an integral part of what Jesus proclaimed in his central message, "I came that they might have life, and have it abundantly" (Jn 10:10). In his teaching and by example Jesus was an empowerer of others. In Mark 10 we are told that James and John requested that when he ruled in glory they be permitted to sit on his right and left sides. We can almost see the gleam in their eyes as they anticipated the power they would have. Note Jesus' response:

> You know that among the Gentiles those whom they recognize as their rulers lord it over them, and their great ones are tyrants over them. But it is not so among you; but whoever wishes to become great among you must be your servant, and whoever wishes to be first among you must be slave of all. For the Son of Man came not to be served, but to serve. (Mk 10:42-45).

By rejecting the use of power to control others, Jesus redefined power by affirming that it is to be used to serve others—to lift up the fallen, to forgive those who fail, to encourage responsibility and maturity in the dependent and to build up the weak.

Jesus sought to empower his disciples in anticipation for his ascension, and he encouraged them by promising that the Holy Spirit would come to comfort them and help accomplish their ministry (Jn 16). Just before his ascension Jesus assured his disciples that they "will receive power when the Holy Spirit has come upon you" (Acts 1:8). Following Jesus' ascension his disciples sought to implement an empowering model of community. Acts 2:44-45 says, "All who believed were together and had all things in common; they would sell their possessions and goods and distribute the proceeds to all, as any had need." The followers of Jesus took his message of servanthood seriously by mutually giving up the very resources conventional power is based on.

Empowering others does not mean yielding to the wishes of another person or giving up your own power to someone else. Rather, empowerment is the active, intentional process of enabling another person to acquire power. The person who is empowered has gained power because of the encouraging behavior of the other. The empowering process facilitates the increase of power in the other. As such, empowerment is the process of helping others recognize their own strengths and potentials, and guiding them in the development of these qualities. It may require that the empowerer be willing to step back and allow the empowered to learn by doing. Empowering does not involve controlling or enforcing a certain way of doing and being. Rather it is a reciprocal process in which empowerment takes place between people in mutually enhancing ways. The empowerer must respect the uniqueness of those being empowered and see strength in unique ways of being competent.

The apostle John points to empowerment when he states, "But to all who received him, who believed in his name, he gave power to become children of God, who were born, not of blood or of the will of the flesh or of the will of man, but of God" (Jn 1:12-13). This text is insightfully exegeted by Ray Anderson (1985) when he notes that power "of blood" is power in the natural order and "the will of the flesh" refers to tradition, duty, honor, obedience and all that is a part of conventional power. It is clear then that in this passage power is given by God and not by either physical or conventional means. The power given by Jesus is power of a personal order—power mediated to the powerless. God gives to sinful and powerless human beings the ability to become children of God. This is the supreme example of human empowering. By relating to human beings as a servant and rejecting the use of power to control others Jesus radically redefined power.

The teaching and behavior of Jesus toward the poor and the powerless also exemplify an empowering model. In the patriarchal culture of biblical times Jesus showed this by honoring children and others who occupied a marginal status in the social structure (Francis, 1996). Paul says that others will know we are Christians by our love. The mark of Jesus Christ that we need to emulate the most is his empowering of others, for this is love in action. The view of authority within the church could be revolutionized if the Christian community began to practice empowering others. Largely because the secular view of power has been widely accepted within the church, authority issues hinder the Christian community from functioning as the body of Christ. Empowerment is the active side of unconditional love and grace. It is the act of using our gifts and strengths to build up the other person. The opposite of empowerment can be seen in the act of using power to control the other. The body analogy for the interdependent workings of the church makes no sense apart from an empowering model. The body functions as a complete whole only to the extent that each part is there for the good of the whole, which means each will contribute to the good of the other. When the good of the other has no priority, empowering ceases to be. The writer of 1 Corinthians 12 takes great pains to stress that the all parts of the body are of equal importance, for if one part suffers then all parts suffer.

The biblical ideal is for reciprocal empowering. I (Jack) took great pride in teaching my son Joel to play tennis. I remember when he improved to the point where he was able to give my game a challenge. By age sixteen he got to the point that he began beating me, but I still won most of the time, and that felt good. By age seventeen he had emerged as one of the best tennis players on his high school tennis team. I found myself in danger of being overtaken by my son, and I was not so sure I liked this. In one of our matches I found myself struggling to return Joel's powerful serve and found myself getting angry. I paused, reflected on the fact that I teach empowerment, looked at the expert player my son had become and said to myself, "Jack, you are a fantastic tennis coach!" The reframing allowed me to actually glory in what my son had become as a tennis player—this is empowerment in action.

My grown son and I still play tennis from time to time. It is no match at all, and Joel tries to disguise the fact that he takes it easy on me. The last time we played, Joel commented on something he had noticed in my form. He said, "Dad, on your forehand I've noticed that you are bending your elbow. You will get more power on the ball if you keep your elbow straight." What goes around comes around. My own son, whom I had taught to play tennis, was empowering me! This is God's ideal for relationship—that the stronger, more knowledgeable or more skilled person in a relationship will use his or her resources for the other so that mutual empowerment might be a reality.

Insecurity causes us to jealously guard against using personal power for the other. Such a view is based on the false notion that power is a limited commodity. This secular view of power drives us to accumulate more and more power while reducing the power of others. The good news for Christians, says Scott Bartchy, is that "according to Scripture, especially the New Testament, the power of God is available to human beings in unlimited amounts!" (1984, p. 13). Such passages as Ephesians 4:11-13 and Galatians 5:22-23 assure that the fruit of the Spirit—love, joy, peace, patience, kindness, goodness, fidelity, gentleness and self-control—are available to all Christians in unlimited supply. The very character of God is available in unlimited supply because God's resources are inexhaustible!

Intimacy: To Know and Be Known

Christianity is unique in its teaching that God has broken into human history to be personally related to us. God wants to know us and to be known by us. Adam and Eve, for instance, stood completely open and transparent before God. In their perfect creatureliness, Adam and Eve were naked and felt no shame (Gen 2:25) before each other and God. Thus Adam and Eve felt an intimacy that allowed them to be themselves without any pretense. They had no need to play deceptive games. Ray Anderson observes that this is "the power of subjectivity expressed as cohumanity. The vulnerability is in the defenselessness each has in the presence of the other" (1982, p. 64).

Throughout the Bible we are encouraged to share our deepest thoughts and feelings through prayer. In Romans 8:26-27 we are told that the Holy Spirit intercedes for us and that God understands our deep sighs or unuttered groanings. Jesus modeled the type of intimacy desirable in personal relationships. At the end of Jesus' earthly ministry he asked Peter three times, "Do you love me?" (Jn 21). Given that Peter had earlier denied Jesus three times, it may very well be that Jesus was giving Peter the opportunity to reaffirm his love to Christ three times. We can imagine the guilt and shame felt by Peter after he had assured Jesus that he would not forsake him. Peter's self was in no condition to resume a reciprocal relationship with Jesus.

Jesus knew this and allowed for the needed healing to take place both within Peter and in their relationship. When our personal relationships become strained due to failure, disappointment and sometimes even betrayal, a similar healing is needed both in our own self and in our relationships. We firmly believe that the two types of healing—inner and relational—go together. We are healed through our relationships, and our relationships are healed as we confess our mutual failings and ask for forgiveness.

Instead of moving toward healing broken relationships, there is a human tendency to deny, withdraw and even hide ourselves. Shame is born out of the fear of being known intimately. When shame is present, even members of the body of Christ put on masks and begin to play deceptive roles before each other. By contrast, in the Genesis description of the pre-Fall human relationships, we find an emphasis on intimacy—on the knowing of the other. Adam and Eve's lack of shame at being naked must be understood at a deeper level than mere physical nakedness. In their created state Adam and Eve were free to be open, honest and who they were before the other. They did not seek to hide by putting on a mask or playing a role; they were free to be whom they were. Following the break in their relationship with God, Adam and Eve felt naked, exposed, shamed, and as a result they tried to hide from God.

When personal relationships are based on mutual covenanting lived out in an atmosphere of mutual grace and mutual empowering, then each person in the relationship is drawn to freely communicate and express him- or herself to the other. The relationship is one of intimate knowing and being known. A concerted effort is made to listen, understand and want what is best for the other. Not only are differences accepted but uniqueness is valued and respected in a way that confirms the other person.

This is how we are to be submissive and loving in relationships. To have any union or partnership or interdependence with another, we must always be willing to give up some of our own needs and desires. It is what it means to be a servant, to empty oneself as Jesus did when he took the form of a servant. When members of the body of Christ come to each other with this kind of attitude and perspective, they will find a common ground of joy, satisfaction and mutual benefit.

For Christian brothers and sisters to communicate feelings freely and openly with each other is contingent on trust and commitment. Then we are not afraid to be intimate with one another. John gives us insight into this in 1 John 4:16, 18: "God is love. . . . There is no fear in love. But perfect love

casts out fear." God expresses perfect love, and we can respond in love because God loved us first (1 Jn 4:19). This leads us back to the unconditional
covenant love that is the cornerstone for honest sharing without the threat
of rejection. As Christians offer their love unconditionally to each other, the
security that is established will lead to deeper levels of intimacy.

Forgiving and being forgiven is an important part of renewal. There is a
need to confess as well as to receive confession. This is a two-way street
that will clear out the unfinished issues between members of the body of
Christ. Being willing to admit mistakes and admit being offended by another
puts a person in a position of vulnerability. In intimacy, however, Christians
need not be ashamed to admit failure and ask for forgiveness and reconciliation. It is desirable that family members verbally communicate feelings of
love and affection toward one another as well as ask forgiveness of and forgive each other. This brings relationships to full maturity.

The previous chapter focused on reciprocating relationships between the
self and divine other. In reality, the model for relationships with human others is the biblical model of God actively seeking to relate to human beings.
This reciprocating relationship is consistently reinforced throughout Scripture. It is most precisely summed up in the words of John: "We love him
because he first loved us" (1 Jn 4:19).

While there are similarities between human relationships and the human-
divine relationship, we do not mean to blur the important difference. The
later is a relationship between the perfect Creator and a fallen created being.
We must not live in the illusion that we can love God unconditionally as he
loves us. When we feel anger toward God and are tempted to blame him,
we must not hold to the illusion that he needs forgiveness for his behavior.
God does not need us to empower him. God wants an intimate relationship
with us, but we must not hold to the illusion that we are able to completely
reciprocate God's intimacy.

The Bible uses metaphors that might help us understand the relationship
between the human self and the divine other. In their book *The Sacred Romance* Brent Curtis and John Eldredge (1997) identify six biblical metaphors
that they believe capture the Christian's relationship to God: Potter-clay, Mas-
ter-servant, Parent-child, Friend-friend and Beloved-beloved. Curtis and Eldredge order these metaphors from the least intimate (Potter-clay) to the
most intimate (Beloved-beloved). These six metaphors are not systematic images or pictures describing the nature of God. Instead they picture the *nature*

of human beings in relationship to God. Each metaphor reveals a different facet of the believer's relationship to God, and as such should be a deterrent against any attempt to oversimplify the complexity of the relationship.

Sin: Missing the Mark in Reciprocal Relationships

Not all relationships will reflect the biblical ideal we have described in this chapter. From a theological perspective sin can be defined as a failure to be in right relationship.

Sin is usually not part of the vocabulary of human development theories. In his book *The Crisis in Psychiatry and Religion* the well-respected psychologist O. Hobart Mowrer (1961) surprised the psychological community by suggesting that sin may be more than psychological distress; it may be an actual offense against God that requires forgiveness and grace. While the thrust of this chapter has been to portray a biblical view of right relationships, in so doing it also provided a relational perspective on sin—conditional acceptance, shaming, controlling and isolating behavior. These miss the mark in reciprocating relationships.

In his book *Reforming Theological Anthropology* L. Leron Shults states, "To claim today that sin really has to do with our essence as persons requires that we speak of personhood in relational and not merely substantial terms. Responsibility, agency, and sinning inherently have to do with community and sociality" (2003, p. 214). Ray Anderson also defines sin in a relational context: it is "defiance of God's gracious relation to those who bear his image . . . [resulting] . . . in separating persons from the gracious life of God" (1990, p. 234). Shults concurs that the "heart of the doctrine of original sin . . . is that each and every person is bound by relations to self, others, and God that inhibit the goodness of loving fellowship" (2003, p. 209).

Shults firmly ties the issue of sin to the broader question of the dynamics of human agency:

> What we call "sinning" has to do with the inability of human activity to establish or maintain a relation to the good it seeks. We desire objects that we hope will bring happiness, and we act in order to secure them. But our acting is overshadowed by an ambiguous relation to goodness, an ambiguity that is intensified as we come to recognize over time that our acting will never be able to secure our relation to those objects that we love. . . . When we act in ways that fall short of the glorious goodness of God (Rom. 3:23), we call this sinning. Persons are formed through their historical, dynamic grasping for good-

ness, and are miserable because of their separation from it. Guilt emerges in relation to this failure of our agency, as we act in ways that depend on our own power to love and secure what we perceived as good. If sinning is understood primarily as that which blocks our relation to the source of goodness, then salvation from sin is not merely pardoning, but also reconciliation in relation to the good. (2003, pp. 214-15)

Shults concludes that a "theology of human acting explores the nature of the ultimate source that secures this relation, and tries to render intelligible the failure of finite human agents to secure the love and good they seek" (p. 215). In this chapter we proposed that the elements that contribute to a well formed and developed reciprocating self are unconditional love, gracing, empowerment and intimacy. While these elements point to the factors that contribute to a secure reciprocating self, the ultimate answer to human sin is found only in God's divine intervention. Only God can offer a forgiveness that will bring about "the renewal of a positive relation between people and God. Forgiveness means restored relation, not merely granting an exception to a moral law. . . . Forgiveness restores an authentic moral history of being in relation" (Anderson, 1990, p. 234). As Shults affirms, this divine intervention can affect human agency:

> As Christians share in the suffering of Jesus Christ, their human agency is freed to participate in the infinitely vulnerable reconciling love of God. Here too in the doctrine of sin we are confronted with an opportunity to return to the relational roots of the biblical tradition and reflect on human acting in light of the Trinitarian God. For Christians, ethical anxiety is alleviated by the atonement effected in the history of Jesus Christ. The whole experience of Christian salvation is structured by the dynamics of the Trinity: "If the spirit of him who raised Jesus from the dead dwells in you, he who raised Christ from the dead will give life to your mortal bodies also through his Spirit that dwells in you" (Rom. 8:11). (2003, pp. 215-16)

Developmental theories share a naturalistic perspective in viewing human behavior as part of the natural order. Thus sin is not a part of their vocabulary. One of the basic assumptions of naturalism is that the principles governing the human species are no different from those governing other species. Utilizing a biblically based teleology to understand human development invites a corresponding consideration of what it means to fall short or miss the mark in human development. In our relationally based model, sin is the relational condition of falling short of being a reciprocating self.

The Reciprocating Self
and Developmental Theory

IN CHAPTER ONE WE INDICATED THAT developmental theories share in common a naturalist assumption. Historically these theories have shaped the way psychologists understand human nature and human development. In spite of teleological limitations, each theory may provide essential insights and confirmation to our model of the reciprocating self. It is far beyond the scope of this book to provide a full understanding of the major development theories. We instead focus on each theory's capacity to contribute to our understanding of the development of the reciprocating self. Given our model, the developmental theories we find most useful are those that conceptualize humans beings as self-conscious agents who are not only acted upon but who are capable of being active agents in relationship, actively participating in the formation of their own environment.

Theoretical orientations that we find most helpful in understanding the development of the reciprocating self are the psychoanalytic (Freud), object relations (Winnicott), symbolic interaction (Mead), and social learning (Bandura) theories. Most of these theorists concentrate on childhood development, seeming to imply that human development ends with the advent of adulthood. This is certainly not the case, as we will see when we examine the life-span development theories of Erik Erikson and Daniel Levinson in part two of this book. Although moral, spiritual and religious development are important aspects of a developing self, these will be the exclusive focus of chapters twelve and thirteen.

Human development has too often been approached from a traditional mental health model that views development as a pathology or neurosis waiting to happen. In his 1998 presidential address to the American Psychological Association, Marty Seligman challenged psychologists to work more from the perspective of positive psychology. In line with the emergent emphasis on positive psychology, we emphasize a positive view of development, emphasizing and elaborating on strengths throughout the human lifespan. In this regard we find a balanced perspective in David Levinson's (1978, 1996) idea that *adolescing* (upward development) and *senescing* (downward development) are both an integral part of the human life cycle. Within a theological perspective, the residual effects of both creation and Fall on human development must be recognized, thus the simultaneous process of *adolescing* and *senescing*.

The Reciprocating Self in Developmental Theories

Most developmental theories consist of systematically organized knowledge that has been accumulated through empirical observation of children. A good theory is like a pair of glasses in that it allows one to focus more sharply on what is being observed. To illustrate this, suppose that representatives of the major theories of child development are viewing a child playing in the family living room. Although the observers will be exposed to the same behavior, they will not *see* it through the same set of eyeglasses. Each observer will perceive the child's activity in accordance with a set of predetermined assumptions about human behavior. For example, the cognitive-development theorist will be especially aware of the particular stage to which the child has developed; the Freudian theorist will look for unconscious motivations in overt behavior; the symbolic interactionist will concentrate on the child's self-concept; and the proponent of social-learning theory will pay special attention to what the child has learned from observing others. Although it is not a conscious process, all of our theorists actually engage in selective perception, viewing the child's actions in accordance with their own general conceptualization of human behavior. We will present the developmental theories in the approximate order they emerged.

Psychoanalytic Theory

Sigmund Freud, the father of psychoanalysis, presented a theory of child development that concentrates on the interplay between biological instincts and parental influence. Although Freud did not use the concept of the self in his tripart depiction of the personality (Freud, 1949), consisting of the id, ego and superego, the ego corresponds to the meaning we give to the self. How similar is Freud's ego to the reciprocating self?

Although Freud's ego can be equated to the self, it is probably more fruitful to ask if Freud's model of the mind allows for the conceptual emergence of the reciprocating self. Freud gives a dynamic model of the mind in which the id is the source of energy present already at the birth of a child, whereas the ego and superego develop as the child is socialized. For Freud there is a high degree of conflict in the mind, with the id and the superego battling each other for control of the ego. The id is amoral, impulsive, ruled by the unconscious and irrational, and demands immediate gratification. The superego, which consists of internalized parental and societal restrictions, is moralistic, seeking to deny the irrational impulses of the id. The superego operates as a type of moral police officer as it attempts to contain the id and control the ego. When the superego gets its way, it rewards the ego by building up self-esteem, but it punishes the ego with a guilty conscience when it does not get its way.

Although a bit of a strain, it is possible to conceptualize the emergence of the reciprocating self within Freudian theory. To begin with, Freud gives a great deal of credence to biological roots in the formation of the self. This is no problem if the self is equated with Freud's ego. However, the self is much broader than mere ego, and an argument can be made for equating the self with the mind in Freud's theory. If this is done we might even argue that by taking into account the self-centered instinctive urges in the id, Freud's model is consistent with a biblical description of the fallen nature of humankind.

In stressing the importance of unconscious and irrational aspects of human motivation, Freud differs from self theories. His fundamental theory of the mind has been referred to as the iceberg theory because it holds that the major part of the mind lies below the surface; only the tip rises to the level of consciousness. The theory is a bit weak in its focus on the importance of extraparental relationships in the formation of the person.

Perhaps the greatest limitation in psychoanalytic theory is the view that human development does not significantly change beyond the early formative years. Freud believed that the first six years of life are vitally important for developing the three parts of the mind and determining how they will interrelate to form personality. According to Freud, during the first six years of life a child is moving through three developmental stages, within each of which a different part of the body serves as the focus of gratification.

First comes the *oral stage*. In the first twelve to eighteen months pain and pleasure are centered in the oral zone. Pleasure is experienced when the infant receives food from a loving mother or sucks on a thumb or some other object. Pain is experienced when the infant is deprived of such oral gratification. Children who are weaned too abruptly or are inadequately nurtured during the oral stage may grow up to be oral-type personalities: greedy materialists, thumb suckers, smokers, pencil biters, excessive babblers and so on. Freud would say that each of these individuals has discovered a substitute form of oral gratification.

Toilet training begins the *anal stage,* at which time control over excretion becomes an important issue between children and parents. Overly rigid toilet-training methods that involve unrealistically high expectations can contribute to the child's developing an anal-type personality: meticulous, punctual, or tied down by petty self-restraints. Or the child may react by becoming the very opposite: messy, disorderly and lacking in self-control.

After toilet training, children enter the *genital stage,* at which time attraction to the parent of the opposite sex and bonding with the parent of the same sex are major developmental issues. Freud explained that boys desire an exclusive relationship with their mother—independent of their father—to the extent that boys subconsciously want to eliminate their fathers (the Oedipus complex), while girls desire an exclusive relationship with their father—independent of their mother (the Electra complex). In a healthy family the love between the mother and father will be unwavering, and the child will eventually conclude that the parent of the same sex cannot be defeated in the competition for the exclusive affection of the parent of the opposite sex. The psychological solution is for the child to seek to be like (identify with) the parent of the same sex and suppress the attraction for the parent of the opposite sex. In a dysfunctional home the weak bond between the mother and father may result in failure to identify with the parent of the same sex.

In traditional psychoanalytic theory the genital stage is the period in which sexual identity is formed. Adult problems that can be tied to unsuccessful resolution of this stage include preoccupation with proving one's masculinity or femininity, confusion in sexual identity, hesitancy to marry and sexual dysfunction.

Between the ages of six and thirteen, children go through the latency stage, characterized by a strong identification with members of their same sex. This is the age of the girls "against" the boys. If healthy conditions have prevailed during the first six years of life, gender identity and self-esteem will firmly develop during the latency stage. But if childhood conditions were less than ideal, there may well be difficulty in relating to others, increasing self-doubt and lack of self-esteem. By puberty the basic personality has been formed; change in personality thereafter are seen as being minimal.

Although psychoanalytic theory is a dynamic-process model, in actuality it gives minimal insight into the formation of the self, which is based on the interplay of the child and its parents. It offers a less than satisfying account of the developing self in relationship with others and, as important, how the self can and does change as it interacts with others. It is also limited in that it only gives explanations of child development. We now turn to the discussion of object relations, which developed out of psychodynamic theory.

Object Relations Theory

While object relations theory is rooted in psychoanalytic theory, it delivers a bit more understanding on *self* development. We find within object relations theory a useful understanding of the development of the reciprocating self. Object relations theories emphasize the development of the self or personality within the context of an infant-caregiver relationship. These theories contend that personality is shaped and formed by the early interactions of an infant (to young child) and his or her most intimate caregiver, usually the mother. Although object-relations theories acknowledge the significance of the phylogenic structure, the biologically determined shape of the unconscious, these theories also convey the significant contributions of the environment, in particular the caregiver.

Object relations theory developed out of Freudian and psychodynamic theory. The most notable change involved a move from *biological* to *interpersonal determinism* and a corresponding change from a *drive* to a *relational* structural model. Melanie Klein is the theorist most noted for facilitating this change. In Klein's theory physical drives are replaced by *psychological and relational drives,* where the developmental focus is on relationships rather than on erogenous zones (e.g., oral, anal, genital) or body parts. The pleasure instinct (libido) was replaced by *love* and the death instinct (thanatos) by *aggression* or *hate.*

The core element in Klein's theory consists of the internalization by the child of its relationship with its mother. In this process a representation of the mother becomes the internalized as an *internal object*. Once internalized the internal object is capable of bringing to the child comfort or pain. According to Klein the internal object is a synthesis of all relational experiences with the significant caregiver as he or she interacts with the child's *phantasy*. Phantasy is an important part of the human unconscious. For Klein, we are all born with an unconscious that comes "loaded" with phantasies, much like a computer comes loaded with software. These phantasies are a part of our unconscious and shape the way we experience relationships. The phantasies are filled with emotions like hate, love, greed, fear and anxiety. According to Klein much of this phantasy is negative. Consequently, no matter how well the caregiver interacts with the infant, the infant most likely will internalize an object with some negativity. Since there is never a one-to-one correspondence between the mother and the mother as internalized, the internal object is a product of *phantasy* plus the *external object* (mother/caretaker).

Most important to the future development of the infant, the internalized object then becomes an organizing principle for future interactions. Children who internalize a good or safe object will feel secure and anticipate that other external objects (other individuals) will form positive relationships. If children internalize an anxious or hateful object, they will anticipate having negative experiences with other relationships.

Klein's work is important because it makes a significant shift from the biological determinism of Freud's psychoanalytic theory to an interpersonal emphasis. From our perspective in the twenty-first century, her theory is still strongly biologically determined, because of the significant role of the phantasy in shaping the internal object. However given the time of her writing, her work brought about a major paradigmatic shift from biological determinism to introducing the significance of interpersonal interaction. That being said, it is important to note that many since Klein have challenged her writing and negated the significance of phantasy. Today it is generally recognized that caregivers have more influence than she gave them credit for.

One such psychologist was Donald Winnicott. Winnicott's work on personality development strongly emphasized the role of the mother (see Grolnick, 1990). In fact he wrote the statement "There is no such thing as a baby, just a nursing couple." In Winnicott's version of object relations theory the mother or caregiver is almost solely responsible for affecting the development of the self. She does so by creating a "holding environment," which refers to a physical and psychological space created by the mother, where the baby experiences a sense of continuity. In the holding environment the infant has a sense of "going on being," for an individual must have a sense of being before doing. It is within this holding environment that the infant has a sense of self and other. Through this environment the infant internalizes the mother as an internal object that gives the infant a sense of security and safety. The holding environment does not have to be perfect, it just needs to be "good enough," reflecting Winnicott's emphasis of the "good enough mother." According to Winnicott the mother does not need to be perfect in order for the infant to develop healthily—just good enough.

The good enough mother is *affectively attuned* to the infant's needs, meaning she is aware of the baby's physical and emotional needs. Although she is affectively attuned, she does not impinge (mothering as smothering) on the child. The good enough mother is also able to find a balance between empathetic gratification of the infant's needs and her own needs. A good enough mother is also effective in *mirroring* the child's behavior and feelings. Such affective attunement can be seen when a mother mimics rhythms and intonations of the child. Effective mirroring contributes to an authentication and validation of a child's sense of self. A good enough mother demonstrates her connection with the child's world through appropriate reactions, neither ignoring nor overwhelming the child. Through mirroring the infant simultaneously experiences self and other and is able to internalize the sense of other as a object.

An adequate holding environment will also include *transitional space*—psychological space within which the child can experiment with fantasy and reality. Such psychological space is needed in order for the baby to react, respond and internalize the good object. Transitional space is the place creativity comes from. As the child develops it also gains the capacity to be alone. This takes place as the self emerges through the process of internalizing the presence of an emotionally attuned but nondemanding other. The capacity to be alone is retarded by both an emotionally absent and an overdemanding other. The capacity to be alone occurs through times of transitional space when the infant can be present to itself. Only in being alone in the company of a significant other can an infant discover his or her own personal life. A *transitional object* is a physical object that helps internalize real external objects. For example, a toddler might find comfort in a special blanket or a stuffed animal. This transitional object acts as a symbol of the caregiver and helps young children internalize a sense of the real external object in the caregiver's absence.

In summary, a good holding environment means a present, mirroring, nonimpinging mother, a transitional space and a fostering of the ability to be alone. Transitional space is created by the nondemanding good enough mother in a holding environment where she is nonimpinging and mirrors the child.

By providing a descriptive understanding of the emergence of the true as opposed to the false self, object relations theory contributes to our understanding of the reciprocating self. The true self is the authentic, spontaneous self, aware and comfortable with his or her uniqueness. As expressed through an infant it entails its own rhythmic and tonal variation of movement and sound. Transitional space allows for the expression of the true self. The false self results from a lack of transitional space. Children with a false self often abandon their own wishes, instead molding their self to external expectations. While all children must yield in a certain degree to external expectations, in its extreme form the result is a fragmented self characterized by the state of not knowing oneself and not being able to be in mutually reciprocating relationships. The major contributors to the false self can be seen in the extremes—*absent* or *impinging* parents.

Figure 4.1 presents a continuum representing the range in the boundaries of the reciprocating self. At the extreme left is the *fortress self* around which are reinforced "concrete" boundaries. The fortress self is highly defended, seeking to be in complete control of all life circumstances. The fortress self results from chronic failure on the parts of parents to meet the child's needs. The fortress self is closed off to others but at the same time needy and wanting others' help and affection. A less extreme version is the *protected self,* who appears to be completely self-sufficient. The appearance can come across as being "better than" or as being a good or perfect person. Although not chronic, the protected self nevertheless has experienced consistently inadequate fulfillment of their needs from parents. The protected self is unaware of others, seeking to cover up their own neediness in relationships.

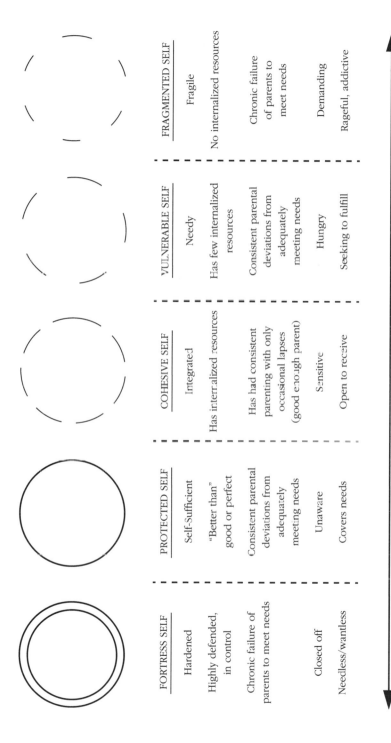

Figure 4.1. Boundaries of the reciprocating self. A modification of a figure developed by Walter Becker.

The *cohesive self* represents the ideal reciprocating self whose personal boundaries are sufficiently protective yet permeable to the influence of others. The cohesive self is an integrated self that has internalized resources sufficient to meet the child's own psychological needs. The cohesive self has had consistent parenting with only occasional lapses—it is a product of the good enough parent. The cohesive self is sensitive to the emotional state and needs of others, open to both receiving and giving nurture in a relationship.

The *vulnerable self* has weak personal boundaries, making this person vulnerable to hurt and harm that may be inflected by others. The vulnerable self is needy because it has few internalized resources to meet its own needs. As with the protected self, the vulnerable self has experienced consistent parental deviations from adequately meeting his or her needs. However, contrary to the withdrawing tendencies of the protected self, the vulnerable self displays a transparent hunger for what others can give. The vulnerable self actively seeks fulfillment from others.

The *fragmented self* is an extreme version of a person with weak personal boundaries. This person is truly fragile with no internalized resources. Like the fortress self, the fragmented self has experienced chronic failure of parents to meet that individual's needs. The external appearance of the fragmented self is one of desperation that can come across as being demanding and even rageful or addictive.

Social Learning Theory

Reflecting a neopositivistic tradition, classic learning/behavioral theorists have argued that any science of human development must purge itself of such mentalistic concepts as the self. However, the father of social learning theory, Albert Bandura, has increasingly brought the self back into learning theory.

Social learning theory is a theoretical offspring of classical conditioning, which is well illustrated by Ivan Pavlov's celebrated stimulus-response experiment. By ringing a bell just before giving food, Pavlov conditioned a dog to salivate when merely hearing the bell. This simple experiment contains the major elements of classical conditioning: the food is the unconditioned stimulus; salivation at the sight of the food is the unconditioned response; the bell is the conditioned stimulus; and salivation at hearing the bell is the conditioned response.

By the mid-twentieth century behaviorism came to be the dominant paradigm in psychology. During the latter half of the twentieth century, behav-

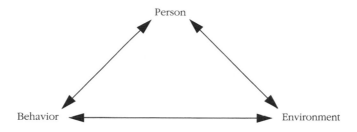

Figure 4.2. Reciprocal determinism

iorism was shaped by the creative research and writing of B. F. Skinner. Skinner (1953) developed what is known as operant conditioning, which is a modification of classical conditioning. Rather than using a stimulus to bring about a desired response, Skinner's model emphasizes reinforcement, that is, a system of rewards for desired behavior and punishment for unacceptable actions. The basic principle here is that behavior is shaped and maintained by its consequences. Operant conditioning has proven useful in bringing about changes in behavior, especially as applied to correcting more basic behavioral problems such as bed-wetting or undesirable habits.

The view of the self within social learning theory can be found most fully within three of Bandura's publications, *Behavior Theory and the Models Man* (1974), *Social Learning Theory* (1977), and *The Self System in Reciprocal Determinism* (1978). Since these publications Bandura has continued to affirm the place of the reciprocal self in social learning theory through his publications.

The initial difficulty in assessing Bandura's view of the self is that he does not specifically define it. That this is so may be the first clue to his distinctive usage of the term. Bandura might feel uncomfortable in conceptualizing the self as a separate entity; to do so might be interpreted as conceiving of the self as a psychic agent that controls action. Instead, Bandura explains that the "self system within the framework of social learning theory comprises cognitive structures and subfunctions for perceiving, evaluation, and regulating behavior" (1978, p. 344).

The "self system" consists of the "reciprocal determinism" in the triadic interaction between *behavior* (B), the *person* (P) as the cognitive and other internal events that can affect perceptions and actions, and the external *environment* (E) (see fig. 4.2). The important point for us to gain from

Bandura's social learning theory is to realize that he has divorced himself from the unidirectional environmental determinism of traditional behaviorism and has adopted a "reciprocal determinism," which sounds most consistent with our model of the reciprocating self.

Bandura's reciprocal determinism allows him to write:

> In their transactions with the environment, people are not simply reactors to external stimulation. The extraordinary capacity of humans to use symbols enables them to engage in reflective thought, to create, and to plan foresightful courses of action in thought rather than having to perform possible options and suffer the consequences of thoughtless action. By altering their immediate environment, by creating cognitive self-inducements, and by arranging conditional incentives for themselves, people can exercise some influences over their own behavior. An act therefore includes among its determinates self-produced influences. (1978, p. 345)

In Bandura's model, learning by observation rather than through direct reinforcement is the norm. Children learn how to behave by observing the consequences of the behavior of other persons. For example, learning not to hit other children on the playground comes primarily by observing that children who do hit others experience some negative consequences, such as getting hurt him- or herself, or being reprimanded.

Social learning theory also emphasizes that children learn from the *modeling* of people who are important in their lives. Parents and other significant others are role models, influencing children by their actions. Comparison of direct learning (reinforcement) and indirect learning (observation and imitation of modeled behavior) reveals that the latter is more effective. Social learning theory advises that resourceful caretakers will model the behaviors they would like children to implement.

In social learning theory the stimulus of change is not found exclusively in the environment, as in behaviorism and classical learning theory. The idea that learning comes through the child's observation and interpretation of behavior implies a self-consciousness and self-determination within the child. Change then can be activated both by environmental stimuli and by the child. Clearly, the self is an integral part of a social learning theory of development.

Symbolic Interaction Theory

Although predating Bandura by some forty years, the father of symbolic interaction, George Herbert Mead, anticipated much that has come to be accepted within social learning theory (*Mind, Self, and Society,* 1934). Mead used the concept of self primarily to refer to a person as an object of one's own activity. A person can act toward anything that is conceptualized as an object; therefore, if conceptualized as an object, one's own self can be acted on. In fact, one way of defining the self in symbolic interaction terms is to view it as the sum total of self concepts that an individual has. Hence, the self consists of the individual's attitudes or plans of action toward his or her own mind and body, which are viewed as objects. As suggested by one interpreter of Mead, the self consists of all the answers an individual might give to the question "Who am I?" (Kuhn, 1954).

Symbolic interaction, more than any other developmental theory, provides a rich understanding of the development of the reciprocating self. In this regard, Stanley Grenz states in his book *The Social God and the Relational Self* that "the social self in social psychology, launched by William James and advanced by George Herbert Mead . . . opened the way to a *perichoretic* understanding of the self-in-relationship" (2001, p. 19). Mead believed that the self only develops in a context of interaction with other human beings. The verification of this can be seen in the documented instances of feral children—cases of extreme child neglect that results in the child failing to develop either speech or social awareness. Some symbolic-interaction theorists go as far as to suggest that infants are not born human but become human through social interaction. As the name of the theory implies it is the symbolic interaction with caretakers that enables the infant to become human in a social sense.

Of all living creatures, human beings are unique because of the vast amount of culture (learned and shared knowledge) that they possess. The accumulation of culture is possible because humans have elaborate language systems. The more elaborate the language system, the greater the potential richness of a culture. The infant is born without language, without culture and without a sense of self or of others. All of these develop as caretakers communicate with the infant.

According to Mead the self develops through three stages (1934). First is the *preparatory stage,* within which the infant is prepared to use language. The purpose of language is to communicate, which can be thought of as occurring on two different levels. Most communication between animals involves gestures. Thus a beaver slapping its tail on the water, a rooster crowing or a dog barking can all be thought of as communication by means of a gesture. On the human level, gestures have meaning, but the meaning is not precise enough to build an elaborate language system. Thus communication in the preparatory stage is one of gestures. *A gesture can be defined as any part of a social act that is a sign for something else.* There is rich communication between parents and their infant through touches, smiles, frowns, laughter and utterances, and these are examples of communication at the gesture level.

The second level of communication is a communication of *significant* symbols. Mead thought that a language system can develop only when oral gestures become significant symbols. *A significant symbol is a gesture that has the same meaning for the creature giving it as for the creature receiving it.* Notice the difference in your emotional reaction between the two questions "Would you like to eat a juicy steak?" and "Would you like to eat a juicy snake?" Yet the difference between the two is a very slight change in sound. The words *steak* and *snake* are significant symbols because of the precise meaning (and resultant feeling) they carry from one person to another.

Parents begin to communicate with their children through gestures—a smile, a soft pat on the hand, a warning glance or the wave of the finger. Words accompany the gesture, and thus children learn the meaning of a word in the context of specific situations. In time a child comes to view the word *from the parent's perspective.* In this way the child first learns its specific meaning (in relationship to a forbidden act) and gradually its general meaning. For instance, once the word *no* is understood in relation to a behavior that has never been forbidden before, the child has learned its general meaning.

Children develop self-concept in much the same way; they see themselves from their parents' point of view. And not only do children see themselves as they think their parents see them, but in defining themselves they make use of their parents' very words. If parents tell their three-year-old daughter Sally that she is good or smart, little Sally will view herself as good or smart. If Greg's parents continually tell him that he is bad as well as stupid, he is likely to view himself as bad and stupid. Children develop their self-concept by *internalizing* their parents' attitudes toward them.

When children are able to communicate through significant symbols, they have entered the second stage of development, the *play stage.* The play stage usually begins between the ages of one and two, and continues for several years. During this period children begin to play (imagine themselves in) the roles of a number of other persons. They play at being Mommy, Daddy, big sister, a policeman or doctor. Putting themselves in the place of each of these individuals, they assume or take on that person's attitude toward them as well. For example, a three- or four-year-old child may move from one dining-room chair to the next and take on the personality (role) of the individual who usually sits in that chair. While sitting in Daddy's chair, little Kathy turns toward the chair she usually occupies and asks in a deep voice, "Did you have fun today, Kathy?" She actually takes on what she believes her father's attitudes are toward her. Having tired of this, Kathy proceeds to the chair where her older sister sits, points to her own chair and says, "You're a crybaby!" In each instance Kathy is adding to her self-concept by taking on what she imagines to be the other person's attitude toward her.

During the play stage, children are limited to taking on the role of only one person at a time. In the process they come to view themselves as they think others view them. Increasingly, there is a sharpening of the child's sense of self as distinguishable and separate from others.

At age three to five children reach the *game stage*. Before reaching this stage it is impossible for children to play certain games because they are unable to take on the role of more than one person at a time, which they can at the game stage. For instance, note the futility in trying to play hide-and-seek with a three-year-old. To play hide-and-seek the child must be able to take on the perspective of both the hider and the seeker. To play a game like basketball or baseball is even more complex—the child must be able to take on the perspective of each team member at the same time.

During the game stage children develop an idea of how they appear to others in general. Thus when a ballplayer strikes out with the bases loaded, she imagines the team's collective attitude toward her. As a child listens to the applause after he has recited a poem at the school program, he gains a general impression of the audience's evaluation of his performance. The cumulative effect of relationships with other individuals and groups is that children continue to take on new and changing attitudes toward themselves.

All of life can be thought of as the process of moving out of certain groups and into others. Of supreme importance to the development of the self is that we acquire a general view of ourself from each group to which we belong. Research indicates that the self is even effected by groups we aspire to be a part of. The "reference group" will effect the self of a graduate student who aspires to be a teacher. Personal identity is found in the groups that we use to define ourselves. Some aspects of the self structure (identity), such as being a male or female, are firm and stable. This particular aspect, which is anchored in gender categories, calls forth gender-appropriate behavior already in the first year of life. Other aspects are formed when children have new experiences. For example, on the first day at school, they begin to identify themselves as students. Through time individual identities are both reinforced and altered. In the end, human personality is the sum total of self-concepts that an individual has experienced and developed through a variety of relationships.

In symbolic interaction theory the self or self-concept reflects what we believe others think of us, and we behave accordingly. Our lives then take on the character of a self-fulfilling prophecy. This contention of symbolic interaction theory is supported elsewhere in child-development literature. For example, it has been found that children who fail in school have, from an early age, had low opinions of their learning abilities, whereas children who excel have developed positive views of themselves as learners.

This point leads us to labeling theory, an offspring of symbolic interaction. It has been discovered that juvenile delinquents are likely to have been told as children that they were no good, worthless and destructive. So labeled, they proceed to behave in accordance with the brands placed on them.

Cognitive Development Theory

Cognitive development theory is similar to symbolic interaction theory in allowing for a conceptualization of the self. Developed by Swiss psychologist Jean Piaget, cognitive development theory has become extremely influential in the United States (Flavell, 1963, 1985). Since Piaget's insights are central to understand infant and child development, his views are presented in chapter six and seven.

Piaget started with the assumption that far from being passive objects in the conditioning process, children *actively construct their own reality*. Once reality is constructed, life experiences are turned into action. Although the concept of the self is not as central in cognitive development as in social learning or symbolic-interaction theories, it provides a rich understanding of the increasing cognitive capacities of children and thus is capable of handling the development of the self.

In many ways cognitive-development and symbolic-interaction theories have many similarities, not the least being the importance they place on language acquisition. All that is needed is the suggestion that at a certain point of development (three to five years) children are capable of viewing themselves as an object. In viewing oneself as an object there are many schemas in which one can define oneself. The *plan of action* toward the self in symbolic interaction theory becomes a *scheme* for the self in cognitive development theory. The focus on relationships is less important in cognitive development than what it needs to be. Discussion of the self as a reflective objection in a maze of social relationships is lacking.

A Concluding Critique of Human Development Theories

The ultimate usefulness of each of the above theories can be measured by the extent to which they are utilized in part two as we describe the *process* of human development and the *context* in which it takes place. Before ending this chapter, however, it might be helpful to critique the human development theories in terms of two criteria central to a biblical model of the reciprocating self—*human agency* and the *relational context for the self.*

Human agency. The question of human agency is related to the issues of human responsibility, freedom and sin. In the last chapter we presented a relational perspective on sin, suggesting that sin is falling short of becoming a reciprocating self. We also quoted Shults (2003) as tying sin to the issue of human agency. In his view sin is the inability of humans to act in a way that will secure goodness and happiness. This is especially true in a relational sense as humans come to recognize that their actions are incapable of building secure relationships with objects of love. When humans act in ways that fall short of the goodness of God, they are sinning. Humans feel guilt when the power of their own agency is unable to secure the good. It is at this point that humans need divine intervention. Ray Anderson states that "as Christians share in the suffering of Jesus Christ, their human agency is freed to participate in the infinitely vulnerable reconciling love of God" (1990, p. 234). Human agency can be transformed as it participates in a righteousness that is not its own but is secured by divine love. We are becoming good as we are drawn into fellowship with the trinitarian God who is love. Then we are formed into the image of Jesus Christ (Shults, 2003, pp. 215-16).

Human agency is far too complex an issue to adequately deal with here. Suffice it to say that an integrated view of human agency must be informed by both theological and psychological wisdom. From a theological perspective human agency must always be understood in terms of persons who struggle to live as fallen and broken beings even though they are created in the image of God. From a psychological perspective human agency must always be understood in terms of persons whose choices are shaped and limited by both their organic base (physiological makeup) and sociocultural environment.

None of the theories adequately takes into account the biblical view that human beings are distinct from all other living creatures in that they bear the image of God (even though this image is marred by sin). The biblical view also holds that the human condition is marked by internal tension. As Paul states in Romans 7:21-24, "So I find it to be a law that when I want to do what is good, evil lies close at hand. For I delight in the law of God in my inmost self, but I see in my members another law at war with the law of my mind, making me captive to the law of sin that dwells in my members. Wretched man that I am! Who will rescue me from this body of death?"

Perhaps psychoanalytic theory comes the closest to providing a view of human existence as trapped in a state of internal tension between good and evil. Freud believed that a child is born with both constructive *(eros)* and destructive *(thanatos)* instincts. This tension becomes even more complex when, as a result of socialization, the superego develops within the child. The tension between the id and superego can be conceptualized as corresponding to the biblical view that sees internal tension as a natural human condition.

Symbolic interaction looks on the self as being caught in a state of internal conflict between the impulsive "I" and the conformist orientation of the "me." However, as explained within symbolic interaction, this tension results from inconsistent internalization of external behavioral norms. The I, as the core part of the self, was internalized in the past, while the me, the more exterior part of the self, is seen as internalized more recently. In the individual's subjective experience, the I is what one really wants to do, and the me is what one thinks others want one to do.

The Bible presents a view of human beings as choice-making creatures who are responsible for their own behavior. Alternatively, built within most development theories is the assumption that human behavior, including decision making, can be explained on the basis of environmental conditioning. Evolutionary psychology, as a noted exception, explains human behavior by means of genetic determinism. The environmentally oriented theories differ significantly, however, in the degree to which they conceptualize humans as choice-making creatures. Whether human beings are mechanistic or active organisms is still debated in the social-science literature.

Although there is great variation in contemporary psychoanalytic theory, Freud's original goal to establish a scientific psychology led him as well to a mechanistic model of human behavior. As Freud stated in *Project for a Scientific Psychology,* "The intention of this project is to furnish us with a psychology which shall be a natural science: Its aim, that is, is to represent psychical processes as quantitatively determined states of specifiable material particles and so to make them plain and void of contradictions" (1954).

Classic learning theory assumes that children are born as clean slates on which social conditioning imprints the cultural script. Within this mechanistic model human beings are viewed as operating on much the same principles as do machines. Thus the behaviorist John B. Watson boasted, "Give me the baby and my world to bring it up in and I'll make it crawl and walk; I'll make it climb and use its hands in constructing buildings of stone or wood, I'll make it a thief, a gunman, or a dope fiend. The possibility of shaping in any direction is almost endless" (quoted in Matson, 1966, p. 30).

Social learning theory, in contrast, leans toward the conviction that children are active organisms who continually act on and construct their own environments. Cognitive development and symbolic interaction theories likewise are based on the assumption that children *act on* and *react to* their environment.

As a whole the professional wisdom on cognitive theories of development has moved closer to what we believe is the biblical view of free will. It would be incorrect, however, to interpret contemporary theories on child development as emphasizing free will to the exclusion of determinism. Rather, the prevailing understanding seems to be that some children and adults are freer than others because their biological dispositions and environmental contexts have combined to provide then with *greater rather than lesser options.* In some homes children have limited cognitive stimulus and moral teachings and, consequently, experience less of the cognitive and moral development that would render them more resistant to the draw of immediate gratification and more able to make decisions based on more long-range consequences.

Contemporary theories generally view children as being unable to take any action apart from the options that are presented by their environment. While we can use the wisdom of child development theories to understand the formation of some of the parameters of human freedom, we must not allow this knowledge to deter us from a scriptural perspective that describes human beings as possessing existential freedom—the capacity to know right from wrong and the ability to choose one over the other. Having said this, we nevertheless feel compelled to acknowledge that due to physiological and environmental conditions, the range of choices among individuals may vary greatly. In *Sin: Radical Evil in Soul and Society* theologian Ted Peters surmises that "our social situation conscripts us into social sin frequently whether we know it or not, whether we will it or not" (1994, p. 287).

The issue of human freedom and responsible choice will be taken up in chapter six when we address the question of a child's age of accountability and continue through to chapter eleven where we raise the question of accountability and responsibility among the elderly affected by dementia and other debilitation conditions.

The relational context of the self. A core assumption in our model of the reciprocating self is that the self is formed and maintained within a network or community of relationships. Developmental theories are consonant with this assumption to the extent that they posit a self structure. This is most central in object relations, social learning and symbolic interaction theories. Whereas child development theories have only recently leaned toward the view that children are active organisms, they have been in continuous agreement that human input is necessary if children are to take on human characteristics. Human behavior begets human behavior. Deprived of human social environment, there is very little in the biological structure of children that would induce them to embrace norms, values or attitudes. On the other hand, when children are nested within human community, they generally take on the attitudes and behaviors of that community.

We learn from Genesis 2:18 that human beings were created by God to live in community: "The Lord God said, 'It is not good that the man should be alone; I will make him a helper as his partner." The need to live in community is a common theme woven throughout the Old and New Testament. Humans require an empowering community of grace that is based on covenant commitment. This foundation leads to an intimacy within which they can experience the secure emotional bonding they crave.

Children need to be nurtured within an intimate family community. The unilateral covenant that parents make with their children can eventually mature and lead to a bilateral covenant. We have argued that this is the biblical ideal. The child-development literature offers two additional suggestions. First, developing the capacity to enter into covenantal relationships is contingent on the child's experiencing unconditional parental love. Research on infants and young children who receive little attentive care confirms this. Sociologist Ira Reiss declares, "The evidence in this area . . . indicates that some sort of emotionally nurturing relationship in the first few years of life between the child and some other individual is vital in the child's development" (1980, p. 36).

Second, child-development theories suggest that human development is contingent on achieving language skills, self-identity and bonding capacity, in that order. The emotional nurturing, which Reiss asserts is imperative, can culminate in bonding ability only if the child is in the process of acquiring language skills and self-identity. Children, of course, need both emotional and cognitive interaction with their parents, a point that we made in the previous chapter.

Conclusion

This has not been a comprehensive overview of developmental theories. Rather, we have selected developmental theories in terms of their ability to inform our model of the reciprocating self. Several developmental theories are limited to more narrow pre-adult developmental age spans—John Bowlby and Mary Ainsworth's attachment theory, Stern's theory of infant self-development, Marcia's theory of ego identity development, and Arnett's theory of emerging adulthood—and thus will be introduced in the appropriate life-span development chapters. Other important developmental theories are relevant to understanding adult development—Erikson, Gould, Vaillant and Levinson—and thus will be introduced in chapters ten and eleven. Before presenting chapters dealing with specific life-span developmental stages, several more compressive theories need to be introduced. Chapter five summarizes three developmental theories that focus on the *socioculture context* within which human development takes place: Vygotsky's social context theory, Learner's developmental systems theory and Bronfenbrenner's ecological theory.

The Reciprocating Self
in Social Context

The child's evolving construction of reality can only be inferred

from patterns of activity as these are expressed in both verbal

and nonverbal behavior, particularly in the activities, roles,

and relations in which a person engages.

URIE BRONFENBRENNER

CHAPTERS TWO AND THREE PRESENTED A theologically integrated model of human development based on teleological assumptions. In chapter four we sketched a general outline of human development in terms of a reciprocating self. We suggested that the reciprocating self carries a telos of theological significance in our tendency for relationship as beings created in the image of God. This chapter serves as a bridge between the reciprocating-self model and the following section where we apply the model to life-span developmental stages. In the process we introduce several sociocultural models that might be used as an organizing framework for understanding life-span development. Each of the theories presented in this chapter share the common assumption that human development must be understood in the context of an individual's total bio-socio-cultural environment and the *relations* between each level.

The social sense of our selfhood is the focus of this chapter. We will attempt to create an integrative dialogue between the science of a reciprocating self and the theological issues that animate it. Specifically, we are interested in how the reciprocating self is "built," a process sometimes referred to as developmental *scaffolding*. First, we will explore the sociocultural theory of Lev Vygotsky, the famous Russian developmentalist. Vygotsky's career, ended prematurely in his late thirties by tuberculosis, had a wide-ranging impact on the study of development in social context. Second, we will summarize Lerner's developmental systems theory, which provides a lens for understanding how the development of the reciprocating self is embedded within interdependent developmental systems. Third, we will consider how we might categorize the many different relationships typically experienced throughout life. We will do this by reviewing Urie Bronfenbrenner's *ecological* theory for development. Bronfenbrenner's theory is timely given our complex and accelerated North American society. New social contexts exist today that could hardly be envisioned even fifteen years ago. As an example, the average American adolescent spends some eight hours per week on the Internet, often participating in "virtual communities" of peers that he or she may never physically meet. In our interest to conceptualize the development of the reciprocating self, diverse social roles and contexts for relationship make a valuable ecological framework. We next give a brief review of how culture constitutes the broadest understanding of the reciprocating self in context. We conclude this chapter by suggesting that our model of reciprocating relationships comports well with Erik Erikson's model of development-span stages, one which we can build on in the next section of this book.

Vygotsky: Social Context and Scaffolding

In its formation the reciprocating self, as an emergent property of cognition, requires others. We might say that the reciprocating self is constructed from *mental representations* that can be sustained over time and in different social situations. Steven Pinker (1994) calls representations the *mentalese* that comprises our thoughts. Representations are symbols, images, feelings or commitments that constitute our thinking. Representations aren't language, but they serve as the "coat hangers" on which language is "hung." A six-month-old infant, lacking the formal ability to speak, will nonetheless construct representations of his or her mother, father, toys, basic feelings and even sibling relationships. Representations are formed around the child's growing sense of a separate self, and the others that live in her world. Representations become increasingly sophisticated through gradual, incremental development as children encounter situations where they find them-

selves "mirrored" through the perceptions of others. The careful reader
might note the similarity between the concept of mental representations and
the insights given by Jean Piaget and George Herbert Mead in chapter four.

It is a foregone conclusion that the first and probably most important representations of the self appear in infancy through experiences with the primary caregiver, usually the mother. The attachment relationship, with its
positive and negative characteristics, will have an affect on the growing
child's ability to extend its self into new relationships. Through adolescence
and into adulthood it is the individual's ongoing catalog of experiences with
others that shapes the reciprocating self, growing into maturity measured by
the ability to love and care for others.

How might representations of the reciprocating self become established
in childhood, adolescence and adulthood? Lev Vygotsky was a contemporary of Piaget who studied children in a hostile and suspicious Stalinist Rus-
sia of the 1930s. Passionately committed to developmental study, Vygotsky
risked his life and reputation to scrutinize Piaget's research as it was being
published. Vygotsky was aware that Piaget's work was biased toward internal processes of development in childhood, generally avoiding relational influences typical of social context. Concerned that Piaget's emerging view of
growth might be overly individualized, Vygotsky applied his energies to un-
earthing social processes in development, particularly those achievements
made on the basis of the child's relationships with others.

To focus his study of how relationships were significant in development,
Vygotsky chose to examine the emergence of language in childhood. The
advantages of language study were threefold. First, language is a *social activity*. While many other animals have the ability to communicate with each
other, the sophistication of human language is unique in the world, permit-
ting a wide variety of expressions and shared emotions that capture the
complexities of human behavior. By studying language acquisition and usage Vygotsky could evaluate the degree to which external relationships,
such as between a child and parent, were significant to development. Moreover, he could compare the relationship between parents and children to
other relationships of potential significance, such as between a child and
peers. Vygotsky rightly hypothesized that relationships were a present but
shifting influence on the child's development. A twelve-year-old girl is much
more likely to be influenced by peers than she would be at age four. Additionally, the kind of influence exerted by her twelve-year-old peers is mark-

edly different than at age four. At twelve, girls create intricate peer associations and alliances, and are beginning to explore opposite-sex relationships. At four the same girls are simply learning how to share toys. Vygotsky's decision to study language acquisition reflected both the magnitude of relational influences and their specific location in the child's world.

Second, language study permitted Vygotsky to study *how children think*. Language is connected to representations of remarkable complexity. The preschooler's simple request for a drink evolves rapidly into the sixth-grader's ability to deduce complicated outcomes and consequences of hypothetical actions, including the relative merits of imbibing highly caffeinated sodas for breakfast. Vygotsky believed that studying language in childhood would allow him to see how the child's relationship with others was influential in changing his or her thought processes. He expected that social influences would be significant in learning, problem solving and in the means by which the child developed representations of the self and other. Probably Vygotsky's best-known work reflects the measure of developmental importance he gave to language acquisition, published in *Thought and Language* (1986).

Third, and most significant to the aim of this chapter, Vygotsky's concern with language enabled him to find out how children *think about the self*. Language is an expression of how we represent the self and others. Again these representations are more or less sophisticated, depending on age and experience. A preschooler is apt to describe herself in somewhat fragmented and concrete terms—"I am a good swimmer, Mom tells me so, watch me dive!" By contrast, a school-aged child is more categorically inclusive but equally concrete in the same description of self—"I am good at sports." In adolescence the abstract capabilities of the brain are evident in self-representation, where youth might describe traits or behaviors that make them unique—"I have a sense of humor; I am a good team leader when the chips are down." Vygotsky knew that language would help reveal the extent to which the child understands him- or herself through reciprocating relationships with others.

Vygotsky's studies of language development in children were remarkable in their scope, meeting Piaget's theory head-on. Vygotsky discovered, as Piaget had before him, that children develop their language abilities out of vocalizations beginning with the newborn's cooing. Between four and six months infants developed more deliberate sounds, including "ba" and "da."

Short words become evident in the second year, with increasingly sophisticated syntax and vocabulary making their appearance through the preschool years. Because the child would often speak to him- or herself without anyone present, Vygotsky, like Piaget, called speech before the age of five years *egocentric*. Piaget had assumed that egocentric self-talk meant that the child was learning to turn outside of the self to engage others in conversation. He maintained that by kindergarten the child would establish an ability to have a real conversation where the other person was fully engaged. Vygotsky rejected this view, arguing that the opposite was taking place. From early infancy, Vygotsky insisted, the child is already interacting with other people in the social world. Even the newborn's vocalizations represent an attempt to communicate with someone else. Instead of developmentally transitioning from the inside-out through the first five years, language acquisition progresses from the outside into the child. The child's egocentric speech represents a point at which relationships and social experiences are internalized and incorporated into the child's ego.

This was a radical departure from cognitive developmental theory. Vygotsky proposed that the child's social context promotes language acquisition rather than the child's ability to first form thoughts that could be extended outward to others. In effect, mental representations of the self are dependent on social context rather than the other way around. Vygotsky's observations meant that people in the child's world were enormously important to development, particularly where those people were involved in the child's growing understanding of the world and the self. Additionally, Vygotsky paved the way for an understanding that *culture* is a significant influence on development insofar as the child is socialized into a particular worldview. Language, as the medium of interpersonal relationships, serves as the primary vehicle for the transmission of cultural information. Vygotsky's perspective helps to explain why children growing up in Japan tend to be more focused on the needs of others than on themselves, particularly when compared to American children (Heine, 2001). Japanese language has few words for the self, but many words to describe other people and their needs.

Vygotsky's contention that development arises from social influence is readily visible in the life of a preschooler. Four-year-old Shawn has just received his first jigsaw puzzle for his birthday. He sits down to work on the puzzle but is quickly frustrated. In the Piagetian view this is the result of the child's inability to solve complex spatial problems related to fitting the pieces of the puzzle together. But for Vygotsky a parent's intervention enables the child's ability to solve the problem. The boy's father, sitting down at the table, offers Shawn some tips. He suggests that Shawn begin with the edge pieces of the puzzle. He points out that matching pieces can be found in the pile because of their shared colors. When Shawn becomes frustrated, Dad moves matching pieces into the boy's field of vision, raising the likelihood that he will discover a successful match. As Shawn gets the hang of the puzzle, Dad gives words of encouragement. In this example it is social context that facilitates cognitive growth rather than the child's repeated attempts and failures.

Vygotsky called the context of Shawn's interactions with his father the *zone of proximal development.* The zone contains the range of tasks that a child cannot yet accomplish without the active assistance of parents and others with greater knowledge capabilities (Vygotsky, 1986). The zone of proximal development makes new possibilities real as the child's skill base is expanded through interpersonal relationships. Skills beyond the child's immediate potential cannot be magically realized within the zone of proximal development. No matter how encouraging, Shawn's dad will not be able to help Shawn master a game of chess. But within the zone of proximal development, Dad can help Shawn develop new problem-solving capabilities that extend from the puzzle. With Mom the next day, Shawn is able to match colored socks with an improved rate of success after incorporating Dad's tip on observing same-colored puzzle pieces. Better, he is able to do this even when a number of socks have similar but slightly different colors and textures. The zone of proximal development implies that as the child learns and masters new skills through relationships, he or she will be increasingly able to independently handle tasks and challenges.

Whereas Piaget thought of the growing child as an independent explorer, Vygotsky thought of the child as a collaborator, learning new skills through interactions with more cognitively advanced individuals. Within the zone of proximal development, strategies such as Dad's use of color-matching with Shawn's puzzle effectively "build" cognitive and self-related processes. Vygotsky called this *scaffolding,* reflecting the construction technique of placing ladders and walkways around a building in order to give workers access to every part of the emerging structure. Caregivers can provide a scaffold of development that optimally extends just slightly beyond the child's abilities, but never so far beyond as to create unreasonable expectations that end in certain failure. Rogoff notes:

> Vygotsky's model for the mechanism through which social interaction facil-
> itates cognitive development resembles apprenticeship, in which a novice
> works closely with an expert in joint problem solving in the zone of proxi-
> mal development. The novice is thereby able to participate in skills beyond
> those that he or she is independently capable of handling. Development
> builds on the internalization by the novice of shared cognitive processes, ap-
> propriating what was carried out in collaboration to extend knowledge and
> skills. (1990)

Vygotsky's theory carries significant implications for the reciprocating self in development. If Shawn's problem-solving abilities are improving within the zone of proximal development, it is additionally likely that the scaffold-ing provided by Dad is helping Shawn to understand himself in new ways. Rather than experience shame for his struggle with the puzzle, Shawn quickly learns that the activity is for discovery, that mistakes are acceptable, and the goal is ultimately to have fun. Shawn learns that his essential self is desirable, leading him to construct new representations of self and other based on his experiences with Dad. These representations will become lodged in Shawn's memory for comparison when future situations require it.

The reciprocating self indicates a high level of interpersonal commitment in its formation. But what happens for children who do not receive this kind of developmental scaffolding? A number of outcomes are possible. Abused or neglected children will, in the absence of consistent scaffolding, develop negative representations of the self and other. Depending on the nature of the abuse and its longevity, the child may develop various protective strat-egies for the self. If Shawn were to be shamed and verbally attacked by his father while working on the puzzle, Shawn would likely withdraw with a deep sense of personal failure. Preschool children who lack adequate scaf-folding are at risk to develop "all or nothing" categories of thinking about the self, such as an internal conviction that "I'm all bad." Harter (1999) notes that abuse frequently results in the child's internalization of social influences on the basis of responsibility. So shame, violence or emotional abuse result in a self that reciprocates negativity to others. This might become evident in a child's bullying behaviors, delinquency or violence.

We might consider the fact that four-year-old Shawn's social context is much simpler than when he will be eleven or eighteen. Advancing age brings increasingly complex social contexts and relationships that potentially scaffold development. At eleven Shawn might have an established peer group, play on various sports teams and participate in his faith community. At eighteen Shawn additionally might be involved as a volunteer in the local convalescent hospital and work for pay as a restaurant server. Each of these environments contain increasingly complicated relationships that Shawn must navigate. As he grows, Shawn's reciprocating self learns to adapt to each social context by acquiring the ability to play an appropriate role. Representations of self and other are configured around these roles and the individuals that populate his relationships.

If we were to speculatively follow Shawn's development into adulthood, we might describe his increasing role as a builder of scaffolds for those younger than himself, such as his own children. In considering Shawn's elderly years we might even describe his need for scaffolding as he finds his physical, intellectual and mental capacities diminishing.

Developmental Systems Theory

Development systems theory (DST) is more of an integrative than a separate approach to human development. We find DST extremely useful because of the similarity in the assumptions made about human development within it and our own model of the reciprocating self.

Ford and Lerner first presented DST in their book *Development Systems Theory: An Integrative Approach* (1992). Used as the basis for life-span development, Lerner presents a more recent version of DST in his book *Concepts and Theories of Human Development* (2002). As is the case for systems theory in general, DST conceptualizes the organization of the human system as an interdependent whole, within which each part (unit or subsystem) is influenced by and in turn influences each other part in the human system as a whole. Although it is hard to do justice to all of the guiding assumptions suggested within DST, we suggest the following:

- Multiplicity of influence. "The individual as a dynamic unit is to be understood as a complex, multilevel organization of biological structures plus biological and psychological-behavioral processes embedded and fused in dynamic interaction with multilevel environments."

- Multiple reciprocal influence. "Individuals' functioning and development results from a dynamic interaction within and between levels of organization of multiple, qualitatively different variables."

- Uniqueness of each individual. "Each human differs from every other human in their genetic endowment, in the environments in which he or she is embedded during their lifetime, and in the dynamic interactions through which genetic and environmental variables are fused in their influence on behavior and development."

- Uniqueness of development. "Human development displays relative plasticity so there is no single, ideal developmental pathway for any person. . . . The nature of the constraining facilitating conditions and of a person's potential developmental pathways change in both predictable and unpredictable ways, making development open ended and probabilistic rather than preordained and rigidly deterministic."

- Humans as active agents. "Individuals influence their own development through their own functioning. Humans are self-organizing and self-constructing, meaning that people are proactive as well as reactive. They selectively engage specific contexts and specific aspects of those contexts from among their potential environments."

- Created for community. "Individuals not only function to establish and maintain coherent intraperson organization so they can function effectively as a unit, but they also function to establish and maintain coherent person-context patterns of organization so they can function effectively as a component of their larger contexts." (Lerner, 2002, p. 184)

Relationalism

Developmental theories are conventionally evaluated on several important oppositional criteria—mechanistic versus organismic, nature versus nurture, and continuous versus discontinuous. Developmental system theory attempts to move beyond such "splitting" of developmental viewpoints into oppositional camps. This is done by emphasizing the importance of understanding the *relationship* between factors contributing to human development. Within DST changing relations are the basic unit of analysis. Neither the individual nor context is emphasized in such theories; rather the individual ← → context relations are the focus.[1] DST is an integrative, fused or relational theory that stresses the mutually influential connections among all levels of the development system, ranging from genes through society, cul-

---

[1] Lerner uses bidirectional arrows to emphasize the reciprocal influence of person on context and context on person.

ture, the designed and natural ecology, and history. In developmental systems theories the reciprocity between the developing person and his or her complex and changing context provides a means for studying and understanding development.

For example, DST argues that components of development, such as nature and nurture, are not the causes of human development. Rather, the *relationship* of the components is what makes human development happen. This view, known as *relationalism,* conceptualizes human development as occurring through the interaction of person and context throughout the life span. The basis for change is anchored in relationships between the different systemic levels—biological, psychological, social, cultural and physical. DST moves us beyond an additive model (heredity plus environment equal human behavior), to an *interactive* model in which the relationship between systems is the primary influence of behavior. There are two features of developmental systems theories that are important to stress in order to understand their use for conceptualizing positive development: relative plasticity and developmental regulation.

Relative plasticity is a concept used within DST that seeks to move beyond the mechanistic versus organismic controversy. Relative plasticity refers to the ability for change across the lifespan and at multiple levels of the system. Although human agency—that human beings are active agents— is recognized, DST also argues that the amount of choice, and thus change, is always constrained by past developments and by present ecological conditions. Thus DST defines human organisms as *relatively* plastic. Relationships between the different levels within the human developmental system both facilitate and constrain opportunities for change. For example, change (learning a new language with native-speaker fluency during adolescence or adulthood) is constrained both by past developments (knowledge of your own native language) and by contemporary contextual conditions (the absence or presence of opportunities to immerse yourself in a new language and culture). Another example might be that I (Pam) am tone deaf. Given the limitations of my voice, no matter how much I intentionally try to cultivate my voice and influence my developmental system so that I might become a rock star, it is not going to happen. Plasticity suggests that I have the potential to change, but relative plasticity conveys that the change is not limitless.

Relative plasticity is explained by malleability and canalization. *Malleability* refers to the capacity (i.e., possibility) of the human being to develop along a vast array of possible trajectories. The range of development for any one individual is vast—from social worker to dictator. *Canalization* refers to the tendency of the human being to adapt to and be shaped by various elements in his or her experience. Canalization points to the *limitations* or narrowing of human responsiveness as a consequence of past experience. Thus, while an infinite variety of development trajectories are possible at birth, this range of trajectories is reduced by experiences that shape the individual. These experiences can be so powerful as to even alter individual DNA coding (Lerner, 2002).

DST represents a modified organismic view of human development. Human beings are viewed as agents who are not only acted on but who act on their environment. Action (direction of influence) is viewed reciprocally: the individual acts on the system while at the same time the system acts on the individual. *Coaction* is a concept used in DST to refer to events that occur in and affect multiple elements of a developing person and its environment.

The mutual influence between individual and context regulate the course of development. When these bidirectional influences maintain or improve the health or well-being of both components of individual ← → context relations, they are termed *adaptive developmental regulations* (Lerner, 2002). From a developmental systems perspective healthy development involves positive changes in the relation between a developing person and a community supporting his or her development. A relationship between an individual and context that maintains and perpetuates the system is one in which the individual acts to support the institutions of society, and the institutions simultaneously support the healthy functioning and development of the individual. Thus it can be said that adaptive developmental regulations involve person-context relations that make positive contributions to self, family, community and society (Lerner, 2004; Lerner, Dowling and Anderson, 2003).

Lerner proposes an explicit developmental teleology. He suggests, "Adaptive developmental regulation results in the emergence among young people of an orientation to transcend self-interest and place value on and commitments to actions supportive of their social system" (Lerner, Dowling and Anderson, 2003, p. 176). Although actions that support a specific social system will vary by culture and era, in short, Lerner proposes that optimal development includes individuals who can reciprocate with their self, family, community and society (Lerner, 2004). In short, from a DST perspective the goal of development is a reciprocating self.

Developmental system theory views the development of the reciprocating self as an *epigenetic* process—development caused by the relations between the individual and the total environmental context. As such, human development always must be understood as *emergent,* as a process that is continually taking place. It is at this point that DST theory addresses the continuity versus discontinuity issue. The emergent process must be understood as qualitative and not merely quantitative change. Lerner (2002) states that human development is best conceived as "successive differentiated change," a phrase similar to how we describe the development of the reciprocating self. The reciprocal self continually emerges, but in its emergent state it becomes qualitatively different from what it was in the past. For example, humans are born as babies, and as we grow we do not just become larger babies. Rather, our personality, body, goals, spirituality and so on change over time because of the mutual relations between ourselves and our context.

Figure 5.1 represents the developmental-contextual view of human development. The central focal point in this figure is the child, represented by the large circle at the left center. The many systemic levels *internal* to the children are represented by the "pie" shapes within the circle—biological, cognitive, personality and so forth. The many systemic levels *external* to the children are outside of this circle. Two-way arrows connecting the child to the school network, the social network, the parent network and the marriage network represent the primary social systems the child is embedded in. The most important of the child's relationships is with the parent, thus the larger circle (within which are the systems *internal* to the parent). Note that each of the other social systems—school, social and marriage networks—are composed of subunits that are subsystems themselves. (For instance, the school network is composed of two units—teachers and classmates—that are themselves social systems.) At the wider level the child is also affected by (and in turn affects) the community, social, cultural and designed and natural environmental systems.

Finally, the developmental context for a child exists within a time dimension. All human development is embedded in history, including the changing context within which the child and the environment interact. For example, along with the changing diets, nutrition and eating habits over time has come a change in the average weight and height of children. The changing

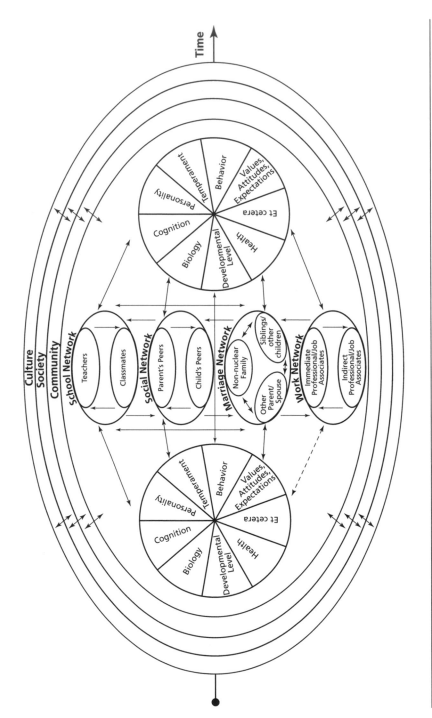

Figure 5.1. The developmental contextual view of human development

historical context has even affected life-span markers, such as the onset of menarche among girls and the emergence of secondary sexual characteristics (voice change and body hair) among boys. The temporal dimension obviously continues to be an important dimension through a person's developmental life span, culminating with increased longevity and sophisticated medical care during the elderly years.

In DST we have an understanding of human beings as inextricably imbedded in their contexts. Thus when it comes to understanding human development, the unit of analysis must be the person-context relation. Although complex, this figure illustrates how DST might be considered a metatheory capable of incorporating many other developmental theories within it. Parenthetically, it might be noted that DST points to a cautionary approach in attempting to build a science of human development based on controlled or "pure" scientific methods. Studying development in so-called controlled environments does not provide information on the relationships between individually distinct people and their unique contexts. What is most needed is the study of human development in real-world settings, those involving people in their natural contexts.

Understanding how people relate to their natural settings is at the heart of the reciprocating self. DST provides a helpful lens for understanding how the self takes shape through the mutual influences between the individual and his or her developmental context. The ideal of becoming an individual who reciprocates with self, family, community and society comports with our understanding of the reciprocating self. Although DST bases its teleological assumption on an evolutionary perspective—providing a theory that is based on the progress of society and individuals through adaptive developmental regulation (see Lerner 2004; Lerner, Dowling and Anderson 2003)—it provides a similar goal to that of the reciprocating self. An obvious difference is the emphasis on a relationship with God in the reciprocating self. However, ecology theory, to which we turn, provides a means for conceptualizing the influence of relationships with God and others on the development of the reciprocating self.

Bronfenbrenner: Roles and Ecosystems

The son of a zoologist, Urie Bronfenbrenner was trained at an early age to observe development in the wilderness. Bronfenbrenner spent most of his career teaching at Cornell University, where he pioneered a theoretical outline of human growth in context. His *Ecology of Human Development* (1979) was something of a watershed event. Prior to that time development was envisioned, as Bronfenbrenner notes with some sarcasm, as the study of strange child behaviors in strange situations. Bronfenbrenner alludes to the famous "strange situation" of Mary Main's attachment theory, an attempt to use an unfamiliar set of events to observe the child's level of security with a primary caregiver. Instead of imposing artificial constraints on the study of development, Bronfenbrenner argued for a naturalistic kind of observation that was grounded in human relationships.

For Bronfenbrenner all people move through various relational contexts, each with unique possibilities that influence development. Moreover, we learn to assume different roles given shifting contexts. An undergraduate student knows that she plays one role with her sorority friends, namely that of fun-loving sister and confidant to her peer group. But the same student knows that her sorority role is not appropriate for her upper-division courses in electrical engineering. With her professors she is serious, studious and task-oriented. Once again, this same student recognizes that neither of these roles is appropriate when she is home for the summer. With Mom and Dad she has a familiar if slightly strained relationship, which is being rene-gotiated as she moves from adolescence into an adult child. The undergrad-uate knows that she "plays" these different roles in each context, yet the wide distance between her various selves does not cause undue stress or concern. In fact, she makes these transitions seamlessly and is barely aware that role transitions are taking place.

Our undergraduate's reciprocating self is able to sustain these various roles because at her core she has developed representations of past expe-riences and relationships that provide her with a sure footing. To put this in Eriksonian terms, she has acquired an *identity*. The strength of Erikson's identity theory is that our core self remains unchanged while moving through a variety of social contexts. Social contexts and relationships in-fluence our identities, but in the presence of well-formed identity, changes are incremental and subject to our opinion of them. While social context is indicated for identity formation, Erikson had no means for interpreting the various contexts through which relationships are established and nur-tured. Bronfenbrenner's key contribution is that he systematized "domains" of relationships, or social interaction, that play a unique role in develop-ment. Bronfenbrenner noted that the basis for stable role-transitioning and the basis for the reciprocating self begins with the *dyad*.

Dyad simply means "two." Bronfenbrenner observed that the child's dyadic relationship with a primary caregiver constitutes a vital social context that becomes a core experience of other relationships. Through a dyadic relationship with a parent, the child learns how to relate more broadly to others. The dyadic relationship is Bronfenbrenner's overture to attachment, assigning special importance to early developmental processes between the infant and a primary caregiver, usually the mother. What distinguished Bronfenbrenner's view of the dyad is that the object of study is not just the child's psychological state but the dyadic relationship itself. Bronfenbrenner notes that

> the ecology of human development involves the scientific study of the progressive, mutual accommodation between an active, growing human being and the changing properties of the immediate settings in which the growing person lives, as this process is affected by relations between these settings, and by the larger contexts in which the settings are embedded. (p. 21)

Bronfenbrenner contends that it is the child's interactions with others that constitute an authentic basis for development. He referred to the growing child's web of social interactions in terms of relational *reciprocity,* recognizing that the child is not a passive agent but acts on his or her environment and is able to change it, even at a very early age.

Consider the following scenario. You are at a doctor's office and have waited for an appointment for over half an hour. During that time you have established a kind of polite distance with most of the people in the room. Intermittently you have had eye contact with many of them, sometimes exchanging smiles. But it is clear that no one is really interested in talking today, even about the weather. Then a young mother enters the waiting room with her eight-month-old infant son. The two sit down a couple of chairs away from you. The infant is adorable, cooing and touching his mother's face. His mother reciprocates, nuzzling him and softly speaking to him. All of a sudden, the waiting room environment is changed. People are smiling as if sharing some kind of insider's secret. Two older women seated across from the mother and son begin a conversation about their grandchildren. The infant drops a toy and a young man immediately reaches across the aisle to pick it up. Even the nurses and administrators in the office are affected—you can hear them talking about their children behind the counter as they do their office work.

Ecologically speaking, the infant in this scene is actively engaged with his environment. He is able to change the collective mood of the waiting room simply through his interactions with his mother. The reciprocity between mother and son are extended to include others, who then act reciprocally with complete strangers or distant colleagues. Bronfenbrenner notes that development is never restricted to a single relationship (such as with the mother) or even a small system (such as a nuclear family). Instead, development is a *nested phenomenon*. Like the fabled Russian wooden dolls, development is nested in various contexts of reciprocal relationships.

In order to effectively pinpoint dyads in their contexts, Bronfenbrenner had to outline boundaries for nested social contexts, or in his terminology, *ecosystems* (see fig. 5.2). The smallest system began with the caregiver-child dyadic relationship. This comprised the *microsystem,* where reciprocal interactions form patterns significant to the child's relationships with others beyond the dyad. Slightly beyond the microsystem is the *mesosystem,* or a system of microsystems. The mesosystem involves two or more participation settings. For a kindergarten girl this might include her relationships with her nuclear family, her classmates at school, her church friends and her same-aged neighbors. For her father the mesosystem would similarly include his nuclear family but also work colleagues and golfing friends. The mesosystem is an intermediate realm of relationships that constitutes a wide variety of intimacy and familiarity.

Beyond the mesosystem is the *exosystem.* The exosystem does not involve the developing person directly as a participant. However, events in the exosystem do affect the developing person. For the same kindergartner Dad's place of work is a part of her exosystem. Her older brother's soccer team is a part of her exosystem. Exosystems exert considerable influence on the developing person but from a distance, usually through some sort of intermediary figure such as a parent or sibling.

The dyadic microsystem is nested even further within the *macrosystem,* or cultural level of reciprocal influence. Macrosystemic influences are evident in the media, the government and the cultural practices that are acceptable to the immediate social context. If our kindergartner found herself growing up in urban Toronto, her macrosystem would consist of cultural variables typical of a large, cosmopolitan city. In such an environment ethnic diversity is common along with a spectrum of wealthy, poor and middle-class economic groups living together in close proximity. Pluralism might be a macrosystemic value operative in her environment. Relative to kindergartners growing up in rural Nebraska, the Toronto girl might have more exposure to various elements of urban life, such as neighborhood crime, crowding and pollution. Note that while Bronfenbrenner's ecological scheme is primarily focused on relationships, the physical characteristics of each system are also emphasized with regard to development. Thus the Canadian kindergartner's exposure to urban smog might make her susceptible to asthma, an influence on her overall well-being and development.

Bronfenbrenner notes that as we grow, we are increasingly enabled to move between systems of relationship and social influence. Like the undergraduate woman living in a sorority and pursuing an engineering degree, we learn through processes of reciprocation how to position ourselves appropriately given the expectations and boundaries of a given context. It is in learning how to manage these role transitions, Bronfenbrenner argues, that we are developing. The challenge of adapting to new environments, roles and relationships requires a self that is plastic or adaptive. In this Bronfenbrenner echoes Piaget, who made a case for cognitive dissonance as the means by which developmental growth occurs. But unlike Piaget, Bronfenbrenner envisions these transitions to be embedded in unique influences of particular ecosystems.

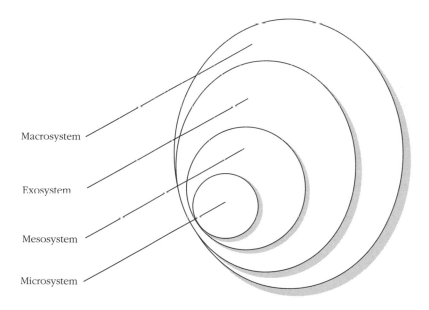

Macrosystem

Exosystem

Mesosystem

Microsystem

Figure 5.2. Bronfenbrenner's ecosystems of social context

We are now at a point where we might pull together our discussion on behalf of the reciprocating self in social context. Representations of ourselves and others are formed in dyadic zones of proximal development where scaffolding enables the child to explore and realize skills. Representations of a reciprocating self are forged in the dynamic web of relationships that characterize the individual's social contexts: from the dyad to family, neighborhood, community and culture. In adolescence the individual learns to sustain representations of self in tension with other selves that play context-specific roles but without compromising the integrity of the core self. In adulthood these representations are solidified in a manner that permits a wide variety of reciprocal relationships, where the individual is able to influence others and their respective contexts. Finally, elderly persons again need scaffolding in order to allow semi-independent behavior where diminished physical and mental abilities make self-care more difficult.

Reciprocating Patterns: Culture and Generations

The reciprocating self is visible in a number of ecosystems, each of which provides different scaffolding for development. Let's take a moment to reflect on the development of the reciprocating self in context. So far we have sketched a fairly individualized reciprocating self, reflecting a Western view of human development and relationships. However, many Eastern cultures think about human development in communalistic terms. We would be wise to ask whether there are communal patterns for the reciprocating self in human development. Put a different way, we should pay special attention to the means by which Bronfenbrenner's cultural-macrosystem scheme results in developmental patterns for large groups. Culture implies a collective way of life and is an immensely important contributor to the formative process of persons within it. Anthropologist Ralph Linton has noted that culture is to a human being as water is to a fish. Linton asks us to imagine a fish that lived its entire life in water. One day swimming upward toward the surface, it emerges into air. The great discovery to the fish, Linton observes, is not air but rather that its entire life was lived in a different substance—water. In a similar sense humans can live their whole lives within their own culture and not be aware of its influence on them. It is not until a person "breaks the surface of culture" by spending time in another, that he or she becomes more fully aware of the macrosystem.

Generational Analysis

Whereas cultures are fairly stable and enduring, they do change over time. Thus it is important to identify the major cultural issues that preoccupy a society during the formative years of an individual. *Generational analysis* represents an attempt to identify cultural phenomena that significantly affect the developmental process. Within life-course theory, this is represented in terms of *historical time* (see Lerner, 2002, p. 236).

The term g*eneration* has been used in a variety of ways, including different biblical applications. The Old Testament word *dor* ("generation") carries the root idea *to go around, to go in a circle, to inhabit or dwell for a time, an age or a period of time*. Thus in Ecclesiastes 1:4, 9-10, we read:

> A generation goes, and a generation comes,
>> but the earth remains forever. . . .
> What has been is what will be,
>> and what has been done is what will be done;
>> there is nothing new under the sun.
> Is there a thing of which it is said,
>> "See, this is new?"

In all likelihood it already existed in the ages before us.

Jesus sometimes referred to his audience as a generation, "Truly I tell you, this generation will not pass away until all these things have taken place" (Mk 13:30; see also Lk 7:31; 17:25). More frequently, Jesus used *genea* ("generation") to address a specific segment of his audience that was distinguished by a common moral characteristic or flaw—"this adulterous and sinful generation" (Mk 8:38), "you faithless generation" (Mark 9:19), and "this generation is an evil generation" (Luke 11:29). The apostle Paul also distinguished "the saints," who as the children of God were to do all things without murmuring and arguing—from the "crooked and perverse generation" among whom they were to shine like stars in the world (Phil 2:15). Taken together we might infer that *generation* usually refers to age differences in understanding, along with different responses to culture. As an illustration we will give overviews of two approaches to generational analysis.

The most comprehensive attempt at generational analysis is found in William Strauss and Neil Howe's book *Generations: The History of America's Future, 1584-2069*. Strauss and Howe identify "a recurring cycle of four distinct types of peer personalities, arriving in the same repeating sequence." They label the four generation types *idealist, reactive, civic* and *adaptive*. The characteristics of each generation are formed by what is going on when individuals reach adulthood. Idealist and civic generations enter the adult years during a period of spiritual awakening, while reactive and adaptive generations reach this phase of life during a secular crisis. Strauss and Howe define a generation as a special cohort group whose births span a basic phase of life, usually about twenty-two years. Thus the generational cycle covers roughly ninety years before it repeats. Each generation is on the stage for a limited period of time, parading unique styles, customs and characteristics.

The last complete generational cycle began with those born between 1860 and 1882. These were idealists who formed the *missionary generation*. This was followed by those born between 1883 and 1900, a *reactive* or *lost generation*. The *civic generation* was born between 1901 and 1924 and is also known as the *G.I. generation* or as "The Great Generation." This was followed by the *silent (adaptive) generation* born between 1925 and 1942. Following the silent generation came the *baby boomers,* born between 1943 and 1960. Boomers initiated a new cycle as *idealists,* redefining the inner world of values and culture. Following the boomers was Generation X, a *reactive* cohort critical of the previous excesses, born between 1961 and 1981. Those born between 1982 and 2003 constitute the new civic generation called *millennials,* but since the tragic events of September 2001, they

Table 5.1. Generational Transitions and Characteristics

Generation	Years of Birth	Characteristics
G.I.'s	1901-1924	World War I, II: hard work; safe; loyal (civic); the Great Depression; cautious; intolerant
Silent	1925-1942	Peace and fit-in; don't question (adaptive); prosperity
Baby Boomers	1943-1960	Large numbers; cause-oriented (idealist); protest war; challenge system; affluence; question authority; electronic media
Generation X	1961-1981	Broken families; feel neglected and lonely (reactive); dual earners; practical education; hi-tech; hesitant to commit
Millennials / 9/11	1981-present	Computer; return to civic values (civic)? the Web

have also come to be known as the *9/11 generation*. An overview of generations is given in table 5.1.

While the Strauss and Howe scheme has merit, an alternative view of generational interpretation was provided by Karl Mannheim (1952). Mannheim's perspective was recently refined by Vern Bengtson, director of the Institute on Aging at the University of Southern California. Mannheim argued that distinctions between "generations" are somewhat arbitrary, but sometimes youth in sufficient numbers experience a *fresh contact* with culture.

Culture is developed by individuals who come into contact anew with the accumulated heritage. In the nature of our physical makeup, a fresh contact (meeting something anew) always means a changed relationship of distance from the object and a novel approach in assimilating, using and developing the preferred material (Mannheim, 1952, p. 294).

Fresh contact with culture most significantly influences youth, distinguishing them as a *generational unit*. Whereas a generational cohort includes all members of a generational age group, a generational unit includes *all members of a generation who have developed a common consciousness and response to a sociohistorical situation*. Generational units develop a *generational personality,* which is recognized and determined by (1) common age location; (2) common beliefs and behavior; and (3) perceived membership in a common generation. It is common life experience that forms generational personality. Obviously, generational personality implies the reciprocating self, not as an individualistic concept but in a collective or shared sense among persons within the generational unit. Intergenerational differences and similarities result from the fresh contact of succeeding generations with accumulating cultural heritage of a society.

Baby Boomers, Hippies and Jesus People

Mannheim's approach to generational analysis is perhaps best understood through the baby boomer generational cohort. Boomers gained their name from the birth boom that immediately followed World War II. Most boomers entered adolescence or young adulthood during the 1960s. Research on the 1960s indicates that young and old did not share the same perception of external reality, and this difference in perception resulted in part from differences in position through the life span (Ahammer and Baltes, 1972; Bengtson and Kuypers, 1971). Youth during the 1960s experienced a fresh contact with a cultural ideal, summed up in a memorable challenge through the acceptance speech of President John F. Kennedy: "Ask not what your country can do for you; ask what you can do for your country."

Boomers nurtured an idealism that was highly critical of what they perceived to be hypocrisy. During the early 1960s, protests formed around the issues of student rights, the war in Vietnam and the counterculture movement led by hippies. Major social institutions such as government, churches, schools, businesses and families were perceived as being overly rigid and unresponsive to change. The hippie movement could best be understood as a reaction against three aspects of the American middle class: *compulsive consumption, passive spectatorship* and *time held captive by the clock* (Davis, 1967, pp. 10-18).

Although counterculture youth shared some of these overarching ideals, many simply dropped out of society, choosing drugs and an alternative, hedonistic lifestyle. Still others became seriously involved in political action against what they saw as an unresponsive establishment. By the end of the 1960s the Jesus People movement emerged as a generational unit within the wider baby boomer cohort.

The Jesus People phenomenon provides an interesting example of the type of influence the macrosystem can have on persons during their adolescence. The Jesus People showcased an unlikely combination of conservative Christian belief system with the hippie symbols of long hair, beards, rock music, castoff clothes and open rejection of the American status quo.

As an alternative Christian movement, Jesus People expressed their beliefs through gospel rock music instead of eighteenth and nineteenth century hymns, and through psychedelic art forms and underground gospel newspapers instead religious publishing houses. Fresh contact with a conservative approach to Christianity resulted (as Mannheim would have predicted) in an identification of religious inconsistencies with an attempt to establish an alternative expression of Christianity.

One of the functions of organized religion is to perpetuate the values of a culture from generation to generation. To an extent the Jesus People altered this process. They chose a theologically conservative protest to the organized church. Jesus People criticized liberal Christianity for its failure to recognize human beings in an alienated state who needed to be rightly related to God. They criticized conservative Christianity for mere lip service to a personal gospel that was often unloving, intolerant and discriminatory. They saw American Christians as obsessed with building expensive and lavish church buildings (the practice that Roman Catholic bishop Fulton Sheen labeled our "edifice complex"). They saw the church as an organization whose objective was to be served, not to serve. For Jesus People traditional church services were archaic, with one-way pulpit communication that allowed no opportunity for dialogue. The Jesus People reacted against this kind of institutional rigidity in a manner similar to the relativistic emptiness of the youth counterculture. Thus cultural influences through the macrosystem are capable of shaping generations, potentially influencing the social institutions that shape future generations and the reciprocating self (Bengtson and Black, 1973; Strauss and Howe, 1991).

Concluding Thoughts: Developmental Theory and Practical Atheism

We have outlined some important theories that help shape our understanding of development. The theories of Vygotsky, Lerner and Bronfenbrenner are helpful in understanding the formation of the reciprocating self. Generational analysis perspectives are highly theoretical in nature, focusing on macrosystemic or cultural factors that influence the reciprocating self. Because this book is interested in practical outcomes, we should step back for a moment and reflect on just what "theory" is and how theory should be considered in a rapidly changing world where social science is often misunderstood.

It is a difficult time for psychology and sociology. The prevailing atmosphere of postmodernism has raised questions over whether social science is a valid field and if the traditional scientific affinity for theory in fact represents singular points of view that are misleading in their universal claim of truth. Defining postmodernism is a tricky thing, but for our purposes *postmodernism* can be characterized as rejecting the assumption that through reason human beings may find universal truth. Beginning with Nietzsche and growing through the work of Foucault, Derrida, Lyotard and Gadamer, postmodern philosophy mounted a frontal assault on the credibility of social science by questioning whether people can be adequately understood through psychological or sociological theories. For the postmodern, the reciprocating self is a potentially dangerous *metanarrative,* or universal claim for developmental processes that cannot accommodate the diversity of human experience. Thus the reciprocating self might represent an imposition of the authors' backgrounds and experiences. In the case of this author

(Kevin), the reciprocating self might reflect a particular ethnic (European), gendered (male) and socioeconomic (middle class) perspective. The reciprocating self may prove completely irrelevant to the African American teenager, the Latina farm worker or the Japanese American internment survivor. In the mind of the postmodern the reciprocating self is limited as a theory of practical significance, apparently reflecting the viewpoint of a single social grouping.

We acknowledge a potentially valuable counterpoint in the postmodern critique of developmental theory, and in particular the reciprocating self as sketched in this chapter. Consequently, we do not propose that the reciprocating self, despite its context-sensitive outlook, is a developmental theory that accommodates all human development in its totality. Yet we are also unwilling to relegate the reciprocating self to the margins of relativism, noting that to do so would be to forfeit our Christian conviction that all truth is God's truth, wherever it may be found. Rather than live unanchored in the middle of this tension, we prefer to take a step toward a solution that in our thinking is *integrative* in its theological consideration of psychology and specifically the reciprocating self.

We suspect that the great debate about whether truth is foundational or relative obscures a more immediate concern. The nineteenth-century Danish philosopher Søren Kierkegaard once remarked that society is constantly tempted to live as if God does not exist. Kierkegaard called this temptation *practical atheism,* noting that Christians and atheists alike are capable of behaving as if God does not exist (Gay, 1998). Kierkegaard noted that even in the Christian church there is much planning and laboring that proceeds as if God were absent or at best a distant onlooker. We are concerned that the modern scientist and the postmodern critic, by making all-or-nothing claims to truth, are at risk of behaving in a manner that is practically atheistic. For the Christian, truth is embodied not as an abstraction but in terms of a relationship. Jesus invites us to know truth not simply as a cognitive, rationalist prescription but in and through his own person. Jesus states that he is the way, the truth and the life. In our estimation the truth noted in any theory, including the reciprocating self, is subjected to reconciliation between what is seen in the developmental worlds of Vygotsky or Lerner or Bronfenbrenner, and what is not seen in the sovereignty of the risen Christ. Indeed, the reciprocating self we have proposed in this chapter remains a witness of these two contexts of exchange and meaning. So the reciprocating self is an ad hoc theoretical position, one that claims not to be universal in any theoretical sense but does make a claim to truth, emerging as it does from a theistic commitment to God's role as architect of all that is true. In our interest to avoid practical atheism we perceive the reciprocating self as a developmental theory that is "both already and not yet." The reciprocating self is already evident in human developmental processes, but it is not yet realized in its theological richness through the reconciliation of human beings in the grace and love of Christ.

Consequently, the reciprocating self should probably be thought of as more than mere theory. We might go a step further to call it a theologically integrative element in our understanding of human experience through social-scientific lenses. It is to this integrative discussion that we now turn in the interest of better understanding an appropriately theistic basis for human development.

Life-Span Stages: An Outline

With this rather lengthy introduction to developmental theory and our theological model, we are now ready to apply the reciprocating self to an understanding of the sequential stages of life-span development. Following the approaches of Vygotsky, Lerner and Bronfenbrenner, we have organized each of the life-span development chapters accordingly. First, we will give a brief overview of the developmental tasks the individual is likely to be working through during the various stages of development. This will be accompanied with a description of the type of scaffolding typically needed during this developmental stage. This helps us to examine the nested contexts development takes place in. Specifically, we begin by describing the microsystem, that level where dyadic relationships are the core focus of attention. Next, our attention moves to the mesosystem, where we examine important group contexts development takes place in. Then we take up the influence of the exosystem on the developing individual. Finally, we examine the macrosystem as a cultural context for understanding human development. The last section of each chapter gives an overview of the potential strengths, limitations and developmental issues of the person as a reciprocating self.

PART TWO

Life-Span Stages

6

Infancy

THE EMERGENCE OF THE RECIPROCATING SELF

THE NATURAL WORLD IS FULL OF SURPRISES. Perhaps nowhere is this more evident than in the life of an infant. Some years ago developmentalists believed that infants were confined to the physical limitations of the brain, in a manner similar to an autistic child. Consequently, infancy was perceived as a cute and inaccessible developmental period. Serious study of infant development lagged behind other life-span stages simply because infants could not tell researchers what it was like to be an infant. Worse, developmental researchers themselves had no memory of infancy. However, it turns out that infant development is filled with remarkable and unexpectedly complex phenomena.

In this chapter we will outline the reciprocating self for infant development, gradually expanding our discussion to consider ecosystemic contexts of influence. Given the importance of establishing developmental boundaries in this section of the book, we will confine our discussion of infancy to the first two years of life. First, we will briefly review biological changes for infants that provide a foundational basis for self-understanding. Second, we will review cognitive changes that enable infants to build and sustain relationships significant to a reciprocating self. In particular, we will focus our discussion on the attachments infants form with a primary caregiver. Third, we will review four different "selves" in infancy. For this discussion we rely on the work of Daniel Stern in *The Interpersonal World of the Infant* (2000). Finally, we will briefly consider the parenting literature in order to understand how unconditional love, gracing, empowering and intimate relationships can be applied on behalf of the infant child. We will extend this parenting overview to a discussion of how the infant self is potentially scaffolded across the ecosystem.

Biological Changes

Although she cannot tell us about it, a four-month-old infant girl is a reflection of the *imago Dei*. Biologically speaking, her ability to act on, sense and perceive the world is fundamentally geared toward adaptability. It is our contention that the infant's physical development is essentially adaptive because changes in her body anticipate relationship with other human beings and God. Whereas many mammals are physically able to defend themselves or run away from a threat just after birth, humans require months to obtain these simple capacities. In fact, the young infant is wholly dependent on a caregiver for defense or flight in the face of danger. The character of infancy is such that even the development of gross motor skills and perception are related to the quality of relational bonding with caregivers. In the absence of a caring relationship infants may suffer profound biological (neurological) impairment or delayed development, a sad lesson observed in the Romanian orphanages of the early 1990s, where a single caregiver might be responsible for dozens or even hundreds of infant children.

It is beyond the scope of this book to provide a detailed review of biological development in infancy. Consequently, our discussion is focused on two aspects of physical growth that are foundational to relationships and ultimately to a reciprocating self. First, we note that as relational beings, humans have the ability to act on their world. At a basic level human action is physically expressed in terms of reflexes, along with gross and fine motor skills. Second, humans are able to sense their world. This may be immediately adaptive in terms of sensing a threat, but more often this means that the infant is developing the capacity to learn from and about his or her environment, including the people that live within it.

Infancy is a period of rapid neurological development. During the initial months of life the brain is forming many new neurological connections known as *synaptic pathways*. The brain is also becoming better connected with the rest of the body through the *myelination* of axons, or basic nerve fibers. Myelin is a kind of fatty insulation that permits neural impulses to travel more freely and quickly through nerves, providing improved responses between the brain and limbs. These processes are just getting underway in early life. As an example the prefrontal cortex of the brain (located behind the forehead and eyes) is known to assist humans in self-regulation and restraint. Because a newborn lacks extensive neurological connections and myelination, this portion of the brain is unable to effectively suppress a cry related to hunger or pain. Later in infancy, changes to the prefrontal cortex facilitate better regulation of these and other impulses. Improved neurological connections and myelination are directly implicated in the development of motor skills.

Reflexes, gross and fine motor skills. Reflexes, or involuntary reactions to external events, are an important aspect of early human survival. Consider the significance of reflexes for the hungry infant. Without the reflexive ability to suck, an infant would be unable to feed, leading to starvation. Associated with sucking, an infant must be able to locate a nipple for the purpose of feeding, a kind of rooting reflex that babies can accomplish from birth. Of course the infant must be able to communicate his or her need for food to a caregiver, reflexively expressed in terms of crying. After feeding, the infant may need to burp, possibly spitting up in the process. This reflex action, known to parents and caregivers the world over, prevents overfeeding. By definition the involuntary nature of reflexes suggests a fairly basic level of neurological development. Indeed, some reflexive behaviors, such as sucking, are visible while an infant is still in mother's womb.

Gross motor skills are premised on reflexes. The infant's ability to wave arms, crawl, walk and jump are eventual consequences of gross motor development. The first two years of life reflect tremendous gains in the sophistication and coordination of gross motor skills. By the age of six months most infants are able to belly crawl with raised head, progressing into full-fledged crawling by nine months. Standing and walking usually come shortly thereafter. The rapidly increasing range of gross motor skills enables an infant to explore the world and to discover many new things. Parental monitoring and supervision are particularly important during this period; infants and toddlers are at some risk of physical harm from electrical outlets, household chemicals, ledges and deep water (e.g., swimming pools).

Whereas gross motor skill development is characterized by sudden accomplishments, fine motor skills are acquired incrementally. *Grabbing* represents one of the most important examples of fine motor development. In the first couple of months an infant is unable to grab objects, although arms may flail at the sight of some desired item. Intentional touching may follow by three months, but not until six months can babies consistently grab and successfully hold on to an object. The highly refined coordination required to grab an object leads to increasingly sophisticated fine motor control; then infants begin to manipulate items within reach. Gibson (1988) notes that the onset of fine motor development enables what she terms the "eye-hand-mouth" exploratory system. Consequently, fine motor development is centrally implicated in the infant's ability to experience and understand the world.

Sensation. A growing infant must be able to navigate his or her environment on the basis of sensation and perception. It is important to note that in development sensation and perception are not synonymous. Sensation and perception are related principles, but have different roles in assisting the infant. *Sensation* refers to the detection of a stimulus, such as when the small bones of the inner ear vibrate in response to sound, sending electrical signals to the brain. *Perception* refers to the brain's process of understanding the meaning of the stimulus. The sound could mean a lullaby or the bark of an angry dog. Both sensations and perceptions are enormously significant to the child's growing ability to make meaning of the world and, in particular, relationships. In the following paragraphs we will review changes in sensory abilities. Perception will be covered in the next section on cognition (see p. 125).

Vision represents one important sensory dimension for the growing infants. At birth vision is poorly developed. Newborns are unable to make clear distinctions because objects in the visual field are blurry and undefined due to a lack of depth perception. However, this rapidly changes. By six months infant vision is about 20/40, reaching 20/20 by twelve months (Haith, 1993). Beyond the simple problem of clarity infants are also developing the ability to focus on an object without a wandering gaze. By three months most infants are able to effectively scan an object and attend to its critical features, making face recognition an easier process. Along with these changes infants learn to follow the movement of an object with greater speed. These changes are central to infants' ability to sense social interactions, providing a basis for interpreting emotions in others.

Hearing is a second crucial sensory dimension for the infant. Unlike vision, hearing is relatively well defined from the moment of birth. Infants are easily startled by loud noises and equally attracted to pleasant sounds (such as a warm conversation between Mom and Dad). Newborns are able to make these more immediate relational connections through hearing that is well developed even when the infant is inside the mother's womb. Remarkably, babies are able to differentiate between subtle differences between sounds used in other languages. Adults in the English-speaking world have difficulty with Thai and Czech vocalizations, but Thai and Czech babies are able to identify phonetic differences with ease (Jusczyk, 1995). This infantile sensitivity to vocalizations may be one reason that children are quickly able to acquire multiple languages.

Taste, smell and touch are all functional sensory capacities for infants. Researchers have noted that even newborns are able to clearly distinguish between salty and sweet tastes. Infants are able to differentiate between the smell of mother versus the smell of another lactating woman. Taste and smell are more sensitive in the first two years of life than at any other age, making first impressions of foods particularly important. It is quite possible that children with picky eating habits were exposed to a narrower range of foods during late infancy than children with a more adventurous palate. Infant exposure to a wider range of foods should, however, be tempered by a physician's advice in order to avoid potential allergic reactions. Touch is also well defined from birth, and by six months infants are able to assess temperature and texture. These sensory aspects of development are essential to the growing brain's ability to understand and predict changes in the environment.

Cognitive Changes

About seventy years ago, cognitive processes in child development were exhaustively described in the parallel work of Jean Piaget and Lev Vygotsky. The brilliant observational research of Piaget provides a sound basis for understanding how infants think about their world. However, Vygotsky's rejection of egocentrism in early childhood was important to an overall understanding of development in social context. Vygotsky was able to revise Piaget's work to include the relational basis of development in a manner reflecting a reciprocating self (see p. 91). First we will review Piaget's contributions to an understanding of infant perception and cognition. From this foundation, we will consider how cognition and emotion are reflected in the infant's reciprocating self through attachments with caregivers. Then, building on Piaget's work, we will revisit the developmental claims of Vygotsky for a dynamic, socially oriented infancy.

Piaget started with the assumption that children actively construct their own reality. Once reality is constructed, life experiences are turned into action. Perceiving an object, an infant instinctively looks at, grabs and sucks it. In the process the child constructs various plans of action or *schemas* toward the object. Schemas are cognitive structures that help organize mental representations related to a particular experience. The schema in turn provides the basis for understanding, whereby meaning is attributed to the experience. Thus a fourteen-month-old infant who is given a wooden block will experiment by looking at it, grasping it, sucking it, banging it and dropping it. In a manner of speaking the child adopts the role of a little scientist, discovering the schema that provides the best fit for the block.

Gibson (1988) notes that moments of infant discovery reflect environmental opportunities for perception and interaction. Such opportunities, or *affordances*, suggest that no two children will form the exact same schema in response to the same stimulus. Returning to the example above, the infant will assess the block on the basis of past experiences, current developmental level, sensory awareness of present opportunities and immediate needs or motivation (Gibson, 1997). The affordance perspective underlines the uniqueness of the individual infant in relation to the ecology of his or her social contexts with their varied stimuli.

Piaget provides a detailed account of perception and interaction in terms of assimilation, accommodation and equilibration. *Assimilation* means that the infant absorbs information in a manner consistent with an established way of thinking. Whatever is perceived is made to fit into existing schemas. It is quickly evident, however, that no new schemas will ever emerge if assimilation is the sum total of infant learning. New schemas must be created through a process of *accommodation*, where existing cognitive structures are altered to make space for new stimuli or schemas. Finally, processes of assimilation and accommodation must be regulated or kept in balance. *Equilibration* represents an infant's ability to efficiently place novel stimuli into existing or new structures that best facilitate meaning and understanding.

Piaget outlined six sensorimotor stages of infant development that provide a kind of developmental "roadmap" to the infant's ability to perceive the world, learn from it and act within it. Stage one (birth to 1 month) is largely reflexive, including sucking, grasping and listening reactions. Stage two (1-4 months) includes more adaptive reactions requiring basic coordination. Thus infants in this stage might learn the different sucking actions required for mother's breast as opposed to a bottle. These are basic, albeit significant, alterations to mental schemas that are accomplished at a remarkably early point in human development.

Infant perception and reaction to objects are foremost in Piaget's observations of stages three and four. The emphasis for these stages is on the formation of schemas that maximize the infants' adaptation to the world. In stage three (4-8 months) infants acquire the ability to actively respond to interesting people and objects, working hard to keep these close by or within a field of view. In stage four (8-12 months) infants begin to work out plans and purposes in response to people and objects in their world. Increasingly sophisticated schemas of the self and other permit infants to form representations of relationships.

Finally, infants begin to show the ability to creatively experience and act on the world, demonstrating the range of assimilation, accommodation and equilibration typical of early childhood. In stage five (12-18 months) toddlers are actively experimenting with people and objects in the world. In stage six (18-24 months) toddlers begin formulating goals that direct behavior, running hypothetical scenarios prior to actually engaging in an activity. Cause and effect are comprehensible to toddlers along with object permanence (the ability to recognize that a person or object continues to exist even when no longer visible).

Attachment

In Vygotsky's view infants are capable of creating mental representations in the first few weeks of life. Even though infants cannot talk about those representations, they are able to mentally re-present the face of a caregiver, the warm presence of the family dog or a mobile hanging over the crib. Indeed, the infantile ability to form representations is documented prior to the acquisition of language (Stern, 2000). This fact has enormous implications for the developing self. If infants can represent symbols and people, then we can assume that they have some kind of working memory. With this memory infants are able to construct representations of their relationships with other people. Far from being the passive protohuman of early developmental studies, an infant has a direct experience of relationships and subsequently of the self.

Obviously, the infant self is much less sophisticated than that of childhood or adolescence. But the foundational attachments made in early life are powerfully influential on later relationships and the development of a reciprocating self. It was John Bowlby (1980) who thought of *attachment* in terms of a behavioral, motivational system for the developing self. Bowlby called this foundation an *internal working model* of relationship. The internal working model consists of an infant's remembered experiences of a relationship and the mental representations that reflect those experiences. Jodie is six months old, too young to have an adult's *episodic memory,* remembered stories that adults tell about particular events, people or places. But Jodie does have an infantile memory that is already accumulating many experiences of an important person—her mother, Tanya. Tanya is a good mother, giving Jodie affection, love and attention to basic needs. Jodie has learned from Tanya that human relationships are for the most part places of safety and comfort. Bowlby suggests that Jodie's internal working model of relationship, influenced as it is by her secure attachment with Tanya, is a representation that can be readily transferred to other people. In brief, Jodie is well positioned to move through childhood with the ability to trust others.

Life circumstances might conspire to complicate this idyllic picture of Jodie's developing infant self. Tanya could be involved in a serious car accident when Jodie is nine months old. Because of her injuries Tanya undergoes a lengthy hospitalization and is unable to directly care for Jodie. Infant Jodie is not yet able to speak, but she is acutely aware that Mommy cannot physically be with her. These experiences result in new memories, changing Jodie's internal working model. Jodie discovers a new set of emotions associated with insecurity in cherished relationships. From Jodie's perspective Mommy is no longer available and may not return in the foreseeable future. Even though Jodie is securely attached to her mother, the girl's internal working model might be altered somewhat by Tanya's hospitalization.

The internal working model of relationship is indicated in the formation of the infant child's reciprocating self. An infant is capable of constructing deeply held beliefs about the self as a result of early encounters with others. We might skip ahead in Jodie's development to late infancy, around twenty-two months. At this point Jodie is a toddler. With her newfound freedom comes opportunity to interact at a more emotionally significant level. Jodie is playing with dominoes in the corner of the living room. Tanya suggests that it might be fun to build a domino "train" that could be tipped over in a design on the kitchen floor. Jodie does not really understand what this means but wants to be with her mother and joins her. Tanya's kitchen domino project soon becomes mildly obsessive, an intricate sunrise that requires more than four hundred dominoes. True to her toddler identity Jodie loses interest after a few minutes and wanders away. She returns to the kitchen a half hour later, wanting to reestablish the connection she had with her mother. By accident Jodie prematurely bumps the dominoes, causing the whole train to tip over in turn. In this pregnant moment Tanya has several parenting options at her disposal, each of which carries implications for Jodie's internal working model of relationships.

Confronted with Jodie's mistake, Tanya could laugh and involve Jodie in the fun of watching the dominoes tip over. Tanya could emotionally withdraw and leave the room in anger. Tanya could yell at Jodie. Finally, Tanya could silently watch and then begin rebuilding the design, ignoring her little daughter. Regardless of which course Tanya takes, the entire episode of the dominoes will become recorded in Jodie's memory and, consequently, her internal working model of relationship. The infant's developing self, emerging from an internal working model of relationship, directly encounters the internal working model of her mother. Tanya and Jodie's relational encounter is *intersubjective* in the sense that the infant's self is subjectively known and experienced on the basis of relationship. Hopefully, Tanya chooses to laugh and involve Jodie in the fun of watching the kitchen floor shimmer with falling dominoes. In this intersubjective encounter Jodie learns that it is her essential self, above all else, that has value to her mother. Nothing can obscure Jodie's worth as a person. If Tanya were to choose another, less caring response to Jodie's accident, the infant might intersubjectively learn that she is flawed, unworthy or undesirable.

If the infant's internal working model of relationship is implicated in her ability to trust people in the future, we might wonder whether attachment quality affects our ability to form a relationship with God in later development. It is unlikely that any researcher will ever be able to resolve this issue with actual infants, owing to communication limitations. However, it is possible to assess attachment quality in adolescents and emerging adults. In a large study of American college students, Neufeld (2004) found a moderate but consistent relationship between attachment quality and relational intimacy with God. With this "retrospective" approach to the attachment issue it appears that internal working models of relationship do affect spiritual formation, although the specific reasons for this remain unanswered (Kirkpatrick, 1999).

The Reciprocating Self in Infancy

An infant's reciprocating self, premised as it is on his or her internal working model of relationship, is general as opposed to specific. The infant does not have the fine memory necessary to reconstruct specific situations and emotions in linear time. Cognitive developmentalists refer to this pre-episodic period as *infant amnesia,* the basis for adult problems in remembering back before the age of three years. But the lack of episodic memory does not mean that the infant has no memory at all. Infant memory is capable of supporting enough schemas of relationships to be noteworthy, even in early development. Building on the attachment perspective of Bowlby and Ainsworth, Daniel Stern (2000) outlined four different self types in infancy. Stern adopted Vygotsky's idea that the self is fully differentiated at birth and that development consists of the self's repeated efforts to establish positive relationships. Stern's framework is a departure from Piaget's idea that the infant is fused with the caregiver at birth and only gradually undertakes a process of differentiation that leads to autonomy.

Emergent self (birth-2 months). Based on observation studies of infants, Stern (2000) argued for a sense of *emergent self* in infants from birth to two months of age. The emergent self is already being organized at birth, possibly even in utero. Unlike the infantile egocentrism of Piaget, Stern believed that the newborn is organizing experience into general schemas of knowing. Specifically, relational experiences are organized toward a sense of the self as a discrete entity. Stern bases the emergent-self concept on studies of newborn infants. MacFarlane (1975) found that even four-week-old children will turn their heads in response to a pad moistened with their mother's milk as opposed to the milk of a surrogate. Siqueland and DeLucia (1969) found that newborns alter their sucking intensity in response to preferences among voices and, additionally, the loudness of those voices. Not surprisingly, infants sucked the hardest for the voice of their mother. These studies imply that newborns have basic memory-retrieval functions in cognition, and that this early memory is capable of supporting internal representations of food and primary attachment relationships.

Stern made some general observations regarding the emergent self of the newborn. First, newborns seek *sensory stimulation.* A newborn infant uses sensory stimulation in order to test the environment. By testing the environment the newborn learns and begins the process of organizing relationships within it. Lee is a two-week-old newborn boy. Even though Lee's eyes are limited in their ability to follow an object, he is able to see faces at fairly close range. Lee's older brother, Antoine, is fascinated by the new addition to his family. Even though Antoine resents the fact that his mother now divides her attention between the two boys, he will spend long minutes gazing down at Lee. He will tickle the baby and hold his hands. When no one else is watching, Antoine will gently sing to Lee. Lee learns from these encounters that Antoine is not his mother. Antoine occupies a different schema in Lee's experience than those of his mother or father. Antoine does not feed Lee, nor is he allowed to pick him up. But Antoine is a close and significant relationship that figures prominently in Lee's limited experience with the world. In the sibling tickle sessions Lee is able to associate stimuli with a new relationship schema and the beginnings of a reciprocating self.

Second, newborns have distinct *biases* or *preferences* with regard to sensation. From stimulation a newborn is able to form perceptions, memories and schemas for sensation. Antoine discovers that Lee will whimper and turn his head away when he tickles the baby by squeezing his legs above the knee. But Lee will regain eye contact when Antoine gently nudges his ribs. Moreover, Antoine quickly learns that Lee loves to be sung to, and that the baby will move his arms and legs more quickly by way of response. Even at two weeks Lee is developing his own preferences, a process that will continue as each brother learns what the other likes and dislikes, eventually exploiting that knowledge for less than noble purposes!

Third, infants learn how to organize the environment on the basis of *emotions*. The emergent reciprocating self is significantly shaped by feelings, a link that will continue for the rest of an infant's life. Lee experiences positive emotions related to nursing at his mother's breast. Because of their feeding times Lee learns that life is not a static or monotone existence. The environment contains people and relationships that are capable of resolving basic needs such as hunger and, additionally, needs related to the self. Lee may experience occasional colic. During these periods of intestinal cramping Lee cries and is not easily comforted. Only at his mother's breast does Lee find relief, not because the cramping has stopped but because the positive feelings of support and closeness compensate for the discomfort, even if he is not actually hungry.

Stern's observations of the emergent reciprocating self imply that infants are aware of their own distinctness based on experienced perceptions, memories and feelings. This is a bold assertion premised on the idea that even the newborn has the ability to form mental representations leading to an internal working model of relationship. At this point we might wonder whether such a developmental argument is purely speculative, given the impossibility of talking to infants about their experiences. How do we know whether newborns are capable of forming mental representations and schemas?

Meltzoff and Borton (1979) designed a study in order to answer this very question. The researchers postulated that newborns would demonstrate a capability for representation if they could transfer one sensory experience to another. In other words, if infants could take an experience of touch and correctly link it to an experience of sight, this would demonstrate the ability to mentally represent an object. To test this idea, three-week-old infants were blindfolded and given two different pacifiers. The first pacifier was smooth but the second was covered with "nubs," small bumps protruding from it. The blindfolded infants were permitted a lengthy suck on each pacifier in order to learn how it felt in the mouth. In the first experiment blindfolded newborns were given the smooth pacifier first and the nubbed pacifier second. Blindfolds were removed and the infants were immediately presented with both pacifiers for comparison. All infants looked intently to the nubbed pacifier they had just sucked. In the second experiment blindfolded newborns were given the nubbed pacifier followed by the smooth one. Once again blindfolds were removed and the infants were presented with both pacifiers for comparison. All infants looked intently at the smooth pacifier they had just sucked. Even at the age of three weeks newborns were capable of mentally representing the feeling of the pacifiers in their mouths, allowing them to make accurate visual judgments (Hayne, 2002).

Sense of core self (2-7 months). The premise of infantile representation led Stern to consider a second type of developing self. Over time infants start to come into their own as social creatures. From two to seven months old Stern noted that infants organized their experiences and memories into increasingly sophisticated representations, leading to what he called a *sense of core self*. For infants in this age bracket, improved motor control makes exploration a reality. Infants' discovery of arms for reaching and the acts of rolling and crawling greatly increase the scope of experiences available to the self. Stern noted that the sense of core self is reflected in exploration and the potential for logical consequences. Without question the core self implies an increasing level of reciprocity with others in an infant's environment.

The emerging sense of core self might be considered in terms of four strategies, each associated with exploration. First, an infant organizes the self on the basis of his or her *agency*. Even at six months an infant is beginning to understand his or her ability to act, to control and to discover unexpected consequences. Monica is a six-month-old girl. She is bright and vivacious, and loves touching faces. Often when she is in her father's lap, she holds his fingers and bounces up and down. When she is close to his face, she feels his scratchy cheek and grabs his nose with surprising force, attempting to rip her father's nose away from his face. In that moment, Monica has little sense of self insofar as her actions are related to consequences. If Monica's father patiently endures his daughter's handiwork, the girl will fail to make a causal connection between her hand, his nose and the state of their relationship. But if Monica's father yells "Ouch!" and turns his head away, she will learns that this connection is in fact significant. Monica discovers that she is an agent, capable of acting on an environment that will reciprocate to her. Albert Bandura refers to this kind of exchange as *reciprocal determinism* (Bandura, 1978, 1998).

Second, Stern outlined the importance of *self-coherence* in the growing sense of having a core self. Self-coherence is predicated on an infant's knowledge that he or she is a whole being. In the nose-adjustment encounter, Monica's father chooses to grimace and gently pull the girl's hand away from his face. Monica learns that her actions precipitate a less-desired response (communicated through facial expression) that alerts her to the reality that she is not her father. Monica did not experience pain as a result of her exploration of Dad's nose. But her father did, and because of her growing ability to relate to others, she learns that her actions are not mutually agreeable. These boundaries are necessary for any relationship in order to help the infant understand the dimensions of the self.

Third, Stern suggests that infants become aware of varied feelings associated with the self in relationships. Stern called this *self-affectivity*. With increased relational skills and a newfound ability to explore the environment, infants encounter a widening number of other people. For Monica, self-affectivity is warm and cozy with Mommy, safe and fun with Daddy, but strangely distant with Grandma, who is not comfortable with children. The infant's growing sense of self suggests an emotional barometer of relational closeness that affects the character of each relationship. Monica learns that all relationships are not equal. Eventually Monica will unthinkingly adapt this knowledge to various roles she will play in her family, her peer group and her school.

Finally, Stern noted that the core-self period contains infants' realization of *self-history*. With increased capability to remember and recall information, infants gain a sense of having a past and a present. Monica comes to realize that she will wake up tomorrow and still be herself. Stern implies that an infant's sense of core self emerges where agency, self-coherence, self-affectivity and self-history are integrated into a larger sense of what it means to be "me." At six months Monica not only knows her name but also that she exists separately from her parents. Yet Monica is empowered by the feelings associated with those relationships to explore new relationships and along with them an increasingly sophisticated framework for the self.

Sense of a subjective self (7-12 months). Incredible as it may seem, infants are capable of learning that they have a mind and that other people have minds too. Even more remarkable, this change is taking place in the first year of life, before most children are forming coherent words and sentences. Stern called this period of development the *sense of a subjective self*. With development infants are learning increasingly sophisticated means to relate to others. With this sophistication comes greater self-understanding. During this period empathy makes its first appearance. Infants learn that they can feel bad for someone else, but also that these feelings can be shared with others (Trevarthen and Aitken, 2001).

Stern's case for a subjective self in infancy relies on the reciprocal concept of intersubjectivity. That is, an infant's self is shaped where its internal working model encounters the internal working model of another, usually the primary caregiver. Murphy and Messer (1977) demonstrated that nine-month-old infants will cease to look only at their mother's pointing hand and will look in the direction that she is pointing. In Piagetian thinking, this is impossible because of the infant's egocentrism. But the Murphy and Messer study demonstrates that when Mom points to something, the infant is able to understand Mom's mind insofar as she is saying, "Look!" Moreover, the same researchers discovered that after looking in the direction of Mom's pointing finger, nine-month-old infants look back at Mom for facial cues that communicate whether or not the child in fact saw the desired object. With a sense of subjective self the infant acquires the ability to figure out whether the focus of attention is shared between child and parent.

This study implies a remarkably sophisticated relational capability in infants, not to mention children's deepening sense of reciprocating self. In effect, through an intersubjective relationship infants are able to understand whether they and their mother are mentally on the same page. For an infant, this means that "me" and "Mom," as discrete minds, can share ideas, intentions and feelings, all before they can talk about them. We wonder how frustrated an infant must feel given the growing capabilities of the subjective self combined with verbal limitations. It is little wonder that infants in this stage of development use loud vocalizations. Developmentally speaking, the acquisition of language must come as a relief.

We can deduce, however, that mother and infant are able to create some helpful communicative strategies in the absence of formal language. Stern notes that mothers and infant children in this stage demonstrate *affect attunement*. Affect attunement simply refers to the nonverbal means by which parent and child communicate shared feelings that reflect the subjective, inner state of the self. Robert, a nine-month-old, is very excited about a new toy and reaches for it. As he grabs the toy, he lets out an exuberant "aaaaaaah!" and looks at his mother. Mom makes eye contact with Robert, scrunches her shoulders and sways back and forth like a dancer. The swaying lasts the same length of time as the infant boy's "aaaaaaah!" Like his vocalization, the swaying is excited, joyful and intense. Affect attunement reinforces the infant's subjective sense of self not as an imitation of behavior, but through communication of mutually shared feelings. Robert is saying, "I'm excited! I love this toy!" In reply, Mom is saying, "I see how you're excited, and it makes me excited too!" This simple affirmation is filled with love. Robert learns that his inner feelings of joy and excitement can be reciprocated (Jonsson et al., 2001).

Sense of a verbal self (12-plus months). Finally, the infant acquires formal language, usually after the first year. The advent of language coincides with a fairly well developed sense of self and other. Rather than waiting for language in order to form the self, Stern argues that language becomes a better strategy for reciprocating organized representations in memory. But with the arrival of language the infant also learns to objectify the self. To put this in a different way, the verbal infant is able to step outside of the self and say, "That's me!" Lewis and Brooks-Gunn (1978) found that before the age of eighteen months infants do not know that what they see in the mirror is their own reflection. Thus fourteen-month-old infants with rouge on their cheeks point to the mirror and verbalize a response, generally about that "other baby." But after eighteen months, rouged infants touch their own cheeks rather than the mirror. The sense of a verbal self means that "me" exists not only internally but externally.

Infant children in the second year of life acquire the ability to play symbolically, with make-believe characters personified as dolls or other actors in fantasy worlds. With language an infant learns new ways of understanding the self and the selves of others. Through reciprocity, ever more sophisticated organization of the self becomes possible. When Dad praises twenty-month-old Nadia with "Good girl!" it activates different representations, schemas and memories than when Mom gives the same encouragement. With Dad, Nadia associates this praise with the situations that usually accompany it. Dad often praises his daughter in this manner when she masters a new task. On the other hand, Mom might use the same phrase when Nadia is playing with other children or at times when good behavior is important. The infant's emerging sense of a verbal self leads to a sharpened internal working model of relationship. When combined with the individual's personality disposition the self is reciprocating.

Parenting and the Infant Self

In the introductory section of the book we discussed several theologically derived concepts that are important to the whole of development. These were *unconditional love, gracing, empowering,* and *intimate relationships* (Balswick and Balswick, 1995). In this section we will reflect on how these concerns are "translated" into the positive development of a reciprocating self. We might approach this task by briefly reviewing some terminology used in the parenting and family studies literature. This literature provides us with a means to apply love, grace, empowerment and intimacy in the varied ecosystems of infant development. Specifically, we rely on the classic work of Diana Baumrind, who conducted detailed studies of children from infancy into adulthood (Baumrind, 1996; Rollins and Thomas, 1979). Thus this section serves as a bridge between our discussion of the reciprocating self in infancy and the nested contexts in which the self might be scaffolded.

How might unconditional love be understood in the developing selves of infants? The parenting literature recognizes the significance of *unconditional love* in terms of *support* for the growing child. Support is just that—the extent to which the parent is emotionally supportive of the child. For the infant's reciprocating self, support is extraordinarily important. From Stern's framework we can conclude that the lack of consistent emotional support for an infant could be catastrophic. Indeed, the tragedy of Romanian orphanages in the early 1990s demonstrates how critical support is to the infant. With ratios of 150 babies to 1 caregiver, infants were often terribly damaged from inadequate support. Lacking an appropriate other with which to create internal working models of relationship, some of these orphaned infants demonstrated reactive attachment disorders, brain damage, learning disabilities and antisocial behavior.

The developmental language of unconditional love suggests that infants should receive *consistently adequate* emotional support. Since this does not imply perfection on the part of parents, we might do better to speak in terms of *the good enough parent* (Winnicott, 1971). Indeed, life is too chaotic to permit more than a consistently adequate benchmark of support. Take Jodie, the nine-month-old whose mother, Tanya, was hospitalized by an automobile accident. For a time Jodie is unable to directly experience her mother's emotional support. Yet there are other caregivers in her world that are able to compensate for this deficit, particularly in a manner that affirms Jodie's reciprocating self. Jodie's paternal grandmother, Anita, comes to stay with the family. Together with her father, Bill, Jodie receives consistently adequate support that permits her not only to grow in her own sense of core self but in the range of relational possibilities that are available to her. Baumrind's research reveals that support is a critical factor in positive early development (Baumrind, 1972, 1991).

How might we understand grace in the world of an infant? *Grace* implies a relationship, particularly one where a less-powerful individual is afforded the space to make mistakes and grow through those experiences. The parenting literature defines this kind of attentive parenting presence in terms of *monitoring*. Monitoring refers to the parent's involvement in the child's activities with a view toward safety and growth. The parent that does not monitor the crawling or toddling infant risks a variety of safety concerns, particularly in relation to places where a child might fall or experience electrocution, drowning or accidental poisoning. Even beyond these basic safety issues, a lack of monitoring communicates an essential unworthiness to the infant's reciprocating self. Unmonitored infants are also ungraced infants, left to their own devices to make mistakes and pay dearly for them in the absence of a caregiver.

For nine-month-old Robert no sense of affect attunement is possible in the absence of a caregiver. In fact, the joy of Robert's new toy is effectively nullified if no one is present to intersubjectively share his excitement. Monitoring means that the parent is heavily invested in the child's waking moments, ensuring safety and a consistent zone of proximal development that affirms the infant's growing range of feelings and preferences. Conversely, we might wonder what happens when an infant experiences too much monitoring. Some overcontrolling parents monitor their infant so closely that the child is unable to effectively know the self apart from the other. The effect of excessive monitoring is to leave the infant with blurred boundaries between the self and other. Consistently adequate monitoring means that the growing infant learns how to position the self in a variety of social situations without undue stress.

How might we understand empowering in the life of the infant? *Empowerment* suggests that an infant is learning to be a capable and appropriately other-focused agent. This does not happen automatically. In the parenting literature, *intervention strategies* refer to preferred techniques to correct children so that they develop character. Rollins and Thomas (1979) further specify intervention around negative and positive strategies. *Coercion* is negative in the sense that it is punitive. Coercive intervention might be physical, emotional or both. Coercion may also include deprivation or removal of privileges. While coercive intervention is not necessary with younger infants, it will become so with the child's increased mobility. Coercive intervention strategies should be focused on creating logical consequences for dangerous or inappropriate behavior rather than as a means of subjugation. Baumrind's research found that coercive strategies, such as time-outs or withdrawal of privileges, were more effective correctives than physical punishments, shame and love withdrawal (1971, 1996). This kind of moderate approach to coercion tended to promote empathy and other-oriented thinking, even in toddlers.

A positive intervention strategy might include induction. *Induction* means that the parent "reasons" with the child about his or her actions, particularly with regard to potential consequences. Consider twenty-month-old Nadia, who impulsively toddles out into the street and is narrowly missed by a car. Nadia's mother, who is terrified, nonetheless recognizes that the toddler has no means of understanding how serious her actions were. Instead of giving Nadia a spanking (physical, coercive strategy), she gets down at eye level and tells the girl in measured tones that to run out into the street means that she could be hit by a car and hurt or killed. This kind of inductive reasoning is effective when combined with a moderate form of coercion such as a time-out. Even if the toddler lacks full understanding of her mother's explanation, a precedent is being set. Through induction the mother is communicating a high degree of worth to Nadia's reciprocating self, along with very serious concern for a dangerous situation. The seriousness of the situation is further reinforced by a coercive intervention. Baumrind found that children who experienced a lot of inductive intervention knew themselves and were able to make better decisions than children who lacked induction. Presumably, induction helps the verbal infant in a process of policing the self away from behaviors that are dangerous or potentially hurtful to others.

How might *intimate relationships* be translated for the infant's reciprocating self? *Control* is an important aspect of human relatedness that figures prominently in parenting behavior. Control is present in any human relationship. Of itself, control is neither positive nor negative but can be handled in a manner that promotes or restricts human intimacy and trust. Extreme examples of parental control often capture national headlines. Unfortunately, most of these examples document child abuse. Moderate examples of control help the infant to differentiate the self from the other, establishing boundaries that will one day be readily transferable into peer relationships. In the parent-child dyad, control is an essential element in creating an effective developmental scaffold (Baumrind, 1991). Given the power differential that is natural to the parent-child relationship, appropriate control is premised on trust, the basic ingredient that makes intimate relationships possible.

Recalling Monica's nose job on her dad, we can note that his response incorporated control that leads to trust. Instead of a harsh, vindictive reaction, Dad makes a measured intervention that helps Monica to better understand what reciprocates intimacy and closeness in relationships. This happens in conjunction with a growing sense of the self as different from Dad, yet still linked with him. An overcontrolling response might include a yell and slap of the hand. An undercontrolling response might be no response at all. Either course fails to help Monica understand herself as both agent and recipient of trust through a reciprocating self.

The Ecology of Infanthood

In this final section we will discuss how an infant's reciprocating self is potentially influenced by successive ecosystems. In particular we will look at infant development in terms of scaffolding. Issues of support, monitoring, intervention strategies and control will be assumed in this discussion.

Microsystem. The microsystem has already figured prominently in this chapter as a means for considering the reciprocating self. We considered the attachment relationship with a primary caregiver and the importance of the dyad in establishing Stern's four iterations of the infant self. Finally, we considered unconditional love, gracing, empowering and intimate relationships from within the parenting literature. Parental support, monitoring, intervention strategies and control all reflect important relational dynamics within the microsystem.

We might think of the microsystem in terms of helping to securely establish an infant's reciprocating self. Because the microsystem is nested within other, larger systemic categories, it is a vitally important place for a growing infant to learn about the self and other in relative safety. Attachment theorists often speak of relationship quality in terms of security. This metaphor makes good sense given that a child's ever-expanding social contexts require increasingly sophisticated role transitions. Thus security in the dyad might be one way of thinking about developmental scaffolding. For example, an infant might grow with an insecure reciprocating self through inadequate parenting practices in the microsystem dyad. A child's internal working model of relationships might be confused by a number of issues, including trust, sharing, emotional support and empathy. This insecurity carries over into real challenges for the individual in middle childhood and adolescence. Such insecurity might result in an avoidant personality, where the child fears rejection. Avoidant children often grow with a deep-seated anger that leads to isolation, chronic pleasing or bullying behavior. Or a child might grow with an ambivalent sense of self, often leading to a manipulative approach to relationships. In the worst-case scenario severely abused or neglected children might be disorganized or disoriented, such as in the case of Romanian orphans.

The highest likelihood of positive development is established in infancy. Secure relations in the microsystem are vital in scaffolding the child's growing sense of what it means to exist, and doubly important, how to exist in relationship.

Mesosystem. In infant development, the mesosystem is not often studied beyond the influence of nuclear families. Some developmentalists have recognized the fact that neighborhood environments, for example, do influence development in significant ways. Neighborhood mesosystems tend to be somewhat removed from the infant's everyday experiences, but they can indirectly exert considerable influence. Infant growing up in a depressed, inner-city neighborhood might inherit the stresses experienced by their parents' struggle to make ends meet and keep the family safe. Stress from socioeconomic deficits, ethnic oppression and other factors can creep into microsystem relations between parents and child, sometimes undermining the parents' efforts at scaffolding a reciprocating self. As an example, it is difficult for a single parent living in a depressed neighborhood to practice much induction with a toddler simply because the child might spend large blocks of time in daycare. The good news is that many parents daily overcome the odds and provide consistently adequate parenting in spite of neighborhood-related stresses. An infant does not require an "ideal" suburban neighborhood in order to develop a strong reciprocating self. In their exclusivity upper-middle-class neighborhoods tend to isolate families from one another, leading to other indirect struggles fostered through the mesosystem. All ecosystems are capable of providing at least some resources capable of nurturing the reciprocating self.

In the developing world the mesosystem typically includes extended family and kin. These aunts, uncles, cousins and grandparents have tremendous influence on an infant's developing self. Positive regular connections with extended relations are important opportunities for a developing infant self, so is exposure to different styles of influence through scaffolding of support, monitoring, intervention and control. This larger sense of "family" or mesosystem carries significant potential to help the infant learn self-understanding through relationship. In our California context, many Latino families place high value on their extended family. Often these families make career sacrifices in order to stay close to extended kin. These cultural priorities for family life are advantageous to the infant's reciprocating self and the language of relationship that he or she will learn by spending time with so many different individuals.

Exosystem. Usually a parent's place of work does not figure into our thinking about infant development. But the exosystem can exert indirect influence on the infant's reciprocating self. In their research on executives and their spouses, Small and Riley (1990) found evidence of adverse spillover from work to the parent-child relationship. Balswick and Balswick (1995) suggested that adverse spillover may be especially problematic among dual-earner parents. Balancing commitment to work and parenting results in some dual-earner parents trying to retain full commitment to both arenas (acrobats), some trying to convince the other to assume more parenting responsibilities (adversaries), and some trimming back involvement in work in favor of joint parenting (allies). A creative example of the latter is Janet, a fourth-grade teacher who chooses to job share her position in order to spend three days a week at home with her seven-month-old daughter, Harriet. Janet's principal and her coteacher are both supportive of the mother's decision, recognizing the benefit for Janet's family life and the benefit of keeping a valued teacher and team member on the school's faculty. Janet's job-sharing schedule will only be for a few years, allowing her to eventually reenter the elementary faculty as a full-time teacher. This kind of exosystemic influence is enormously helpful to Harriet and the scaffolding of her reciprocating self. The infant is the indirect beneficiary of the support her mother receives in her workplace. Consequently, we can expect that Janet is more easily able to offer support to Harriet with the knowledge that she is supported in her commitment to be a consistently adequate mother.

In European countries it is increasingly common for parents to job share. Moreover, many European countries place a premium on early infant scaffolding by giving paternity and maternity leave to young parents. This is in contrast to the United States, where reduced paternity and maternity leave is the norm, and working parents are expected to take advantage of paid childcare solutions for their infants. We do not have space here to critique the developmental advantages and disadvantages of these two approaches to infancy and family. But it is clear from an exosystemic perspective that the European situation offers better support for the developing infant simply through the supportive environment experienced by the parent in the workplace. In economic terms American policy-makers would do well to weigh the costs of paternity and maternity leave next to the long-term repercussions of parents who do not feel supported by their work environment. Such parents are likely to be less loyal to their jobs and colleagues, and more likely to move to a new job, thereby creating additional transition stressors for the family system.

Macrosystem. How might culture affect the infant's reciprocating self? There are many different possibilities in our accelerated, information-laden Western society. Given space limitations, we will briefly focus on television aimed at early childhood. Most toddlers are fascinated by television, particularly those programs that are populated with age-appropriate characters. In the United States *Barney & Friends* is a popular show aimed at toddlers and preschool-aged children. In England *Teletubbies* fills a similar niche. Generally, these shows are not fully absorbed by children under the age of two. Toddlers simply do not have long enough attention spans to take in a thirty-minute program. But within their limited attention span, toddlers are still influenced by television. TV characters become representations that at times figure prominently in toddler play. Often, a Barney doll or Teletubby character can become central to the toddler's expanding capability for creative play.

Do these programs influence an infant's sense of reciprocating self? Few studies have been done in this area. Yet this dearth of research does not mean that the question is unimportant. Although the *Barney* program employs an educational psychologist as a consultant, we should know more about how the program influences the growing infant. At least superficially, television's ability to scaffold the reciprocating self is minimized by its lack of direct, relational interaction. Children may *relate* to a program and its characters, but *lack a relationship* with those characters. Herein lies the rub. Television can become a poor substitute for the scaffolding of a child's reciprocating self because it superficially appears to occupy the child's attention, at least for a time. But television is not a dynamic, reciprocating entity. The child is only a recipient rather than a contributor to television. This lack of reciprocity does nothing to help a child learn new contexts and languages for relationship reflecting his or her internal working model. Support, monitoring, intervention strategies and control are not on the agenda for television or its characters. Thus while a child may extract some bits of "learned" information from a program, he or she will gain little by way of self-understanding in relationship.

Concluding Thoughts

We have outlined a number of issues related to the reciprocating self in infancy, beginning with biological and cognitive factors in development. Through the work of John Bowlby and Daniel Stern we have made a case for four different reciprocating selves from birth to age two. We have attempted to describe how love, gracing, empowerment and intimate relationships are experienced through the language of the parenting and family studies literature. Finally, we used Bronfenbrenner's ecosystemic model to consider how the reciprocating self might form in various social contexts. Much of this work may come as a surprise to readers who assume infancy to be a relatively unremarkable period of egocentrism. We believe, however, that the developmental literature makes a compelling case for an active infancy. The depth of our argument will be tested as we expand it through childhood and adolescence.

7

Childhood

THE RECIPROCATING SELF
GOES TO SCHOOL

MARK TWAIN ONCE OBSERVED THAT IT would be better for humanity to be born at the age of eighty and then develop *down* the life span, eventually becoming children! This kind of backward growth implies that everyone would begin life with the wisdom of age, a considerable advantage when navigating the challenges of childhood. Twain's joke speaks to the many complications of growing up. Indeed, his humor might be prophetic, given an accelerating American culture that places significant pressures on modern children.

It is probably unfair to romanticize the childhood of Twain's day in the mid-nineteenth century. As in our time Victorian parents placed considerable achievement expectations on their children, whether this meant doing a good job with chores on the family farm, dedicating oneself to a trade or working to help their financially struggling families. The difference between Twain's world and ours is that today's child is increasingly asked to achieve apart from immediate family concerns, to "make it" in a highly individualized America. The pressure of achievement in childhood extends to school performance, extracurricular activities, sports and peer leadership. It is more than likely that these pressures exert an influence on the child's reciprocating self, particularly as he or she gains a deeper sense of identity as a person created in the *imago Dei*.

How do children develop a coherent self through the din of Game Boys, screaming soccer parents and mass-marketed pop music? In this chapter we will consider the developmental scaffolding of childhood through the age span of three to eleven years. To accomplish this we will break our discussion into two sections. In the first section we will consider the biological and cognitive characteristics of early childhood (3-7 years), also known as the *play years*. In the second section we will review biological and cognitive characteristics of older children (7-11 years), often referred to as the *school years*. Next, we will move on to explore the child's reciprocating self in terms of *attachment, risk and resiliency* and *parenting issues* related to unconditional love, gracing, empowering and intimate relationships. Finally, we will take a look at the child's ecosystem, focusing on issues relating to the family and the child's role in society. In particular, we will consider *divorce* and *discrimination*.

Play Years: Biological Changes

Early childhood is a period of rapid biological development. Extending from infancy the brain continues to establish synaptic pathways that are accompanied by ongoing myelinization. Children in the play years become increasingly effective in their reactions to stimuli, and they also demonstrate improved control of their responses. A five-year-old boy is better able to handle the frustration of a playmate's stubborn refusal to share toys than he was at age two. While conflict is likely in this situation, the boys will be more apt to handle things verbally rather than immediately resorting to a temper tantrum.

An interesting aspect of brain development in the play years involves a bundle of nerves known as the *corpus callosum*. The corpus callosum connects the left and right hemispheres of the brain, serving as a kind of information pathway for communication between hemispheres. Children in the play years experience rapid myelinization and growth of the corpus callosum, greatly expanding the range of coordinated activity. Further, growth of the corpus callosum facilitates better processing of stimuli and past experiences. This is one reason that children in the play years are somewhat less at risk for injury than toddlers. The five-year-old is able to anticipate a red stoplight signal at an intersection without impulsively jumping into the street.

Increased coordination and improved processing are immediately helpful to the young child's ability to recognize letters on a page or to handle a pencil for the purpose of writing. These changes make it possible for the child to link speech with written language, making connections between letters and sounds that anticipate reading. By age six the brain is mature enough to move ahead with formal instruction in reading, writing and mathematics.

This should not serve, however, as a hard and fast threshold on the road to literacy. Indeed, there is evidence that reading to two- and three-year-old children significantly aids brain development, leaving a child well positioned for formal reading instruction in kindergarten.

Gross and fine motor skills are rapidly improving for the young child. An activity such as riding a bicycle is out of the question for the two-year-old toddler, but it becomes a real possibility for four- or five-year-old children. Cultural conditions and expectations result in variation between gross motor accomplishments in the play years. In Canada, many children begin ice skating at two or three, becoming remarkably competent skaters by kindergarten. In Polynesia five-year-olds are able to swim in waves or climb rock formations that would intimidate many Western adults. Much of the gross motor accomplishments typical of the play years occur in the context of social interactions with peers rather than direct instruction from adults. The dynamic relational aspect of play yields dividends in terms of the young child's ability to master complex activities and sports in a manner that scaffolds the social dimensions of the reciprocating self.

Children in the play years are able to handle increasingly demanding tasks that require fine motor skills. A good example of this developmental progression can be found in the art produced by preschool children. At two, most children tend to create rather undefined masterpieces, with little recognizable form. By three and four, many children begin drawing people, first as potato-head bodies with pipe-cleaner limbs, then with more sophisticated and realistic heads with proportional torsos. Eventually, young artists improve their work to include hair, ears and other facial features. Improved use of color and detail is typical of this progression, reflecting better fine motor control and the ability to express what is already represented in the mind. Additionally, increased myelinization allows children in early childhood to eventually master buttons and zippers when getting dressed, and effectively handle silverware at mealtime. Frustration with these tasks is gradually replaced by a sense of accomplishment, whereby the child gains confidence in his or her fine motor abilities and problem-solving skills.

Play Years: Cognitive Changes

We will use Piaget's observations of children in the play years as a foundation for Vygotsky's reflections on cognitive development. Piaget maintained that the primary difference between the toddler and play years is the preschooler's ability to think symbolically. The young child acquires the ability to interpret various symbols in the environment, including the family dog. *Dog* refers to more than just an animal; it also includes an entire domain of knowledge including barking, playing fetch and neighborhood walks after dinner. A child in the play years can identify meanings associated with dogs that are beyond a toddler's range of interpretation. For example, a five-year-old knows that dogs are *household pets,* a concept that is elusive to toddlers.

Piaget referred to the play years as a period of *preoperational thought.* Although the newfound symbolic ability of the young child is a hallmark of the preoperational period, Piaget's work tended to focus on what children in this age bracket could not do rather than what they could accomplish. Preoperational children are not logical, in Piaget's view, because of their tendency to focus thought on one aspect of a situation to the exclusion of everything else. Such *centration* means that preoperational children cannot combine conceptual categories in a way that make logical sense. In the preoperational child's mind, wolves and coyotes are not related to dogs because these animals do not live in the house as domestic pets. For Piaget this kind of one-track thinking reflects egocentric tendencies typical of the play years.

A well-known example of centration is found in Piaget's experiments with young children's understanding of *conservation.* Piaget found that when children at the play age were confronted with an identical volume of milk in a squat glass and a tall, thin glass, the children insisted that the tall glass contained more milk. Preoperational children were unable to understand the concept of volume, instead focusing on the height of the milk level as an index of quantity. Piaget's observations, while useful, are directed toward highly individualized processes that appear to limit development on the basis of cognitive capacities. Throughout this book we have emphasized the relational aspects of the reciprocating self. Given our earlier theological discussion regarding the underpinnings of the reciprocating self, we view Piaget's work as a worthy beginning toward a more complete, contextual understanding of child development.

In chapter five we discussed the social and relational bases for development in terms of Vygotsky's cognitive theory. We considered the means by which relationships *scaffold* cognition in early childhood, specifically through a *zone of proximal development.* For Vygotsky, scaffolding and proximal development are based on the idea that children are *apprentices* to others in their social context. The child looks to others in order to better understand the world and the way it works. For Vygotsky recognition of the child's inability to recognize the same volume of milk in glasses with different shapes is less important than the fact that when learning the truth of the situation, the child turns to a nearby adult and asks why. The child's cognitive development is significantly supported by interactions with receptive, patient adults willing to provide age-appropriate answers. With their rapidly expanding linguistic capabilities, children are able to communicate with adults in such a way that ideas and concepts previously out of reach become accessible.

One important consequence of social learning for the young apprentice is that he or she acquires the ability to understand mental processes in others. Building on infancy, children in the play years are able to generate an increasingly sophisticated *theory of mind*, knowing that others have thoughts, beliefs, preferences and desires. This can have immediate positive implications in terms of empathy. A five-year-old is more than capable of understanding a friend's despair over a treasured cat that ran away. Conversely, the same five-year-old is now able to understand that his younger sibling doesn't like spiders, exploiting that knowledge by teasing the sibling with a plastic tarantula. Interestingly, developmentalists have found that general language ability is correlated with the child's ability to understand the thoughts of others (Moore, Pure and Furrow, 1990). The reciprocating self, understood in terms of relationships with others, suggests a theory of mind built on language.

Language abilities change rapidly for children in the play years. Initial acquisition of vocabulary proceeds slowly, but by three years children begin to acquire new words to describe a myriad of external situations and internal feelings. One possible explanation for this rapid progression of language is that children develop a process for mapping the meanings of words in relation to other words. This kind of strategy makes use of analogies, resulting in somewhat flexible definitions for a given word. A child might hear a preschool teacher mention a teal-colored piece of chalk, understand that *teal* is a kind of color, but not know specifically what kind or what to look for. Words are mapped and understood on the basis of context and relationship with other word meanings. The reciprocating self is shaped by new words that create categories for a five-year-old to understand him- or herself as a valued child of God.

School Years: Biological Changes

Without a doubt the school years can be a wonderful and carefree life-span stage. Biological changes to the brain and motor skills continue, enabling children to succeed in sports and to accomplish increasingly complicated intellectual feats. However, the same period of life can be stressful and difficult. Stress and subtle changes in the American lifestyle have had negative consequences for the physical development of children. American children in the school years are among the most obese (per capita) among Western nations, displaying a number of weight-related medical problems and disorders. At the same time, children in the school years are notoriously unforgiving of physical differences in others. Freckles, hair, skin and weight can all be the objects of criticism or teasing. Our discussion of biological development must become increasingly sensitive to the child's growing social capacity and reciprocating influences, particularly given the heightened importance of the peer group.

Physical growth slows somewhat in the school years, causing a kind of filling out for many children in middle and upper grades. Genes are a significant factor in how children carry their weight. In affluent countries well-fed children will easily achieve their genetically determined height for a given age in childhood. However, an increasingly sedentary American lifestyle combined with cheap and easy junk food options have created a situation where many children are overnourished, to the point of obesity. By some estimates 30 percent of American children in the school years are medically obese, heightening risk for a range of orthopedic and respiratory ailments (Dietz, 1999). Children reciprocate the eating habits and basic self-care of their parents, siblings and peers. Stressed-out parents who are unable to promote healthy nutrition at home can directly influence biological developmental processes in school-aged children by modeling that junk food is an acceptable solution to problems. When combined with popular, sedentary pastimes (e.g., video games and TV), this kind of scaffolding can have significant effect on a child's health.

Sports and group games provide healthy opportunities for children to exercise in a social context, promoting good health, coordination and diverse relationships for a reciprocating self. Brain development and motor skills for school-aged children are enhanced with involvement in activities such as gymnastics, soccer and dance. Children acquire improved hand-eye coordination through sports, demonstrating better reaction times and increased flexibility. Such activities can greatly support the development of a mature reciprocating self, to the extent that children may learn they are a whole, complete being created in God's image. With their bodies, children discover they can make valuable contributions as an accepted member of a team. They learn that life is a gift from God, something to be celebrated individually and for the sake of others. We suspect that a critical issue in children's ability to apprehend this truth relates to the degree of competition and expectation placed on them in sports and group games. The zone of proximal biological development in the school years is optimized when children are given challenges that are realistic (achievable). Unrealistic or impossible expectations can lead to negative reciprocity, where a child repeatedly fails and eventually gives up or withdraws.

The brain develops rapidly during the school years. Often, children at this stage of life are presented with intelligence tests and other means of identifying intellectual aptitude. There is increasing conflict among developmental psychologists over the value and crosscultural generalizability of tests such as the Stanford-Binet and the Wechsler Intelligence Scale for Children (WISC). In some cases these tests can be used to stereotype children without a full appreciation of their unique gifts and abilities. In the past results from these tests have been used as a basis for comparison between children, sometimes with unfortunate results.

By the time a child reaches the school years, he or she begins to demonstrate a particular style or set of preferences for learning and academic achievement. Gardner (1983) recognized this aspect of middle and late childhood, proposing eight different "intelligences," or aptitude profiles. In a sense these profiles reflect the uniqueness of God's creative purposes in each child. Gardner identified *linguistic, logical-mathematical, musical, spatial, bodily-kinesthetic, interpersonal, intrapersonal* and *naturalistic* intelligence aptitudes. The linguistic learner is heavily invested in writing, reading and verbal interaction. The logical-mathematical learner enjoys numbers, counting and organizational activities. Musically oriented children often sing spontaneously or incorporate music into mundane everyday activities. Spatial learners design elaborate forts, dollhouses and Lego creations. Bodily kinesthetic learners build and work with their hands. Interpersonal children are powerfully social and often gravitate toward positions of leadership and influence. Intrapersonal children are thoughtful and reflective, sometimes surprising adults with sophisticated wisdom on a spectrum of issues. Naturalistic individuals thrive in the outdoors, combining an aesthetic appreciation for nature with an ever-expanding knowledge of detail. In Gardner's scheme no child is stereotyped by any intelligence type; each child combines more or less aptitude across all eight categories. An appreciation and sensitivity to each child's unique profile of aptitudes reciprocates his or her sense of personal worth and value in a manner that is less geared toward achievement at the expense of others.

School Years: Cognitive Changes

Children's cognitive abilities improve markedly throughout the school years. Memory is one area that changes dramatically. In the play years children often struggle to recount what happened yesterday. But in the school years children develop the ability to remember events in great detail, sometimes reproducing the entire plot of a book or movie. School-aged children have a developed *episodic memory* that is able to place life events into a personal narrative that becomes a significant foundation for the reciprocating self. *Procedural memory,* or the ability to repeat sequences of behavior or learning, also improves. Children in the school years become adept at free throws in basketball and timed multiplication tests in class. Memory-related successes are fostered in part by the school-aged child's improving ability to pay attention. Children in later childhood can be selectively attentive to a teacher or coach, listening intently even when peers are talking around them. This kind of concentrated focus greatly helps children acquire and retain information.

Piaget referred to the school years as a period of *concrete operational thought.* The concrete operational thinker is now able to master problems of logic that confound children in the play years. A nine-year-old boy is able to deduce that the volume of milk in squat and tall glasses is quite possibly the same, and he can design a mini-experiment to prove it. The same boy is also able to understand that things can be reversed back to their original state. Play-aged children are unable to comprehend that addition is the opposite of subtraction, and that equations can be reversed to produce the same number. The school-aged child's ability to handle these basic logic issues opens the door to rapid learning in mathematics and problem-solving.

Without a doubt, one of the most noticeable characteristics of the school years is a child's growing affinity for peers. Improved theory-of-mind capability makes more intricate social allegiances and associations possible.

Some gender differences may become obvious in this process. Boys may establish fraternal group identities where they understand others to value activity for a common purpose, frequently through sports. Girls do the same, but with sometimes different criteria that reflect a broad range of interpersonal understanding. Girls may form complex alliances, in-groups and out-groups during the school years, demonstrating well-developed abilities to understand what others are thinking and desiring. Expanded theory-of-mind ability combined with a lack of personal experience makes children in the school years highly impressionable. Peer pressure becomes a potent force in the middle grades, a surprise to many who consider this to be an adolescent phenomenon. The school years are a critical period for the reciprocating self, a kind of peer-oriented proving ground that can validate or inhibit social development.

The school years are a period of remarkable linguistic growth that mirror an increasingly complex set of social relationships. Children in this period of life must navigate home and playground relationships. With improved language abilities children in the school years are able to tell jokes to their peers and recognize when these might not play well at home with Mom or Dad. Puns and other word games become cognitively possible, enabled by a larger and more specific vocabulary. The social basis for language acquisition is expanded in the school years in part through the many new and complicated relationships that must be constructed with peers. Children in this period may create context-specific dialects or language codes with their peers as a way of maintaining group membership and establishing boundaries apart from adults. Slang makes its first appearance, becoming more common by the time children reach adolescence. These cognitive changes anticipate an increasingly advanced ability for relationships and, as a consequence, added depth and breadth for a reciprocating self.

The Reciprocating Self in Childhood

At this point we will pull together our discussion of biological and cognitive foundations of childhood to more intentionally consider the reciprocating self. We will sketch several developmental issues relevant to the reciprocating self in childhood. First, we will consider how *attachment* plays out in childhood, particularly in the development of the self. To do this, we will look at how the self might be structured or organized in the mind of the child. We will also consider how a child's experience of the self in real-life relationships might clash with internal ideals through comparisons with others. Second, we will review *risk and resiliency* factors for the reciprocating self in childhood. Finally, we will look at *parenting issues* and the formation of the reciprocating self, paying attention to children's theological identity as *imago Dei*.

Our review of biological and cognitive changes in childhood hints at remarkably complex changes to the reciprocating self in development. These changes reflect an evolving social and relational sophistication in the child. The increased social complexity of childhood ushers in new challenges for the reciprocating self in development. Rolando is seven years old, a second grader involved in soccer and baseball. Even at his relatively tender age, he is a gifted goal scorer on his soccer team. His father, Efren, is a well-meaning but overly enthusiastic supporter on the sideline. Often Efren will bellow encouragement or express disappointment to Rolando from the sideline. While he plays, Rolando must balance expectations from his father and his teammates, particularly in a big game against an undefeated team. The manner in which Rolondo resolves these tensions is related to his mental representations of his relationships along with his ability to trust others based on experiences of care in early life.

Attachment. Bowlby (1980) proposed an *internal working model* (IWM) of relationships with others. The IWM consists of mental representations (symbols) of the self and other in relationship. We may expect some developmental changes to the IWM in the mind of a seven-year-old. With a growing episodic memory, or ability to remember events and experiences, Rolando is developing the ability to link specific memories with particular people. He is able to make some preliminary judgments about new situations on the basis of what he knows from older, more established relationships. Fortunately, Rolando had good care in his early life and is able to trust people fairly easily. But because he is only seven, Rolando is still unable to make fine distinctions between his own qualities and the qualities of others. His representations of self with Dad are accumulating, recently characterized by several tension-filled moments when Efren yelled from the sideline in soccer games. While Rolando's representations of self with close friends are positive, he is increasingly anxious in light of team expectations for goals scored in tough games.

Internal structure. Harter (1999) notes that children in Rolando's age bracket are able to make rudimentary links between representations of the self and others, but these links are typically opposites that demonstrate all-or-nothing thinking. Some admired adults in Rolando's world may occupy a special place of nearly heroic status. Indeed, this is probably true of his relationship with his father. In Rolando's eyes Dad looms large as an authority figure and also as a hero to be emulated and worshiped. If it turns out that Efren is a gifted weekend mechanic, Rolando may ask to be involved in his father's restoration project on an old Ford Mustang. His relationship with his father carries a strong "Dad can do anything" emphasis, which can lead to profound mentoring opportunities or more conflictual competitive interactions. If Efren happens to be insecure, he may try to compete with his son even when the two are engaged in a friendly game of catch football. If such a relational pattern persists, Rolando may form an IWM that includes an *oppositional,* or competitive, interpretation of his relationship with father. In the all-or-nothing world of the seven-year-old boy, Efren's hero status may be juxtaposed with an oppositional understanding of Dad as the competition to be rivaled and eventually surpassed.

Accuracy. Rolando's reciprocating self develops from aggregate experiences of relationships with others. Yet as he forms self-understanding, he may do so with some initial assumptions that adults would probably call naive. This is normal for childhood. At seven, Rolando's view of self is typically positive, with some blatantly obvious inaccuracies (Harter, 1999). Rolando knows that he is an excellent soccer player and a top scorer. This could translate to exaggerated braggadocio on the playground or peer-group conversations that extend these achievements into other arenas beyond what is likely or immediately possible. Thus Rolando may conclude that because he is a second-grade soccer star, he will probably grow up to become a professional player and make millions of dollars. He will live in a pricey Malibu mansion and drive a Mercedes. While there is a possibility of this happening, Rolando may have a better chance of winning the lottery. Rolando's episodic knowledge of himself in relationships is still fairly limited.

Comparisons to others. Rolando's reciprocating self reflects increased comparisons that he is able to make based on experiences of relationship within his IWM. Additionally, comparisons are made easier by his newfound ability to compare the Rolando of the present to the Rolando of the past. Rolando knows that just two years ago he could not play soccer and was unable to score goals. In fact, as a kindergartner Rolando could hardly kick the ball straight. Rolando is able to compare himself to the Rolando of the past as a matter of reference, helping him to better apprehend the Rolando of the present. Moreover, as a child moving into the school years Rolando is increasingly oriented toward his peer group, and this becomes an unceasing source of comparison. He will compare himself to classmates on scholastic performance, video game prowess and, of course, on the soccer field. Around the age of seven, the childhood penchant for *fairness* makes its full-blown appearance, becoming the ultimate mitigating factor in all peer-group comparisons. Rolando's IWM evolves to accommodate a self that is "fairly" constructed on the basis of honorable principles. In his mind Rolando's success on the soccer field is legitimate, not only on the basis of goals scored but because he plays the game without cheating.

Sensitivity to others. Along with Rolando's heightened awareness of peers through comparison, his IWM is accommodating the opinions of others at new and more sensitive levels. More than just a gross yardstick for comparison purposes, Rolando is newly aware that his peers make *judgments* regarding his performance. With this knowledge comes Rolando's implicit use of others' standards in helping him to establish his own benchmarks. Rolando's peers expect that he will score goals. This weighs heavily on him and adds to the considerable heft of Dad's expectations for success. Rolando's reciprocating self is increasingly tuned in to the values that other people place on his gifts and performance. It is quite possible that this heightened sensitivity will result in some anxiety. The boy might anticipate a big game for an entire week before the actual event, knowing that his peers are counting on him and his family is watching. Rolando's IWM may shift on the basis of his success or failure at the fateful soccer game depending on the degree to which Rolando's reciprocating self relies on peer opinion and family expectation.

Risk and resiliency. What will help children thrive whether the context is one of education, therapy or discipleship? The complex interplay between the reciprocating self and others makes developmental predictions hazardous at best. We all remember child and adolescent peers who had "everything going for them" and yet ended up in prison, involved in troubled relationships or enduring financial failure. We also know children from difficult or abusive backgrounds who managed to make it anyway. How might we assess the direction of Rolando's development of a reciprocating self, recognizing that only God knows the precise details of his future?

In order to construct a more realistic basis for understanding why some kids succeed where others inexplicably struggle, psychologists outlined a theory of *risk* and *resiliency* in development. Leaders in this field include Emmy Werner at the University of California, Davis, and Anne Masten at the University of Minnesota. For these theorists *risk* represents any factor in a child's world that jeopardizes healthy development. Risk might be "internal" in the sense that issues related to the child's physiology or psychological makeup might hinder normal development. A crack baby with low birth weight and cocaine-induced neurological damage carries numerous internal risk factors. Risk might also be "external" in the sense that unhealthy relationships or environmental conditions might derail normal development (Benson, 1997; Masten and Coatsworth, 1995; Werner and Smith, 2001). A six-year-old girl living in poverty might have limited access to adequate health care and proper nutrition. These issues represent external risk to the girl's development. By contrast, *resiliency* represents any factor in a child's world that promotes healthy development. Internal resiliency might include intelligence or moral restraint. External resiliency is indicated in supportive family relationships and mentors.

I (Kevin) teach the risk-resiliency model to psychology graduate students using the analogy of a two-platform scale (like those found in a middle-school science classroom). The scale is like a seesaw, weighted at either end by risk and resiliency factors respectively. All children, no matter what their background or situation, have at least some risk and resiliency factors. For educators and clinicians working with children, the primary challenge is to make sure the resiliency side of the scale is heavily weighted. When risk and resiliency hang evenly in the balance or are tipped toward the risk side of the scale, children are in danger of developing psychopathology or other symptoms of normal development gone awry (Wenar and Kerig, 1999).

In seven-year-old Rolando's situation we can assume that the boy's resiliency factors outweigh his risk factors. Despite stress associated with overly enthusiastic parenting from the sidelines and pressure from his teammates, Rolando manages to score one goal in a big game that his team loses in the end. The game in many ways reflects real life—some triumphs are also accompanied by failures that must be socially integrated into a mature reciprocating self. Rolando is a reasonably happy child with a variety of personal gifts and a fairly supportive home environment. However, this assessment is no guarantee for successful development. As with the attachment discussion, we are interested in briefly exploring how risk and resiliency offer insight into Rolando's circumstances along with his future development.

Risk. Risk can be overt, such as in the case of neglectful parenting or even something more subtle. It may be that Rolando is a firstborn child. Several developmental studies have revealed that birth order does have implications for child development. In particular, firstborn children tend to be more competitive and potentially more anxious (Falbo, 1981). This may result from the firstborn's tendency to internalize and appropriate parental expectations more keenly than other siblings. If true, this fits well into our earlier discussion of heightened sensitivity to others manifest in Rolando's self-understanding and IWM. Rolando's firstborn status, combined with parental and peer expectations for success, could lead to excessive worrying or anxiety. Whereas birth order in itself is not necessarily a risk factor, in the presence of other mitigating issues it may present some risk to Rolando's reciprocating self.

Rolando's relationship with his father might imply risk if Efren's competitive streak causes him to shame the boy. Shame can be corrosive to Rolando's developing self as it mirrors back to him messages of failure and rejection that can be difficult to overcome. In the event that Rolando's relationship with his father continues to grow in its oppositional nature, the boy may export the motif of "Rolando as failure" into increasingly more relationships through a revised IWM. The tendency for shame to dominate a child's self-understanding over time could become a self-fulfilling prophecy in adolescence and adulthood. This can be expected to show up in all of the domains where Rolando considers performance to be important such as academic work, peer relationships and sports.

Resiliency. Rolando appears to have many resiliency factors. Rolando is intelligent and has a fun, gregarious personality. Rolando experiences secure attachment with his mother, and at a core level he perceives himself as fundamentally good. These traits have been known and reinforced throughout his childhood experiences to date. We might surmise that Rolando's preschool and kindergarten teachers picked up on these positive factors and helped draw them out further. We can also guess that Rolando chooses well-adjusted peers as friends, increasing the likelihood that his positive qualities will be reciprocated. Rolando has been shown respect as a child within his family context and is learning to extend this respect outward to include peers and other adults.

Rolando is blessed with a supportive mother and extended family. This is particularly significant given Rolando's Mexican identity. Family is of paramount importance in Mexican culture. The Roman Catholic Church of Mexico has encouraged large families. Traditionally, these extended networks of kin played an enormous role in the socialization of Mexican children. Rolando is part of a third-generation immigrant family that is largely acculturated to American society. Indeed, none of his immediate family speaks Spanish. However, expectations for extended-family support are still tremendously powerful, evident in the many relatives that regularly attend his soccer games. Consequently, Rolando is the beneficiary of a range of supportive relationships that create resiliency for self-understanding and the organization of his IWM.

It appears that Rolando's two-platform scale is weighted toward the resiliency side. Rolando's future development is likely to continue normally. Earlier, we implied that Rolando might use increased peer affiliation as a compensation for his oppositional relationship with his father. This serves as a good example of resiliency factors overcoming risk in a child's overall developmental course. Children with a considerable number of resiliency factors are generally able to prevail in the midst of adversity and failure (Masten and Coatsworth, 1995; Werner and Smith, 2001). In summary, we might expect to see Rolando's growing peer network complement other deficiencies in his relationship with his father. As an intelligent and sociable individual, Rolando is able to adapt in ways that keep a predominantly positive perspective on his reciprocating self, particularly as this develops in relationship with others. Hopefully, the friction in Rolando's relationship with his father will be fleeting, and eventually it will reflect other positive influences for Rolando's reciprocating self.

Parenting. We have already discussed the significance of *unconditional love, gracing, empowering* and *intimate relationships* in human development, and the specific connections between each of these factors with *parental support, monitoring, intervention* and *control,* respectively. Now we will discuss each of these areas with a view toward finding an optimal profile of parenting behaviors that scaffold the reciprocating self as it develops in childhood. This search for effectively balanced and consistently adequate parenting takes us back to the work of Diana Baumrind (see p. 134). After her decades-long study of families, Baumrind concluded that parenting exists along a continuum of types. At one extreme are *permissive* parents, characterized by low support and low control. At the other extreme are *authoritarian* parents, who use excessively high control but are low in their support of children. Children tended not to thrive in either of these environments. In the middle of the continuum Baumrind noted a group of parents that combined high support with high control, upholding an *authoritative* parenting style that was very effective (Baumrind, 1971).

Support. Through the unconditional love of parents children acquire a reciprocating self that is secure, knowing that physical and emotional needs will be addressed. High support is a hallmark of authoritative parenting. Shortly before his death the famous theologian and psychologist Henri Nouwen observed three subtle deceits in our thinking about the self. These are typically learned in childhood through parents, peers and cultural influences. They are (1) *I am what I have,* (2) *I am what I do or achieve,* and (3) *I am what other people say about me.* Nouwen reminds us that these are empty promises for an authentically reciprocating self. Only the unconditional love of God in Christ is able to provide the stable knowledge that a child has value and worth in the universe. In our view the most significant contribution of parental support in childhood is to reinforce for each child his or her essential *belovedness* as an individual treasured by God.

The authoritative ideal is without question the most demanding and costly kind of parenting. Children's support needs often come at inopportune times. Sick children keep parents awake through the night. Broken limbs may require lengthy home stays. Today's children are involved in an extraordinary variety of activities, many of which require parental taxi services. Help with homework, chores, peer problems and spiritual concerns all enlist the involvement of mothers and fathers. In the rapid-paced environment of the United States, parents must balance career requirements with attendance at sporting events and performances that are enormously significant to young participants. True to the unconditional love of authentic parental support, many parents make quiet, daily sacrifices on behalf of their children, a kind of *kenotic* (emptying) commitment that follows after the example of Christ.

Monitoring. The play- and school-aged child requires grace. The authoritative parent places a premium on monitoring child activities, but not in a manner that obscures growing independence. Of course, monitoring strategies change across the range of childhood. A five-year-old boy will require direct supervision for play dates with a good friend. Care must be taken to ensure a safe environment and age-appropriate toys. A ten-year-old girl will not require the same kind of monitoring. Parental supervision will be necessary, but monitoring for the independent, grade-school-aged child reinforces commonsense understandings about household rules and safety, along with encouragement to explore new activities. To an extent this balancing act is specific to cultural and environmental conditions. It may be safe for the ten-year-old to ride her bike down the street to a neighbor's house to play or her parent might have to give her a ride, depending on local context. The grace extended by parents through this kind of monitoring recognizes that the zone of proximal development includes both challenge and safety, a delicate equilibrium requiring emotionally involved fathers and mothers.

Some parents of school-aged students choose to home school their children. The reasons for this decision vary widely. A common justification for home schooling involves parental concerns regarding the values learned by children in the public education setting. The home-school approach affords the parent the ability to more closely monitor the child's development and the social influences that shape the reciprocating self. We appreciate the logic of parents wishing to grace their children with values and character traits that reflect biblical priorities. Regardless of whether the child ends up in public or home-school settings, we suspect that it is this parental prerogative to use monitoring as a gracing force for values integration that promotes positive development in the child's reciprocating self. Parents with strong, positive values will model these to children through their monitoring, demonstrating forgiveness, patience and fidelity in situations too numerous to measure. Whether the child attends public school or stays at home, the gracing parent helps the child to reciprocate relationships of respect and dignity, affirming the *imago Dei* in others.

Intervention strategies. The authoritative parent uses high support and high control to empower a reciprocating self in childhood. Recall from chapter six that there are two kinds of intervention approaches in parenting. These interventions serve as one means to providing control or structure to the child's developmental scaffolding. *Coercive,* or negative, interventions are commonly understood as punishments, including physical retribution or withdrawal of privileges. *Inductive,* or positive, interventions focus on reasoning with children over the anticipated consequences of an action. Baumrind (1971, 1996) noted that effective, authoritative intervention strategies with play- and school-aged children tended toward withdrawal of privileges with abundant inductive reasoning. Harsher coercive strategies were less evident in this group. Her findings raise the curtain on an old debate over interventions and positive development. What kind of interventions empower the reciprocating self in the child?

One way to address this question is to find out how parent interventions affect child behavior in social settings, specifically with regard to the most controversial interventions in *hitting* and *spanking*. A well-known study by Strassberg, Dodge, Pettit and Bates (1994) tracked 273 children (4-6 years old) in order to consider the relationship between intervention strategies and child aggression toward peers in kindergarten. Child aggression was outlined in terms of (1) *instrumental aggression,* such as fighting over toys; (2) *reactive aggression,* such as physical retaliation toward peers; and (3) *bullying aggression.* Children were sampled from families that used three different strategies, including *no hitting or spanking, spanked only* or *hitting and spanking both*. On instrumental aggression there was no significant difference between any of the three parent-intervention strategies. However, a powerful effect was revealed for reactive aggression. Children who were spanked were more than twice as likely as children who were not spanked to physically retaliate against kindergarten peers during disagreements. Further, bullying aggression was strongly predicted by those children that were both hit and spanked relative to the other two strategies. Thus the most extreme coercive intervention strategy (hitting and spanking) appeared to promote bullying behaviors and elevate the likelihood of physical retaliation against peers. Spanking seemed to facilitate a reflexive reaction in children to perceived threats of attack, resulting in a low threshold for self-control in immediate conflicts with peers. Overall, peer aggression was lower for children who were not hit or spanked relative to the other intervention strategies (Strassberg et al., 1994). It seems clear that the parent's choice of intervention is to a significant extent reciprocated in the child's self relative to conflict behaviors with peers.

Should this serve as an argument for permissive parenting that avoids coercive interventions? Not necessarily. Over the years a number of authorities have weighed in on the contemporary American controversy over parental intervention strategies. Christians have made passionate, biblically informed arguments weighted toward the use of both highly coercive and permissive interventions with children. Among our students in a Christian seminary and a university graduate school we have noticed a similar range of opinions, typically generated on the basis of personal experiences as children. Some of these opinions appear to be local to denominational interpretations of the Scripture. We have argued in this book that interventions should be oriented toward the positive development of a reciprocating self in the child, empowering him or her to more fully experience identity as Christ's beloved. For us, Baumrind's findings regarding high support and high control (intervention strategies) as optimally configured for positive development fit with our view that children are kingdom citizens ready for discipleship (Mt 18:1-4). Selection of intervention strategies should uphold a mandate of discipleship in our relationships with children. Discipleship implies correction as guidance embedded within an ongoing, committed relationship that reflects the parent's intimacy with Christ. This differs from correction as an imposition or exercise of power that diminishes the child's essential identity or value as a bearer of the *imago Dei*. Given this perspective we find it impossible to justify hitting a child for any reason. The use of other less extreme coercive interventions, such as spanking, are more ambiguous, subject to the measure of accountability parents are willing to accept in their own relationship with God. Baumrind's work suggests that time-outs and withdrawal of privileges are creative intervention strategies that effectively empower children to fully experience their belovedness.

Control. Control presupposes intimate relationships that foster positive values and respect for others. Intervention strategies represent one aspect of parental control. In a cognitive sense control exercised through *boundaries* and *rules for conduct* functions as a second developmental scaffold. Certainly the growing child's capacity for self-control is an important feature for a mature reciprocating self. If Baumrind is correct, authoritative parents must create structure in boundaries and rules for conduct that enables children to explore and make mistakes without violating the parent's fundamental, unspoken promise to the child that "I'll be there for you." It is the primacy of the child's relationship with his or her parent that makes control effective. In the absence of parental control children are unable to effectively form boundaries in relationships, a problematic situation in adolescence and emerging adulthood. Boundaries assume that others exist separately from the self and that others are worthy of respect. By the same token, rules for conduct extend respect to others whether through the courtesy of a shaken hand or decent table manners.

The Ecology of Childhood

It is commonly observed that as children change, their environment changes
with them. At times development works hand-in-glove with environmental
shifts, but this is not always the case. Human systems tend toward stability—
also known as *equilibrium*. Equilibrium is that state where persons and relationships within a system are as stable as they are capable of being
(O'Connor and Ammen, 1997). When change is introduced to a system,
however, the system reacts and equilibrium is disrupted. Individuals or relationships within the system may move to oppose or block the change. It
is in these situations that we can learn much about how development happens. In this section we will consider how the child's self is influenced
within nested ecosystems. Rather than deal with each ecosystem and its potential influence on the reciprocating self in childhood, we will use the remaining space to frame an ecosystemic discussion of several important
childhood issues. We will discuss changes to the reciprocating self on the
basis of disruption to equilibrium within the ecosystem. Specifically, our discussion will focus on *divorce* and *discrimination*.

Divorce. It is a sobering fact that nearly 60 percent of American marriages will end in divorce. This reality has created a surge of research in psychology regarding outcomes for every aspect of child development before,
during and after a married couple separates. Additional research on children
living in single-parent homes and the effects of blended, or reconstituted,
families (through second and third marriages) has provided data on implications and consequences of divorce. Significant theorists in the divorce literature include E. Mavis Hetherington at the University of Virginia and Paul
Amato at Pennsylvania State University. While there are many other theorists
in the field, these scholars represent rather different poles on a continuum
of the issue. Psychologists and family-studies researchers in general tend to
frame their own positions relative to the two poles.

Hetherington (1993; Hetherington and Kelly, 2003) maintains that divorce
is not necessarily harmful to children in the long run. She bases her argument on extensive and brilliantly conceived outcome studies of boys and
girls in the United States. For Hetherington divorce often improves living
conditions for children. In the predivorce environment, children are exposed to intense emotional conflict between parents, sometimes escalating
into violence. Hetherington's argument centers on the fact that after divorce,
conflict is typically reduced with an overall positive effect on children's ex-

perience of each parent. As a result, children are better able to form a reciprocating self that is grounded on trust, intimacy and love. In effect, Hetherington's argument would classify divorce as a potentially resiliency-
promoting event.

Amato (1993; Amato and Keith, 1991; Amato and Booth, 2000) suggests
that divorce is harmful to child development for both the short and long
term. Amato's empirical research is the equal of Hetherington's, documenting a range of variables in the study of American children. Amato maintains
that divorce, with its fragmentation of the nuclear family, effectively under-
mines the child's self-concept, leading to depression, anxiety and a host of
psychological and relational difficulties. In adapting to shared custody or
single-parent situations, children are bereft of coherence in their experience
of parenting, having to balance potentially conflicting allegiances. From this
body of literature divorce may be understood as harmful to the reciprocating
self and better thought of in terms of risk to the child.

We contend that divorce is more likely to function as a risk than as a resiliency factor in the development of a reciprocating self. The disequilibrium
created by divorce within the microsystem and mesosystem is often accompanied by a fault-finding period, perpetuated through the modern legal system where decisions are made regarding child custody along with division
of property and monetary assets. Recalling our earlier discussion, the child
tends to conceive of the self and other in all-or-nothing terms. Black-and-
white thinking can easily lead the child to internalize blame for the divorce
and its repercussions, commonly observed in the mantra, "it's my fault." Because play- and school-aged children are developmentally unable to make
fine judgments regarding the self and parental behavior, it becomes easier
for the child to conclude that his or her own inadequacies are to blame. If
he or she is unable to move beyond a position of self-blame for Mom and
Dad's actions, it will become increasingly difficult to trust others. Some children who have lived through divorce compulsively work to please parents
or authority figures. This is not to say that divorce is an irreparable catastro-
phe for the child's reciprocating self, but this should be carefully and sensi-
tively considered through family communication, therapy and relations with
extended kin.

Discrimination. As with divorce, the effects of discrimination on the
family and the growing child's reciprocating self can be profound. We recall
that seven-year-old Rolando's family is third-generation Mexican American.

This means that for three generations his family has lived in the United States. Nobody in Rolando's immediate family speaks Spanish. Moreover, it turns out that Rolando's father, Efren, went to a prestigious American public university. The family is thoroughly acculturated to American society and earns a high standard of living. Nevertheless, non-Caucasian ethnic groups are still objects of discrimination in mainstream American society. It may be that Rolando's mother, Rita, is called a "brown" in a derogatory manner by a senior businessperson in the office where she works. This event deeply hurts Rita. Efren is enraged. For several days the couple discusses potential options to confront the individual, including litigation. During this time the stress level in Rolando's household multiplies tenfold. Rolando learns of the situation when he eavesdrops on a phone conversation between his mother and her sister. After the conversation Rolando asks his uncle about the meaning of *brown* and why this term is so hurtful to his mother.

In the aftermath of Rita's conflict at work, we can clearly see how increased stress levels might ecosystemically play out through the family. Both parents are angry, hurt and anxious. These emotions are typical of a heightened arousal state in the body. In this situation they are unlikely to sleep well, a problem that Rolando subconsciously picks up on. Efren's frustration may additionally fuel his antics on the soccer field and his pressured expectations of his son's performance. In this environment Rolando's reciprocating self might be affected. Rolando learns, perhaps for the first time, that he is perceived as different from other children. The exosystem of his mother's workplace and the broader macrosystem of American society reflect something back to Rolando that he was not previously aware of. He is of Mexican descent. Rolando previously thought of this identity as a source of pride, particularly around Christmastime when his friends would envy the homemade tamales his mother packed in his lunch. Now, however, Rolando understands that the wider ecosystem may not be as friendly to his ethnicity as he once believed.

The impact of this event upon Rolando's IWM depends greatly on how his parents handle it. If Efren and Rita choose a *stress-sustaining* solution to the workplace problem, we can expect fairly dramatic changes to Rolando's reciprocating self. Developmentally, Rolando cannot make fine distinctions in his core self. Consequently, residual hostility in his home surrounding the event might considerably affect Rolando's ability to trust others. He may understand himself in a less positive light and make quicker value judgments regarding the perspective and opinions of others. His IWM appropriates a view that, on the whole, Caucasians are untrustworthy, representing insidious elements of the system that his family struggled to overcome.

If Rolando's parents choose a *stress-reducing* option to deal with the situation, the event becomes a different kind of learning opportunity for the boy's IWM. In this latter scenario Rolondo learns that some (but not all) people in wider society harbor unfortunate and hurtful biases against non-Caucasians. Despite this, the goodness of Rolando's identity as a Mexican American will prevail and is worthy of the respect Rolando has already experienced both within his family and without. In terms of his self-understanding, Rolando adjusts his IWM to include a small category of persons unfriendly to his Mexican heritage. But in the main the implications of the event are less detrimental in terms of Rolando's ability to trust others.

Note that for Rolando the best developmental outcome relies on how his parents handle the long-term fallout of the discrimination event. There can be no question that such a scenario will create stress in the family. This is a legitimate ecosystemic response to a change in equilibrium. But for a seven-year-old boy, the best response on the part of his parents is not necessarily related to the measure of justice meted out in the workplace. Rolando's developing self is learning that not everyone is supportive. The critical issue is the extent to which he will expand this view of people to include a few or nearly everyone, increasing the likelihood that his greater sensitivity to others causes him to absorb negative self-attributions. North American society is increasingly global and multiethnic, making situations such as Rita's workplace discrimination a valid issue of developmental significance.

Concluding Thoughts: The Reciprocating Self in Childhood

We have reviewed biological and cognitive changes for both play- and school-aged children. We explored the contours of the reciprocating self in childhood, particularly through *attachment, risk and resiliency,* and *parenting issues in development.* We then attempted to obtain a wider view of development on the basis of changes to the child's ecosystem, including *divorce* and *discrimination.* In our overall interest to outline positive principles in development, we underscored the importance of helping children understand their fundamental worth as sons and daughters of God. This becomes especially important in a consideration of adolescence, a crucial life-span moment where issues of identity become particularly important.

Adolescence

MORE RECIPROCITY THAN YOU THINK

AT FIRST GLANCE THE PERIOD OF ADOLESCENCE seems to have little to do with reciprocity. In general, people perceive adolescents as being pre-occupied with themselves—their identity, their clothes, their friends and their music. Parents often ask, "What happened to my sweet eleven year old who used to like to curl up with me and read *Harry Potter,* or who would hold my hand as we walked down the streets? Now, the only give and take she seems to be interested in is taking from my wallet!" A colleague at Fuller Seminary recently wrote a funny anecdote in their Christmas newsletter about the similarities between cats and teenagers. He noted that neither cats nor teenagers turn their heads when you call their names, nor do they like to be seen with you in public. (When was the last time you saw a cat being walked on a leash?)

The media does not help this rather negative portrayal of adolescence. More frequently than not, the stories featured in the news media include those of teenage violence and delinquency (Damon, 2004). Additionally, our media-saturated culture broadcasts violent and oversexualized images of ad-olescents and role models for adolescents. The word *wholesome* does not exactly come to mind when thinking of performers topping the charts (e.g., Brittney Spears, Eminem, Pink). Regardless of era, teens are of course known for their loud music, outlandish clothes and rebellious spirit—whether this be the greasers of the 1950s, the flower children of the 1960s, the punks of the 1980s or the Goths of the 1990s. Every era is characterized by a style and means of rebellion. Although the more extreme groups do not include all young people of an era, they do significantly influence the way the media portray and the public perceives youth. The general stereotype of adolescence is that biological changes of puberty create a developmental disturbance of emotional and social turmoil and problem behaviors. Research demonstrates that all too often adults are influenced by these negative stereotypes of teens, and they so fear the young people in their own community that they are reluctant to engage with them (Scales et al., 2003).

Although this perception of adolescents is less than favorable, in our society we are somewhat sympathetic to this period known for its awkwardness and rebellion. Personal memories remind us of what an awkward and difficult period of life adolescence can be. Memories such as shifting relationships with parents, adjusting to rapid physical growth and raging hormones, negotiating peer pressure, and navigating the waters of relationships with members of the opposite sex are enough to make anyone relieved that they have survived the period. In addition psychologists have significantly contributed to this unfavorable perception of adolescence. Since the time of J. Stanley Hall (1904), who stated that "human development included a period of *Sturm and Drang* [German for 'storm and stress'] between childhood and adulthood," storm and stress has characterized what many people in Western culture believe about the essence of adolescence. Furthermore, the current status of social-science research illustrates psychology's preoccupation with the negative aspects of adolescence. Studies of violence, suicide, depression, eating disorders, delinquency and substance abuse are found in disproportionate numbers compared to studies examining aspects of positive development in young people (e.g., caring, spirituality, leadership).

Although the popular and academic portrayal of adolescents suggests a more self-absorbed period of life, the concept of the reciprocating self challenges us to ask deeper questions: During the period of adolescence, how do individuals develop the capacity to be in reciprocating relationships characterized by the mutual encounter of two differentiated individuals? How is the *I* developing in relationship to *others?* How do adolescents reciprocate with other individuals, their families and society? What do the dangerous risk-taking behaviors often associated with adolescence have to do with the emergence of the reciprocating self?

This chapter will consider how the developmental tasks that take place during adolescence relate to the emergence of the reciprocating self. More physical, cognitive and socioemotional growth may take place during adolescence than during any other period of life. We first provide a general overview of the major facets of adolescent development and then examine how aspects of individual development contribute to the sense of uniqueness or particularity present in a person capable of being in an authentic mutual relationship. Such facets of individual development include identity development and differentiation. Then we explore issues of adolescent development that promote relationality and reciprocity by looking at the roles of intimacy and moral, spiritual and civic development.

Adolescent Development

Adolescence, as a period of life, has only been recognized in the last century. As noted previously, Hall (1904) was the first person to name the significance of a unique stage of development between childhood and adulthood. Since its inception adolescence has been traditionally defined as the period of life between childhood and adulthood that commences with the onset of puberty and ends with the commitment to adult roles. As such, adolescence has typically been recognized to begin around the age of twelve and then conclude somewhere between eighteen and twenty-two, at which point persons presumably move into the labor market, get married and begin families. As recently as the 1960s the transition into adulthood was well defined in most Western industrialized countries. On finishing high school, adolescents either went to college, got a full-time job or joined the military. For the most part people married in their early twenties and began families almost immediately (Arnett, 2000).

However, at the commencement of the twentieth century the onset of adolescence began earlier due to complex social and biological factors that contribute to children starting puberty at an earlier age than one hundred years ago (Arnett, 2000; Mortimer and Larson, 2002). For example, the average age of menarche has dropped from fifteen to sixteen years in the mid-1800s to twelve to thirteen years for young women today. Consequently, adolescence in the Western world is now recognized as beginning between the ages of nine and ten. Not only is adolescence starting earlier, but rapid demographic, sociocultural and economic trends have extended adolescence well into the twenties. Throughout much of the twentieth century only a limited number of fairly defined pathways from adolescence into adulthood existed. This is no longer the case; youth today are faced with many different educational/training, employment and partner/spousal options.

Most youth today can expect to have as many as four quite different occupational careers, anticipate living in a different community than the one
they grew up in, and have multiple intimate partners. Consequently, more
preparation is required as people make many vocational and relational commitments. In order to prepare adequately for the diverse labor market, more
youth are spending more time in postsecondary education. At one point a
G.E.D. or surely a B.A. or B.S. degree prepared most for employment. However, today more young people are preparing for their careers by pursuing
master's or doctorate degrees. In many cases education expenses and lack
of full-time employment cause young people to be financially dependent on
and in some cases living with their parents until their mid-twenties. Additionally, the median age for marriage and childbearing is now in the late
twenties. Consequently, it is more accurate to understand adolescence ending in the mid-twenties when young people make a commitment to adult
roles—namely, *marriage* and *employment.*

We discuss the expansion of adolescence at risk of alienating a significant
number of our readership, given that this book is largely used in higher education. It has been our experience that our students do *not* initially appreciate being referred to as adolescents. However, it has been our experience
that as a discussion ensues about the task of forming identity, defining a
sense of meaning and purpose in life and establishing intimate relationships,
our students often recognize themselves as wrestling with some of the major
developmental issues of *later* adolescence.

Many theorists have proposed systematic ways of thinking about the developmental challenges, opportunities and risks of adolescence. Erik Erikson's (1968) life-span model has been one of the most prominent models to
identify the developmental tasks of adolescence and the other life stages. Although Erikson names *identity formation* as the definitive developmental
task of adolescence, for individuals aged ten to eighteen his theory also includes the importance of developing a sense of *mastery* and *intimacy.* Other
scholars have also included *autonomy, sexuality* and *achievement* (e.g.,
Carnegie Corporation, 1989) as important components of adolescent
growth. A recent publication by the National Academy of Science (Eccles
and Gootman, 2002) report that in many different cultural groups these challenges involve the following more specific tasks: (1) changing relationships
between adolescent-aged children and their parents in order for youth to
take on a more mature role in their community; (2) exploring new personal,

social and sexual roles and identities; (3) transforming peer relationships into deeper friendships and more intimate partnerships; and (4) participating in opportunities and experiences that facilitate future economic independence and interdependence.

These adolescent developmental tasks need to be understood as taking place in complex web of social, cultural and historical settings (e.g., Bronfenbrenner, 1979; Ford and Lerner, 1992; Lerner, 2002). Optimal adolescent development depends on (1) the physical, psychological and cognitive assets of the individual; (2) available social supports; and (3) the developmental fit or appropriateness between each of the social settings and the young person. Development occurs within a dynamic system including individual factors, contextual influences and the fit between the individual and their context. With rapid and numerous changes occurring over the course of a few years, an increased potential for both positive and negative outcomes arises. Although most young people make it through this developmental period without exceedingly high levels of stress and strain, many do not. The complex interplay of individual issues, whether biological, cognitive or socioemotional, and contextual influences have significant ramifications for the emergence of the reciprocating self. In this next section we provide an overview of the developmental issues that may help or hinder the development of the reciprocating self.

Biological Changes

A thorough review of the biological changes associated with puberty is beyond the scope of this book, but given the significance of these changes we feel it is important to provide a brief overview of major issues, including the presence of hormones and brain growth. The activation of hormones responsible for pubertal development prompt a significant growth spurt, the emergence of primary and secondary sex characteristics, the onset of fertility and the experience of increased sexual libido in most early adolescents (ages nine to thirteen). Recently, research has explored how hormonal changes occurring in early adolescence might relate to changes in behavior commonly associated with adolescence. Although there is some evidence for direct effects of hormones on such behaviors as heightened sexual feelings, mood swings and aggression (Adams, Montemayor and Gullotta, 1989; Brooks-Gunn and Reiter, 1990; Caspi et al., 1993), these relations are quite complex. Hormones and other biological systems interact with genetic predispositions and social experiences in multifaceted ways.

For example, it has been suggested that the gender differences associated with the onset of depression, eating disorders and aggression may be connected to differences in patterns of hormonal changes associated with puberty. However, evidence suggests that such mood and behavior patterns lie in complex interactions between life experience, gender-role socialization, genetically linked vulnerabilities and changes in hormonal systems (Eccles and Gootman, 2002). An illustration of this point is the research findings that the early onset of puberty for young white girls is often problematic and linked with increased rates of eating disorders, depression and involvement in problematic behaviors. (As an aside, early onset of maturation is advantageous for white boys, particularly with respect to the athletic participation and social standing in schools.) In addition, early maturation is not associated with these problematic behaviors among black girls. These gender and ethnic differences are better understood in light of many ecological factors, rather than merely examining the role of hormones. It has been suggested that early pubertal maturation may be particularly problematic for white American girls because the changes associated with puberty, like gaining weight, are not valued by many white Americans, who often yearn for a slim, androgynous female body (an image promoted by the media). In addition, research suggests that because of increased sexual attention from boys and men, young girls who enter puberty earlier fall in with older peer groups. It has been suggested that these young women base more of their identity on their relationships with boys and men and less on developing individual competencies (Magnusson, 1988; Stattin and Magnusson, 1990).

In addition to affecting the growth of the physical body, hormonal changes are associated with emotions related to sexuality. The biological changes of puberty both increase young persons' interest in sex and their awareness of others' perception of them as sexual objects. Both physical and emotional changes can have a significant affect on development. Sexual behavior increases dramatically during early to middle adolescence. The most recent report from a national study of American adolescents, the National Longitudinal Study of Adolescent Health (Blum, Beuhring and Rinehart, 2000), indicates that 16 percent of seventh and eighth graders report having had sexual intercourse and that this number increases to 60 percent during the eleventh and twelfth grades. Accompanying these age-related sexual activities are the increased frequencies of pregnancy and sexually transmitted diseases—both of which profoundly affect the future trajectory of a young person's life.

In addition to biological changes related to sexuality, new research reveals that the brain undergoes important growth and change during adolescence. Until recently brain development has typically been understood to be completed within the early years of life. Cutting edge research based on series of brain scans reveal that the brain continues to develop into adolescence. Neurologists think that the frontal lobes of the brain, the part of the brain responsible for functions such as self-control, judgment, emotional regulation, organization and planning may undergo the most significant amount of change during adolescence (Begley, 2000). The presence and activation of this part of the brain can have significant influence on the maturity of a young person, potentially affecting moral decision-making and educational and social outcomes.

Cognitive Development

The most significant cognitive changes that take place during the period of adolescence involve the increasing ability for young people to think abstractly. Abstract thinking includes being able to think hypothetically as well as consider the real and actual, to process information in a sophisticated and complex manner, to consider multiple dimensions of a problem at once, to take other people's perspective and to reflect on oneself. Such abstract thinking is the cornerstone of Piaget's formal operational thought, assumed to begin during adolescence. Although the scholarly community still debates whether cognitive processes emerge in qualitatively different global stages as Piaget described, most researchers are convinced that these kinds of thought processes are more characteristic of adolescent cognition than the cognition of younger children. Current research suggests that the development of these cognitive skills emerges gradually over the entire adolescent period and depends on individual factors and opportunities and experiences to use and practice them (Keating, 1990).

Cognitive skills greatly affect the way young people interact with the world. They affect a young person's capacity to learn, which can have important ramifications for their academic success. Information-processing skills (topic-specific thinking and problem solving), cognitive learning strategies (conscious strategies used to learn new information) and metacognitive skills (the conscious monitoring of one's own learning and problem-solving activities) also change over the period between the onset of puberty and adulthood. These skills also require intentional practice for their development.

In addition to learning, cognitive abilities also affect a young person's self-concept and understanding of others. The adolescent years are critical to the formation of a self-concept, which refers to a consistent definition or understanding of self. An understanding of self includes physical and psychological self-descriptions, stable social-personality characterizations of self, and the tendency toward conceptual integration of diverse aspects of self into a unified self-system (Damon, 1983). Abstract thinking, especially self-reflection, is necessary to attain a self-concept. A young person must have the ability to reflect on themselves and discriminate what makes them unique from others. Defining their relationships and roles with their family, friends, community and society is an important part of this process. The ability to assess the future and consider what possibilities are available to them is an important aspect of coming to a deeper understanding of themselves in the social and cultural settings in which they live.

The higher-order cognitive processes discussed above allow for young people to increase their perspective-taking skills. They have the increased capacity to consider what other individuals may be thinking or feeling. They become more interested in understanding others' psychological characteristics. Friendships begin to be based more on perceived similarity in these characteristics. Although friendships are more often based on similarity, adolescents can benefit from a curiosity to understand perspectives of different types of people. For instance, a young person's ability to consider the perspectives of individuals from other ethnicities or cultures is an important facet of developing an openness to diversity or a sense of multiculturalism.

Social-Contextual Changes

During adolescence many changes occur in the young person's social context. These primarily include changes in friendships and peer groups, transition in parental relations and school transitions.

When we think of adolescents, we think of the significance of peers—peer groups, peer pressure and so forth. During this period young people become much more peer-focused. This is evident in the increase of peer-related social, sports, religious or other extracurricular activities and in the increase in the importance of romance and sexuality in peer relationships.

Having previously addressed the romantic and sexual aspect of adolescent peer relationships, here we focus on the emerging prevalence and influence of peer relations during adolescence.

Most adolescents attach great importance to the activities they do with their friends. To the chagrin of their parents and teachers, activities with peers, peer acceptance and appearance often take precedence over school activities (Wigfield et al., 1991). Because social acceptance is so important during adolescence, friendship networks during adolescence are often organized into relatively rigid cliques that have a different social status within school and community settings (see Brown, 1990). The existence and commitment to these cliques probably reflects a young person's need to differentiate from family and establish their own sense of identity and place in this world. Belonging to a group is a way to define oneself and also gain a means of affirmation.

Ironically, in the attempt to establish their own identity and to exert their individuality, adolescents often join with a peer group to such an extent that they act, talk and dress exactly like their group. Generally, joining in conformity does not typify differentiation. However, this process might be understood as a way of practicing individuality that can lead to individuation. It is as if youth are practicing being their own person free from their families. They exert their individuality to the extent that they can try out a new identity or expressions of self apart from their family, yet they are not capable of doing so completely on their own. Perhaps as a result they find a group of "individuals" with whom they can practice. Although the youth might be distinguishing themselves from their families, they typically do so in an identical manner. In short, perhaps the community or unity of the group enables them to practice being unique within their families.

At the risk of dating myself, I (Pam) recall when I entered a new school during sixth grade. I quickly figured out that to fit in and belong, which of course I desperately wanted to, I had to acquire some brightly colored Gloria Vanderbilt or Calvin Klein jeans. A girl who did not have purple, green, royal blue or some other such color pants (complete with comb in the pocket and the right labels) was not part of the group. I recall repeatedly begging my mother to get me a pair of such pants. Despite her most rational and reasonable discussion with me regarding the ridiculous cost, issues of stewardship and the reality of peer pressure, I could not be persuaded. Finally she acquiesced to taking me shopping at Carson Pirie Scott. I will never forget the trip.

She bought me one pair of pea-green Gloria Vanderbilt jeans. I thought I had arrived! I could hardly wait to wear my new pants to school the next day. What might appear to be a bothersome or frivolous trip to the department store was potentially a developmentally rich experience. In that trip to Carson Pirie Scott I was simultaneously differentiating from my family and asserting my own taste (or lack thereof!) from my mother, but at the same time I was bonding through conforming to my new peer group.

Conformity to peers raises susceptibility to negative peer pressure as well (Brown, 1990; Ruben, Bukowski and Parker, 1998). Although much has been written about the prevalence of peer pressure and its negative effects on youth, most researchers do not accept the simplistic view that peer groups are primarily bad influences during adolescence (Eccles and Gootman, 2002). In fact, adolescents more frequently agree with their parents' views than their friends' views on major issues such as religion, politics, importance of education and morality (Ruben, Bukowski and Parker, 1998; Smetana, 1995; Smetana, Yau and Hanson, 1991). However peers have more influence on such things as clothing style, music and activity choice. In fact, youth tend to spend time with peers who hold views similar to those of their parents on the major issues above.

Family Relations

As adolescents begin to gravitate toward their peers, they become less attentive to their families. An adolescent can be understood as a sort of satellite that is changing from orbiting around the family planet (desatellization) to the peer planet (resatellization) (Balswick and Balswick, 1999). The time, activities and emotions of school-aged children revolve around the family. During adolescence, however, this changes. Relational energy and time begin to revolve around their friendships. This transition is very natural and normal. And, significantly, the extent of actual disruption in parent-adolescent relationships is not as great as we might expect (Collins, 1990; Paikoff and Brooks-Gunn, 1991). As young people grow up they seek more independence and autonomy. They may begin to question not only family rules and roles but also religious and social norms. Such questioning often leads to parental conflict—especially around issues of appearance, dating and chores. Despite conflicts over these smaller issues stated above, parents and their adolescent children agree more than they disagree regarding core values related to education, religion and politics.

Research demonstrates that parents play a very important role in the lives of their adolescent children. Although adolescent children may act out, adopt an "attitude" or appear disgruntled with family life at times, teenaged children need their parents. Having a strong sense of shared values, beliefs and goals with parents is strongly related to moral outcomes among youth (King and Furrow, 2004). Youth who are more altruistic and empathetic toward others report having higher levels of these shared values and trust with their parents. Youth who receive more parental monitoring, meaning their parents exert clear boundaries and expectations for their children and are aware of their coming and going, report less delinquent behaviors and higher academic success. Research also demonstrates the significance of parental influence on many areas of life such as religiousness (King, Furrow and Roth, 2002; King and Mueller, 2004).

Not only do adolescent children need their parents' attention, affection and supervision, but they desire it. In my (Pam's) own research I have been continually surprised to hear young people talk about how important it is that their parents set curfews, be available for them to talk and give them guidance in their academic, social and religious lives. For example, I recall two rather promiscuously dressed sixteen-year-old girls who participated in a focus group. One explained, "You see, we're just teenagers, and we need our parents to tell us what to do! We need curfews. We need to know when to come home." The other added, "Yeah, like, sometimes we actually want to come home, and if our parents don't tell us we have to, then we won't have an excuse to go home, or not to go to certain parties." In amazement at what I was hearing, I responded, "Did I hear you right? You want curfews and to be told what to do?" One responded, "Yeah, we're only teenagers. We don't always know what to do. And if our parents tell us what to do and pay attention to us, we know that they love us. We need that. We might not always act like it, but that's what we want." The rest of the group nodded and smiled in agreement. These girls clearly articulated a message that I have heard time and again. Adolescents do not always act like they want boundaries and structure, and they might kick and scream about it on occasion, but they strongly desire that their parents not only pay attention but to be active in the choices that they are making.

The way children differentiate themselves within their families varies by culture. More typical of white middle-class families in America is a decline in the amount of time spent interacting within and outside the home. Scholars understand this distancing in relations between adolescent and parents as a natural part of the developmental process. This distance plays an important function for youth, allowing them to do more things on their own, to experiment and to discover their own competencies. In American culture this fosters the highly valued process of individuation from parents. This is not the case in all cultures. For example in most non-Western cultures and in both Hispanic and Asian communities in the United States, this distancing occurs less frequently, and when it does occur, to a lesser extent (Larson and Verma, 1999; Mortimer and Larson, 2002). In other cultures, youth take on more responsibility not by differentiating from the family and making more decisions about their own lives, but rather by taking on greater responsibility for their family and for increased participation in family decision making and family support.

The Role of Adults

As youth progressively differentiate from their families, they seek the support of and guidance from other adults. Adult support can take place through formal mentoring programs or in natural relationships in school, neighborhood or a congregation. These relationships are most effective in promoting positive outcomes in youth when they are characterized by trust, positive social interaction, communication and having a sense of shared values (King and Furrow, 2004). Similar to parents, mentoring adults need to not only provide affection and encouragement but also are most effective when they provide guidance, empowerment and accountability.

A study of individuals who demonstrate an extraordinary commitment to caring for those in their communities report having adults in their life who came alongside of them and affirmed their gifts and vision, encouraged them in their service to others and helped them clarify their beliefs (Colby and Damon, 1995). At a "Youth Sunday" in a church in the Los Angeles area, one senior in high school pleaded with the adults to engage the youth in the congregation. His message implored the congregation to come together and be like a family. He beckoned the adults to talk to the youth—even if they seem intimidating and listen to loud music. His message was clear that the youth longed for adults to engage them. Another senior girl articulated the potential impact adults could make on youth. She communicated to the adults that youth need to know that they matter. She talked about how potentially influential the adults in their congregation could be on the youth.

She thought that if the adult members of the church trusted and believed in the youth and treated them with more potential than as "weirdos" who dress strange and listen to strange music, then they would be empowered to do something for their society through God. She wanted to hear that she mattered to the adults. These youth clearly articulated to the adults in their congregation that they both long for and need adult support. They need their genuine interest, encouragement and guidance so that they can become contributing members of our society. I believe that underneath their pleas is their desire to be known. Adolescence is an intense period of growth in which young people need the presence of others.

The Reciprocating Self During Adolescence

How do various aspects of adolescent development relate to the emergence of the reciprocating self? In this section we will first consider how these issues factor in to the development of a unique, differentiated self. Then we will examine how they enable this self to participate in mutual relationships with others.

Emerging particularity. It is hard to talk about the particularity of adolescents with a straight face. Let's face it; adolescents can be extremely particular! Much of adolescence is about a child becoming his or her own unique person. Independence, autonomy, differentiation and individuation are all crucial aspects of adolescent development. Most often adolescence is when young people begin to get a stronger and clearer sense of their unique self. For the first time they begin to differentiate themselves from their families and begin to develop a firmer self-construct and identity. In doing so they explore different types of activities, behaviors and dress.

Identity. The formation and consolidation of a sense of self, or identity, is central to the emergence of a reciprocating self. As youth struggle toward identity cohesion, they actively search for a sense of self. They embark on this psychological endeavor in order to consolidate and understand their experience of self as well as identify the self in terms of familial, vocational and societal roles (Erikson, 1950). Personal goals, values, worldviews and a sense of meaning and purpose are integrated into an individual's understanding of self. This quest is marked by yearnings and behaviors that simultaneously bond youth to or locate them within something bigger than themselves and affirm their sense of uniqueness and independence.

Erikson (1968) explained that identity development was based on a psychosocial crisis in which adolescents have the opportunity to explore different identities. This period of exploration is referred to as *moratorium* and is natural to this stage of life. Successful adaptation to this identity crisis is accomplished by making an enduring commitment to an identity and the roles associated with it. The virtue of *fidelity* results from the commitment to an identity. For Erikson, fidelity is an unflagging commitment to an ideology that transcends the self and brings about genuineness, sincerity and a sense of duty to others. In this sense, identity development is crucial to the reciprocating self because it provides an individual with a sense of self and commitment to others.

Differentiation. A major developmental task that takes place during adolescence is differentiation. Through differentiation young people wrestle with their identity; personal beliefs, values and goals; and boundaries with families, peers, and romantic partners. During this process, young people may experiment with different identities, they may explore different belief systems and try out different worldviews. They begin to formulate their own short- and long-term goals for their life. One way young people discover and set boundaries between them and the closest people in their lives is through risk-taking.

Risk-taking and rebellion are characteristic of the period of adolescence. Such behavior is often viewed as troublesome or dangerous and something that must be thwarted. However appropriate risk-taking can play an important role as young people attempt to differentiate themselves from their families, explore boundaries with society and bond to their peer groups. Emerging research by Jay Giedd and colleagues (see, e.g., Giedd et al., 1999) suggests that brain development occurring during adolescence may also contribute to rebellious and dangerous activities. Adolescent risk taking can range from harmless (e.g., teepeeing a friends house or piercing a belly button) to harmful (e.g., drunk driving or substance abuse). That being said, risk-taking always involves some risk. Taking risks allows for young people to assert their own autonomy, explore social boundaries and experience commonality. It is important for adolescents to have safe and constructive outlets for this necessary action. Youth programs can provide a service to youth and parents by offering appropriate forms of risk-taking behaviors. For example, youth groups often participate in wilderness experiences where young people have the opportunity to jump blindfolded off a forty-foot pole or to repel down one-hundred-foot cliffs. These activities, when properly supervised, can provide safe but risky-enough adrenalin rushes that allow youth to explore identity, push boundaries and eventually differentiate.

As individuals wrestle with issues of identity, meaning, beliefs, goals and their own behavior, they gain a clearer sense of self in relationship with those around them. In "Buberian" terms, they gain a clearer understanding of where the *I* stops and the *Thou* begins. Such an understanding of self is necessary for mutually reciprocating relationships. There can be no give and take if one does not know what one has to give.

Emerging relationality. Although individuation is a strong theme in adolescence, relationships are as well. Identity and differentiation provide a crucial component to adolescents' capacity for relationships. The sense of self that emerges enables the young person to begin entering into relationships with peers, parents and other adults as authentic, unique individuals. Although it is tempting to say that identity formation and differentiation are foundational to intimacy, this is not necessarily the case. Even Erikson (1968), who claimed that the identity crisis occurs developmentally before intimacy, recognized that this developmental process does not occur in an absolute linear fashion. Erikson contended that during all stages in life, individuals are working on all eight crises. Although he argued that during adolescence identity development is the most pressing issue and that resolving it to a significant extent is necessary in order for a person to move on to successfully resolve the crisis of intimacy verses isolation, he recognized that relationships greatly influence a sense of identity. There is some evidence that adolescent girls are more likely to be working on intimacy more than identity (Damon, 1983). Even more so than Erikson, scholars today generally agree that identity and intimacy evolve together.

Interpersonal Relationships. To an adolescent, relationships are not just something, they are *everything.* Adolescence is strongly characterized by its social susceptibility (Feldman and Elliott, 1990). Intense bonding occurs between adolescents and their peers, intimacy grows in both same-sex friendships as well as in romantic relationships and parents continue to play a crucial role of providing support and guidance. Not only does reciprocity/relationality manifest itself during adolescence in an interpersonal manner, but adolescents demonstrate their reciprocity in a give-and-take with the greater good. Central to adolescent development is moral, spiritual and civic development.

Moral, spiritual and civic development. Adolescence is marked by a time of biological growth that facilitates the development of cognitive abilities resulting in an individual who has new sensitivities, perspectives and reasoning abilities. These new or expanded capacities allow for the adolescent to engage with his or her world in a new way. For example, enhanced perspective-taking facilitates the increase of empathy, a moral emotion associated with moral action and behavior. D'Aquili and Newberg (1998) hypothesized that a part of the parietal lobe on the nondominant side of the brain may underlie the experience of the transcendence of self that is necessary for such investment in the "beyond-the-self" social world. In addition, increasingly abstract thinking promotes the ability to consolidate and commit to a sense of identity, allowing for the sense of moral, civic and spiritual identities to develop.

These new abilities promote experiences of transcendence in adolescents. They become more aware of others and society. As adolescents grow in a sense of fidelity, they gain a sense of purpose in life, a sense of belonging and commitment to others and society as a whole (Furrow, King and White, 2004; Lerner, Dowling and Anderson, 2003; Markstrom and Kalmanir, 2001; Markstrom et al., 1997). Lerner (2004) argues that adolescence is characterized by a transcendent or spiritual sensibility that propels young people to contribute to the common good.

Research demonstrates that youth have an immense capacity to care for families, friends and members of their community; they are engaged in volunteer activities and make commitments to religious communities and to God (see, e.g., the works of William Damon, Daniel Hart, Kevin Reimer, James Youniss and Christian Smith). Such research reveals that adolescents are not in fact the selfish creatures that the media and traditional stereotypes convey. Adolescence, rather, is often marked by exuberant transcendence, where young people take considerable efforts to contribute to their friends, families, communities and societies. (For further discussion on moral and spiritual development see chaps. 12-13).

Although at first glance adolescents appear to be self-absorbed, awkward and rebellious, we see through the lens of the reciprocating self that this developmental period is characterized by rapid development of both a unique and authentic self as well as the ability to participate more fully in mutually reciprocating relations. Models of development that do not capture the depth and complexity of this stage do a disservice to our understanding of adolescence. One emerging approach that helps capture positive adolescent development more fully is the concept of *thriving*.

Thriving. A thriving young person is a youth who makes the most of his or her own potential and circumstances, has a meaningful and satisfying life, actively contributes to the common good and is on the pathway to a hopeful future (Lerner, 2004; Lerner, Dowling and Anderson, 2003; Scales et al., 2000). Such youth make the most of themselves and their circumstances. They not only have a sense of meaning and personal fulfillment, but they demonstrate a commitment to the community or society in which they live. In short they are not only doing well personally or growing as an *I*, but they are giving back to others. Such youth, despite setbacks or negative experiences, are on a positive developmental trajectory.

These young people have an appropriate sense of self. They have a clear sense of their identity, sufficiently knowing who they are and what they stand for. They have a sense of purpose and meaning that motivates and directs their actions. In addition, their personality is marked by as sense of positivity that comprises both a sense of optimism and joy. The sense of purpose and positivity contribute to tenacity that enables them to overcome obstacles. Also central to thriving is a future orientation, which involves having expectations for oneself. Such thriving young people are adaptable and resourceful. They have the ability to access their personal assets and mobilize external resources available to them through family, community, school and neighborhood. In addition they can adapt to changing situations and can modify their expectations and dreams for self.

An important component of thriving is realizing one's potential. From the perspective of thriving, all youth can be successful. However, success looks differently based on their unique gifts and circumstances. Thriving youth make the most of who they are and what they have access to. For example, a young girl who is physically disabled would not thrive in the same manner as a young boy with great physical strength and dexterity. In addition, having different resources available also affects how one might thrive.

Finally, central to an understanding of thriving is making a contribution to the common good. From the perspective of thriving, optimal development is not about individual success, achievement or subjective well-being. Thriving can include those things but also involves a commitment to giving back to society in some manner. Lerner, Dowling and Anderson (2003) describe idealized personhood as a developmental teleology in which individuals experience reciprocity with their family, their community and larger society. Lerner (2004) understands thriving young people to be on a developmental trajectory that will enable them to be in ever-increasing reciprocating relationships. We would add that a thriving young person is in a reciprocating relationship with God as well. The moral, civic and spiritual development that occurs during adolescence enables youth to reciprocate in these different domains.

Reciprocity on the Way

Although adolescence is a formative time for the reciprocating self, it is important to recognize that both thriving and the capacity to reciprocate are a process. Paul reminds the Christians in Philippi "that the one who began a good work among you will bring it to completion by the day of Christ Jesus" (Phil 1:6). We are all works in progress, and adolescents are no exception, perhaps more obviously so. Although young people at this stage make tremendous growth in their capacities as reciprocating selves, they are not complete. From our teleological perspective, in the end—when Christ comes again—we will become complete reciprocating selves, fully able to participate with the new humanity in Christ. We will not only experience unity and communion with one another but also be drawn into the dynamic life of the triune God and participate in the reciprocating glorification of the Father, Son and Holy Spirit.

We need to remember that adolescents are not yet there. At times they come across as competent and confident, and at other times immature and hopeless. We must remember that they are on their way. During this period, the *I* grows in leaps and bounds in the context of the *Thou*. Identity takes shape in the processes of differentiation, experimentation and relationship-building. At this stage relationships grow in intensity, yet they can quickly fall apart. Adolescents try new things. At times they are brilliantly successful and shine; at others they stumble and fail miserably. This is all part of the growth process. With all the rapid growth there is as much potential to go right as there is to go wrong. Although youth are undoubtedly resilient, the self is in process—under construction, so to speak. Just like any structure under construction the adolescent self needs scaffolding support. The adolescent self needs a certain amount of structure around it, providing guidance and stability as it firms its sense of beliefs, values and identity. Although the adolescent needs a certain amount of structure and support, the developmental scaffold is different from that of a young child. The scaffold must continue to provide guidance, values, beliefs, boundaries and expectations.

However, the scaffold at this stage needs to begin to come down, enabling the adolescent freedom to explore and experiment in order to differentiate and develop their own sense of self. If the scaffold remains rigid and high, the young person will not have the opportunity to explore and achieve identity commitment. He or she will not have the necessary space to differentiate—or for "full unfolding," to use Jürgen Moltmann's (1996) words. They can grow overly dependent on others to dictate their belief, values, self-concept and preferences.

Adolescence has long been viewed as a difficult stage in life. No doubt the highs are higher and the lows lower, but too often adolescents are wrongly viewed as delinquents, dangerous, awkward or problems waiting to happen. A quote from a 1950s newspaper makes this point. In an interview with a junior in high school, a journalists concludes, "All too frequently these days, teenagers are portrayed as gawky, not-quite-adults who sit around drug stores, race around in hot-rods, cause trouble or stand around in groups on street corners discussing boys, girls, clothes and cars" (Pettingell, *Park Forest Star,* 1959). Although the issues facing society in the twenty-first century are more dangerous, such menacing behavior does not characterize all adolescents. The reciprocating self provides a means for understanding the hard developmental work that adolescents go through as they attend to becoming more clearly defined selves. The outward-appearing independent behavior is part of the journey toward interdependence. Because this journey is not without its perils, young people need company on the way to assist and guide them as they explore the terrain of life. As the journalist points out, many adolescents contribute much along the way: "But many young people are serious-minded, well-informed, forward-looking citizens, participating in and donating to school and community activities." With the right support and encouragement, young people will emerge as more fully capable reciprocating selves.

Emerging Adulthood and Young Adulthood

THE SOLIDIFYING OF THE RECIPROCATING SELF

MY FRIENDS AND I (PAM) WERE VERY EXCITED to graduate from college. We were equipped with our Stanford degrees, had a sense of call from God to various forms of work and ministry, and had one another for support. But many of us were not quite sure what to do or where to go. We felt like well-trained athletes after an intense season of training. We were crouched in the starting blocks, equipped with state-of-the-art cleats. But when we heard the starting gun and burst forth from the blocks, we realized the race could be run in many directions. For many in their early twenties this frustrating feeling of potential combined with lack a of directional clarity is common.

At the turn of the twenty-first century, psychologists have begun to recognize a new stage in the life span—*emerging adulthood.* Jeffrey Arnett has identified emerging adulthood as the stage of life falling between adolescence and adulthood. Emerging adults, generally classified as starting in the late teens and enduring through the mid-to-late twenties, do not experience themselves as adolescents, nor do they feel comfortable describing themselves as adults. For most young people in industrialized cultures, this time period is marked by profound change and importance. It is often a time of exploration of vocational and love interests. In industrialized countries young people pursue education and training that will equip them for occupational success and achievement the rest of their adult lives. In addition, this is a time to explore relationships and intimacy.

A central aspect of emerging adulthood is exploration and experimentation. Unlike adolescents, emerging adults experience more independence and less parental monitoring than they did as children or adolescents. Unlike adolescents, society expects them to be responsible and accountable. Most do not have the commitments (e.g., marriage, parenthood, career) older adults do. Consequently, they have much freedom and take the opportunity to explore the possibilities afforded in work, love and worldviews. Although this is common among young people in industrialized cultures, it has not been the case for all times and cultures. Cultural norms, expectations and opportunities may limit the extent to which emerging adults are able to use this period for independent exploration.

The Theoretical Roots of Emerging Adulthood

Although "emerging adulthood" is recognized as a new period of life, psychologists—without identifying it as a distinct life-span stage—have alluded to the uniqueness of this period from the late teens to early twenties. For example, in his writing about the period of young adulthood, Erikson (1950, 1968) discussed a phenomenon he called "prolonged adolescence." He commented that industrialized societies provided a psychological moratorium for young people, during which the young adult was free to experiment with different roles without undue pressure to commit until a particular niche was discovered. Arnett comments that, without naming it, Erikson seems to distinguish a stage that has qualities of both adolescence and young adulthood yet is neither one. "It is a period in which adult commitments and responsibilities are delayed while the role experimentation that began in adolescence continues and in fact intensifies" (Arnett 2000a, p. 19).

The work of Daniel Levinson also alludes to this period of emerging adulthood. He called ages seventeen to thirty-three "the novice phase" of development and suggested that the dominant task of this phase is to move into the adult world and build what he called a "stable life structure." Young people experience much change and instability as they explore various relational and vocational possibilities. And during this period, they move toward establishing ongoing love and work commitments that become part of their life structure. Levinson acknowledged the theoretical similarities between his conception of the "novice phase" and Erikson's formulation about role experimentation and psychological moratorium. (For further discussion of Levinson see chap. 11.)

Emerging Adulthood: The Demographics

Demographic changes in the time of marriage, parenthood and vocational commitments in the past several decades have established the period of emerging adulthood as typical for young people in industrialized cultures. Postponing these traditional commitments until the late twenties or often during the thirties allows the late teens and early twenties to be available for exploring possible life directions.

Among people experiencing emerging adulthood the common demographic is variability. Emerging adulthood is characterized by so much change that nothing is normative demographically. This is in sharp contrast to adolescence and young adulthood. During adolescence there is little diversity in many demographic areas. Over 95 percent of American youth aged twelve to seventeen live at home with at least one parent. Over 95 percent attend school, while 98 percent are unmarried and less that 10 percent have a child of their own (U.S. Bureau of the Census, 1997). Similarly, young adulthood is characterized by strong demographic norms. By age thirty, 75 percent have married, roughly 75 percent are parents and less than 10 percent are enrolled in school (U.S. Bureau of the Census, 1997).

In between these two periods a person's demographic status is not predictable. Arnett (2000a) explains that the demographic unpredictability and diversity of emerging adults aged eighteen to twenty-five is a reflection of the experimental and exploratory quality of the period. Emerging adulthood, more than any other stage in life, affords the individual a wide array of opportunities. Some choose to continue education, some travel and explore, some pursue serious jobs, some live at home, some cohabitate, some marry, and some do not. Young people at this stage are not constrained by social norms and role requirements, making their demographic status of residence, employment and marriage unpredictable.

Here are some statistics to help paint the picture of how varied American emerging-adult experience is. Roughly one-third of emerging adults go to college and live away from home after high school. This time away at college is "semiautonomous," where college students live in a combination of independent living and continued reliance on parents (Goldscheider and Goldscheider, 1994; Goldscheider and Davanzo, 1986). Most college students take on new forms of responsibility for independent living (e.g., their laundry, hopefully) but in many cases parents remain responsible for others. About 40 percent leave their parental home for independent living and full-time work. A study in the mid-1990s found that about two-thirds cohabitate with a romantic partner (Michael et al., 1995). Still others remain at home to work, attend college or a combination of the two. Today in America only about 10 percent of males and 30 percent of females live with their parents until marriage (Goldscheider and Goldscheider, 1994). Roughly 40 percent of the current generation of emerging adults will move back into their family home and then out again at least once during this period of life (Goldscheider and Goldscheider, 1994).

School attendance also demonstrates a picture of variability. With higher rates than ever before, over 60 percent of high school graduates now enter some form of higher education (Bianchi and Spain, 1996). However, only 32 percent of twenty-five to twenty-nine year olds have completed four years of college (U.S. Bureau of the Census, 1997). For emerging adults today, college completion is being pursued in a less linear fashion, where work and periods of nonattendance may break up times of full-time attendance. For those who do graduate from college, one-third enroll in graduate school the following year (Mogelonsky, 1996). This demographic diversity is reflective of the emphasis on change and exploration of the period of emerging adulthood. As young people make enduring commitments to love and work, these demographics begin to stabilize.

Subjective Uniqueness of Emerging Adulthood

Demographics not only statistically illustrate differences between adolescents, emerging adults and young adults, but emerging adults report that they feel distinct from the two surrounding life stages. They do not see themselves as adolescents, nor do they feel entirely comfortable calling themselves adults. Arnett (2000b) found that when asked if they have reached adulthood the majority of Americans in their late teens and early twenties answer ambiguously: "In some respects yes, in some respects no." These findings suggest that for the most part, emerging adults perceive themselves as having left adolescence, but not completely having entered young adulthood. It is not until the late twenties and early thirties that two-thirds of young people report feeling like they have completely transitioned into adulthood. That still leaves one-third not feeling like an adult by their early thirties.

Why would young persons in this age group feel this way? Perhaps it is related to the demographics previously discussed. Maybe this age group does not feel adultlike because they do not have a stable residence, or because they are still in school, or because they have not married. Surprisingly enough, research suggests that for late teens and early twenties these are not the top criteria for feeling like one has reached adulthood (see Arnett, 2000a). Such transitions as marriage, parenthood, finishing school or settling into a career rank at the bottom of importance of transitions that qualify a person as an adult. Since these demographic transitions seem to have little to do with emerging adults understanding of what it means to become an adult, what does?

The characteristics that seem to matter most to emerging adults are not demographic transitions but rather personal qualities of character. Studies reveal that the two top qualities young people report making them feel "adult" are (1) accepting responsibility for one's self, and (2) making independent decisions. A third basis that ranks consistently near the top is becoming financially independent (Arnett, 2001b).

These criteria for making the transition into adulthood emphasize the significance of self-sufficiency in emerging adulthood. During these years new levels of independence and opportunities for exploration and experimentation allow self-sufficiency to be developed. Accepting responsibility for one's self, making independent decisions and financial independence give the young person a sense of self-sufficiency. It is when young people have confidence in themselves that they transition out of emerging adulthood and into young adulthood. For most Americans this is accomplished by the late twenties (Arnett, 2001b).

Emerging Adulthood and the Reciprocating Self

Given our understanding of the reciprocating self, how does emerging adulthood function in the development of the individual who is able to be in mutual, reciprocating relationships with others where they experience simultaneous intimacy and individuality? Current theories and research suggest that independent exploration and a growing self-sufficiency are characteristic of this stage. Opportunities to explore relationships and different vocational options allow a young person to know themselves better—define their interests, recognize their natural talents and abilities, experience their relational strengths and weaknesses. In many ways emerging adulthood functions much like adolescence in the emergence of self. However, given the increased levels of independence and options, the emerging adult has more opportunities for exploration. At this point in life parental scaffolding is almost completely removed. Late teens and early twenties are often responsible for their own curfews and whereabouts. Some of them are working and have discretionary income that allows them to pursue experiences of their choosing. Furthermore, by this point in life they have acquired more skills and relationships that open doors for a larger variety of work and recreational experiences.

Consistent with the theme of experimentation and exploration, the little research available on risk behavior suggests that several types of risk behavior peak during emerging adulthood, not adolescence. These risk behaviors include unprotected sex, most forms of substance use and driving while intoxicated or at high speeds (Bachman, Johnston and O'Malley, 1996). Such behaviors reflect the emerging adult's resistance to settling down into roles and responsibilities of adult life. Erikson described "locomotion" as an important component of identity development during adolescence. Locomotion refers to a young person's tendency toward sensation-seeking. This is the need to experience the physical self to the fullest extent and simultaneously challenge social rules and norms. Consequently, experiences that qualify as sensation-seeking, or locomotion, are often considered dangerous, novel and intense. Emerging adults generally have more freedom to pursue such experiences than adolescents because they are less monitored by parents and have more resources at their disposal. They experience more freedom than young adults because they are less constrained by the responsibility of roles such as parent or spouse.

By providing opportunities for exploration and experimentation, emerging adulthood gives way to the emerging self. As the self nurtures a more salient self-concept through exploring love relationships, work, risk and worldviews, the self becomes more capable of reciprocity. Identity is a crucial aspect of the self, and in some ways emerging adulthood is much like adolescence, only with less scaffolding. Let us consider how identity takes shape during emerging adulthood. Arnett (2000a) contends that emerging adulthood is the period of life that offers the most opportunities for identity exploration in the areas of work and love. Although Erikson (1950, 1968) suggested that adolescence was the period to resolve the crisis between identity and role confusion, he also argued that Western industrialized societies allowed for "prolonged adolescence" for necessary identity exploration. Although research on identity formation has focused on adolescence (ten to eighteen years), many studies have shown that identity achievement is rarely attained by the end of high school and extends through the late teens and twenties (Waterman, 1982).

If we look at two main areas of identity exploration—love and work— we will see how identity exploration begins during adolescence and continues on into emerging adulthood. Identity development involves testing various life possibilities and gradually moving toward making enduring decisions (Arnett, 2000a). In regard to love, American adolescents generally begin dating in their early teens. These relationships typically last only a few weeks or months. Although they can be an important source of companionship, they are viewed as recreational and rarely come with the expectation of being lifelong relationships. In contrast, during emerging adulthood, explorations in love become much more serious and intimate as couples more often take seriously the potential for emotional, spiritual and physical intimacy. Such relationships last longer than during adolescence and are more likely to include greater intimacy, sexual intercourse and sometimes cohabitation (Michael et al., 1995). Adolescent romantic relationships are much more transient whereas relationships in emerging adulthood tend to raise more serious questions of identity, "Given the person I am, what kind of partner do I wish to spend my life with?"

Similarly, adolescent work is characterized by transient and tentative explorations, but emerging-adult work generally involves more serious and focused explorations. Although the majority of American adolescents work part-time, their work experiences do not provide them with knowledge and expertise related to their future occupations. On the other hand, during emerging adulthood young people intentionally pursue work experiences focused on preparation for enduring careers. Emerging adults intentionally seek out opportunities to explore identity issues that allow them to discover what kind of work they enjoy, are good at or find meaning in.

Not all emerging adults pursue focused and serious relationships or work experiences. For many the absence of enduring roles and commitments makes this stage of life unique in allowing for a high degree of experimentation and exploration. Consequently, some people have a variety of romantic and sexual experiences (while parental supervision is reduced and there is little social pressure to enter marriage). Emerging adulthood also affords an opportunity to take advantage of unusual or risky work or educational opportunities. Consequently, many emerging adults pursue short-term volunteer or missionary work and others take opportunities to travel and explore other cultures. These experiences allow for rich opportunities of identity exploration, expanding the emerging adults' ranges of experience prior to making more enduring choices of adulthood.

Distinguishing Between Emerging Adulthood and Young Adulthood

How are emerging adulthood and young adulthood different? Is it necessary to distinguish between the two periods? Arnett (2000a) builds a case for two unique periods. His research confirms that eighteen- to twenty-five-year-olds generally do not consider themselves as having reached adulthood, while the majority of those in their thirties do. The majority of youth eighteen to twenty-five are in the process of preparing for long-term careers through education and training, whereas most in their thirties have chosen an enduring career path. Most in this younger period are not married and are childless, and most in their thirties are married and have children. The term *emerging adulthood* captures the change and growth that characterize the gradual transition that young people make during this period as they mature toward young adulthood.

If exploration and experimentation characterize emerging adulthood, then what characterizes young adulthood? Stability. Erikson specifically addresses the significance of stability in relationships, and Levinson articulates the importance of building one's life structures during the young adult stage. We will discuss the pursuit of stability in young adulthood through relationships and work.

Erikson identifies the crisis of "intimacy versus isolation" as the predominant focus of young adulthood. He proposed that when a young person successfully resolves his or her identity crisis and role confusion, he or she is able to forge intimate relationships. He reasoned that once a young adult has established independence from his or her parents and can function as a productive person in society, he or she would be able to enter into relationships with satisfying intimacy—a closeness experienced without the fear of losing oneself in the intimacy. Not being able to achieve intimacy with others results in isolation, where the young adult chooses to withdraw from relationships in order to preserve ego identity.

The basic strength or virtue that resulted from a positive adaptive re-

sponse to this crisis is love, which Erikson conceptualized as a mutual devotion to shared identity that permitted a fusing of self to another without
losing oneself. The late theologian James Loder (1998) beautifully articulates
this kind of intimacy: "Love implies a nonpossessive delight in the particularity of the other."

A major developmental task present in the early adulthood transition is
differentiation. Differentiation is a continuing process in the formation and
reconstruction of the reciprocating self. Perhaps more than at any other time
in life, persons in the early adult transition are trying to figure out where
their family's values, beliefs and morals leave off and where their own begin; they are striving toward self-sufficiency. At its core differentiation has
to do with *identity,* with asking and successfully answering the question,
Who am I? Are my values and beliefs really my own? Is this "me" talking
and acting, or am I merely playing out a role my family expects me to play?
Youth who are enmeshed with parents—those who have not developed
sufficient boundaries around their self structure—will have a very difficult
time in finding their own separate identity. Family therapist Karl Whiticker
suggests that youth who are too enmeshed with their families may need to
leave in a huff.

In Eriksonian terms the differentiated young adult has a solid sense of
identity and is able to sustain intimate relationships. One of the marks of
young adulthood is marriage, and differentiation is essential in order to successfully select a mate and maintain a marriage.

Selecting a mate. With young adults, a most important demographic
change has taken place in regard to marriage. Whereas the age of first marriage was approximately 23 years for men and 20.5 years for women in 1960,
it has risen to 27 years for men and 25 years for women in 2000 (U.S. Census
Bureau, 1997). During this same period the annual divorce rate (number of
divorces per 1,000 married couples) rose dramatically, from 9 in 1960 to 21
in 2000. While the divorce rate has not risen in recent years, it has plateaued
at this high level, meaning that if present rates continue, approximately four
out of every ten marriages will end in divorce.

Corresponding to the change from a premodern to a modern society is a
change in the nature of marriage. The *institutional marriage* of the past was
a union between two families, with parents actively involved in the selection
of a spouse for their children. The major functions of this marriage centered
on economic well-being and the production of children. The *companion-*

ship marriage of the present is primarily a union between two individuals who are in love and have personally selected each other. The major function of this marriage is companionship and personal fulfillment derived from the relationship shared together.

The simplicity of the parentally arranged marriage system in traditional societies has been replaced by the complexity of a mate-selection system that relies on the participants to detect true love. Given the distorting emphasis on romantic love in contemporary popular culture, this is a daunting task placed on young adults. Thus we offer an attempt to better understand the love-detection process placed on young adults.

In his attempt to sort out the complexity of romantic love, Roger Sternberg (1986) has suggested that complete love includes three dimensions. These include *commitment,* which is the cognitive component, *intimacy,* which is the friendship factor and emotional component, and *passion,* which is the motivational component. Balswick and Balswick (1999, pp. 58-60) have suggested that Sternberg's model might be integrated with the three types of love known in ancient Greek culture and used in the New Testament. They suggest that *agape* (self-giving) corresponds to commitment, *philia* (brotherly love) corresponds to intimacy, and *eros* (physical desire for one's beloved) corresponds to passion.

In the participant-run mate-selection pattern of modern societies, passion is likely to dominate at the beginning of courtship, followed by a surge in intimacy and culminating in a commitment as a couple contemplate the possibility of marriage. We suggest that while all three dimensions of love are important for a Christian marriage, courtship that begins with commitment to the other person establishes an environment in which intimacy and passion can grow to full maturity after the marriage has been consummated. The ideal relationship will exhibit equal amounts of commitment, intimacy and passion before two people marry.

Parenthetically, this model of love also allows us to conceptualize forms of love that might not be complete enough for marriage. Thus when the self-giving love of commitment to a person is present, but passion *(eros)* or intimacy *(philia)* is lacking, there is hope that these dimensions grow with the relationship. When intimate friendship is present, but commitment *(agape)* and passion *(eros)* are lacking, then a decision to marry seems premature. When passion *(eros)* is dominant, but commitment *(agape)* and intimacy *(philia)* are lacking, then infatuation rather than mature love is present.

While most young adults today would not choose to marry someone who they did not love, most would not marry on the basis of love alone, giving some thought to the issue of personal compatibility. Compatibility however does not merely mean being alike, for a marriage in which partners were exactly alike in every way might not make a strong marriage. There are two differing theories on mate selection: one suggesting that *like marries like,* and the other that *opposites attract.* Research on mate selection reveals that in reality both theories are true. Persons tend to initiate relationships with those whom they are alike in regard to *endogamous* factors—sharing a similar social background such as race, ethnicity, religion, education, occupation and geographical proximity. Relationships that move beyond this stage are then tested by another set of factors known as *homogamous* factors. Homogamy refers to persons being similar in regard to personal characteristics and interests, such as political beliefs, specific religions beliefs, moral values, hobbies, intelligence, height, weight and physical appearance. This set of factors can be considered the second "filter" through which a few relationships progress to a more serious phase. The third filter is know as *complementary needs.* For the relationships that reach this level of seriousness, opposite personality characteristics increasingly come into play. It seems that individuals tend to select a mate who has strength where they have a weakness. Thus research suggests that opposites tend to attract in regard to such personality factors as dominance-submissiveness, introversion-extroversion, and nurture-succor. Needless to say, some adjustments are probably in store for the couple that has extreme differences in a personality characteristics. The most attractive characteristic may become an irritation as the marriage develops or as one of the spouses grows in an deficient area.

At the beginning of the twenty-first century there are signs of a movement away from the certainty given by both traditional religious systems and scientifically based thinking when it comes to marriage. Postmodernity represents a radical response to the Enlightenment rationalism found in modernity. It embraces many flavors of truth, depending on one's personal experiences and group identities. Postmodernists reject the supposedly universal laws of nature as grounds for accepting or rejecting the priorities of certain life structures, because reality is viewed as multilayered with many ways of knowledge. Although postmodernity can be a useful corrective to the "certainties" of modernity, which promoted human reason as the basis for constructing meaningful life structures, it too can be problematic when taken to the extreme—that there is no reality except what is constructed by one's own experience.

The effects of postmodern thinking on the choices made by young adults can be seen in the emergence of a variety of alternative marital and family forms. Marriage is an option, but only as a conditional arrangement that can conveniently be terminated if it proves to yield insufficient self-fulfillment. There are a variety of ways a person can chose to be a parent while rejecting marriage—single motherhood, artificial insemination, single-parent adoption and community-based living are a few examples. For the 1 to 3 percent of the population who are homosexual in orientation, a choice can be made to openly build a same-sex relationship rather than to build a heterosexual relationship and secretly live as a homosexual. Our purpose at this point is not to address the moral implications of each of these examples but to point to the nature of life-structure choices available to persons in postmodern societies.

Vocation and the dream. In addition to love and intimacy, commitment to work and vocation is the other recognized developmental task of young adulthood. For Levinson (1978) young adulthood is characterized by actively constructing one's own life structures. The "novice phase" is a transition and experimental stage occurring within emerging adulthood in which a young person explores his or her place in the world, relationally and vocationally. In young adulthood the individual places a more serious focus on developing and eventually committing to a career. For Levinson these acts involve attempts to make a space for oneself in the world.

The sequence in which a person's life structure is built will vary, depending on the priority one gives to education and occupation as opposed to marriage and beginning a family. Some of the most salient tensions and frustrations experienced by young adults emanates from the desire to "have it all"—a higher education, a successful career, a strong marriage, deep bonding with one's children and an affluent life style. With high energy, young adults may launch into each, not realizing the amount of investment demanded by each life-structure situation.

The tension can be especially great among young women as they seek to balance marriage with a rising career, and at the same time hear the ticking of their biological clock that warns them that they need to begin a family. However, "having it all" stills seems possible during young adulthood, so we will postpone our discussion on this issue until the next chapter. The key developmental issues for most during young adulthood center on selecting a mate and education/occupational decisions.

An important aspect of making a place in the world is what Levinson calls the "dream." The dream is a vision of the future that gathers up deeply held personal feelings and translates them into images of the self in the adult world "out there." The dream is shaped by an individual's present perceptions of him- or herself and what he or she is open to in the future. The dream has a transitional quality as it acts as a guiding vision for the future. According to Loder (1998) the dream is conjured up as a resolution to the developmental conflicts of the ego. It incorporates issues surrounding occupation, intimate relationships, marital adjustment, singleness, parenting and lifestyle. The dream acts as a guide for the young adult, providing a vision for the resolution of these life issues. The dream provides inspiration and motivation for pursuing vocational and relational paths that hopefully will result in the attainment of the dream.

For example, from an early age a young boy might have a "dream" to be a teacher and to one day help disadvantaged inner-city children. This vocational vision might serve to guide him as he navigates educational choices. The dream carries with it a sense of devotion that inspires him to stick with his dream despite challenge and obstacles. For instance, his parents may not approve of his decision to relocate to a more "dangerous" neighborhood in order to be accessible to his students and school. The dream can provide a sense of conviction that propels him to persevere with his commitments.

It is crucial that the dream is a person's own. If the dream is handed down from parents or imposed by a social or cultural order, it will lack integrity and misguide the young adult seeking his or her way in the world. The integrity of the dream depends on expressing an individual's innermost passion about him or herself and vision for the future. Often in enmeshed families it is easy for adult children to dream their parents' dream for them. They might pursue a certain career or even a certain marriage partner because their parents' expectations are so deeply engrained in them that those expectations have become the dream. This is often true of adult children of overbearing parents or for those who became parentified children, where they had to take on the role of an adult within their family for various reasons. Such adults have a hard time dreaming their own dreams. Living out someone else's dreams can have grievous consequences for the adult. For example, an adult who carries out her parents' dreams and wishes for her and pursues a career in software development, only to realize (consciously or unconsciously) years later that she longs to work with and serve people intimately, will not only experience grave dissatisfaction and tension but may experience anxiety and depression as well.

It is also important that the dream is realistic. The dream offers no help when we have an unrealistic impression of ourselves. Forgive the illustration, but I am reminded of one of the earlier episodes of the TV show *American Idol,* where "emerging adults" from around the country auditioned in their home towns in hope of being invited back to Hollywood as the next potential American idol. Mixed in among the extremely talented were the not so talented individuals. A few of these individuals were certain that they would be the next American idol, oblivious to the fact that they had absolutely no musical talent whatsoever. These "dreams" are more like fantasies or delusional fantasies that mislead people and often result in disappointment or feelings of failure.

A mentor is important to making the dream a reality. Mentors are those who understand and share the importance and potential of the dream. They can practically connect the dreamer and the dream with the real world out there. They do this by giving realistic feedback and helping shape the dream in such a way that maximizes the potential of the dreamer and encourages realistic assessment. In addition, mentors use their position in the world to influence the world and open doors on behalf of the dreamer. For example, a professor might recognize a student's dream to pursue academics. Inviting the student to participate in a research project would be one way of influencing the world "out there" and making the dream more of a reality.

Connecting vocation with intimacy, Loder (1998) talks about the importance of sharing the dream. Intimacy depends on sharing a dream with someone who can respect, enjoy and enrich one's own dream. Intimacy occurs when a special person can help an individual feel the power and depth of the dream as realistic. The dream can be shared between close friends or between spouses. It is important in relationships that one person's dream does not dominate. Often dysfunctional relationships occur because one individual is a great dreamer and the other needs someone else's dream to follow. The latter ends up supporting the dream of the partner, and he or she often ends up resentful. In some cases, one partner will have a dream and be too threatened to recognize the other's dream.

Deepest intimacy occurs when individuals empower others in pursuit of their dreams. In marriage it is optimal when the spouses are able to merge their dreams to co-create a dream that guides and sustains their lives as a couple. In keeping with the reciprocating self, this does not mean abandoning one's own dream but having space in the relationship to empower one another's dreams as well as be close enough to dream together.

Conclusion

Today, scholars recognize that emerging adulthood and young adulthood are two distinct stages of the life span. Some scholars contend that emerging adulthood is a luxury of the educated and middle or upper classes, arguing that only those who stay in school and remain childless have the opportunity to experience it. Although this may be the case, it still applies to a significant amount of the American population and needs to be taken into consideration.

From the perspective of the development of the reciprocating self, emerging adulthood is helpful in that it highlights an especially poignant time of development of the self. In some ways it takes the issues of adolescence a step further, providing time and opportunity for young people to intentionally pursue the development of the self. In a recent editorial in the *Los Angeles Times* on the topic of emerging adulthood commented that this period of life was "a heretofore nameless nether world of angst and hope." This quote correctly gets at the active and profound questioning and searching as well as the hope and possibility that characterizes this period. Emerging adulthood might be described as a crucible, where the self takes shape in the fiery furnace of transformation.

Young adulthood is less about the emergence of self and more about the self in action. Most young adults have a solid sense of self; they have made at least initial commitments to vocation and often to love and relationships. If intimacy is not pursued in a marital relationship, young adults often establish enduring friendships with members of the same and opposite sex. During this time the self is actively reciprocating, investing in a vocation as well as in relationships. The self is found in mutual relationships and is preparing for the next more generative stage of life.

Middle Adulthood

THE GENERATIVITY OF
THE RECIPROCATING SELF

THIS CHAPTER FOCUSES ON THE PERIOD OF TIME beyond young adulthood and before the elderly years, which roughly spans the fourth through sixth decades of life. Commitments to work, marriage, parenting, elderly parents and friends all constitute dimensions of a person's life structure in which the reciprocal self in relationships is continually shaped and reformulated. The internal reshaping of the self corresponds to the external middle adulthood process of "responsible scaffolding." The major responsibility in the majority of social institutions—family, religious, educational, political, economic—fall on persons who are in their middle adulthood years. Involvement in each institutional life structure demands a participatory role in "scaffold development." Persons in middle adulthood constitute the "backbone of society," on whose backs fall the major responsibilities of life. Responsibility constitutes the source of many of the anticipated fulfillments, as well as the developmental tensions and issues among persons during this period. Issues to be addressed in this chapter include midlife crisis, emotional intelligence, change or decline in intelligence and the development of wisdom.

Theories of Adult Life-Span Development

Since it is assumed that most human development takes place during the formative years, considerably less attention has been given to adult development. That which has been done has been guided by the theories of Erikson, Levinson, Gould and Vaillant. Although Levinson's theory has gained the most attention, the studies of Gould and Vaillant actually predate the work of Levinson.

Gould's phases of life. Based on both clinical data and responses to questionnaires by 524 nonclinical adults, Gould (1978) suggests seven chronological phases of life. *Sixteen to eighteen years:* adulthood begins when the desire for autonomy moves youths away from parents and toward closer relationships with peers. *Eighteen to twenty-two years:* individuals seek to deepen family-type relationships with peers as a way of resisting their family's attempt to "reclaim" them. *Twenty-two to twenty-nine years:* individuals work at being competent adults, begin to "really live," but are guarded against extreme emotions as they build for the future. Role confusion is characteristic of those from *twenty-nine to thirty-five* as individuals begin to question commitments to marriage or work as well as their own purpose and goals in life. This is a time when persons seek continuity between what they do and who they are. Those from *thirty-five to forty-three* characteristically feel they do not have enough time to accomplish all that needs to be done. The time squeeze is not only felt at work but also in relationship with their children, with whom they are fast losing influence. *Forty-three to fifty* is a settling-down stage in which people learn to accept the limitation imposed by time and destiny. At this age a person wants to gain a better feel for his or her relational and affection needs from family and friends. A continuing quest for meaningful personal relationships characterizes the period from age *fifty to sixty*. This also is a time of warming and mellowing toward children, parents, spouse and friends. Gould's suggested phases of life contributes a richness to understanding the changing nature of the reciprocating self through the life span.

Vaillant's adaptation to life. Based on a longitudinal study of ninety-four male Harvard College graduates, George Vaillant developed an adult life-span model that he characterized as *adaptation to life* (1977). Utilizing a variety of research methods Vaillant reported that his study confirmed the major developmental task proposed in Erikson's theory. Vaillant's longitudinal research was especially effective in demonstrating the accumulative effect of positive or negative stage-specific life-span effects. He reports, for instance, that whereas about half of the subjects who had experienced poor childhood environments were among the thirty worst outcomes in their fifties, only 17 percent with poor childhood environments were among the thirty best outcomes in their fifties. Other confirmations of the accumulative hypotheses are the importance of achieving intimacy during young adulthood for marital stability later in life, and the contributions of a stable marriage and rich friendship network to achievement in the sphere of work. Like Erikson and unlike Gould and Levinson, Vaillant conceptualized adulthood in broad life periods. Vaillant's research suggests that the development of the reciprocating self must, at least in part, be understood in terms of accumulative strengths or deficiencies.

Levinson's seasons of life. Daniel Levinson utilized qualitative analysis as a basis for identifying "the seasons of a man's life" and "the season's of a woman's life" (see *The Seasons of a Man's Life* [1978]; *The Seasons of a Woman's Life* [1996]). Levinson gathered information through intensive biographical interviews that could be described as a story-telling, narrative approach. Although methodological details are curiously absent from *The Seasons of a Man's Life,* Levinson indicates in *The Seasons of a Woman's Life* that the book is based on twenty hours of interviews for forty-five women, which translates to two to three hundred typed pages for each. As with his sample of men, professional women were overrepresented in his women's sample (fifteen each of homemakers, career women and academic women were interviewed).

Levinson has expanded the adult developmental stages from those suggested by Erikson, Gould and Vaillant by viewing the adult life cycle as a sequence of eras. Each era has its own bio-psycho-social character and makes distinctive contribution to the whole. Persons might be understood as active participants in constructing their own life structure. Adult development takes place within four eras, with five-year cross-era transitions. (See table 10.1 for a graphic depiction of Levinson's developmental model.)

Levinson believes that adult development can best be understood as individuals seeking to find their niche in society. By creating their life structure individuals are actually constructing their own "life space." The underlying pattern or design of a person's life at a given time might be considered to be a "snapshot" of a person's life structure. Development can be up (adolescing) or down (senescing), as both processes go on at the same time throughout the life span. The speed with which one moves through each era differs within the life of each person as well from person to person. One person, for example, may get "stuck" in the early adulthood era, while another finds him- or herself restless and eager to move on the next.

Table 10.1. Levinson's Developmental Model

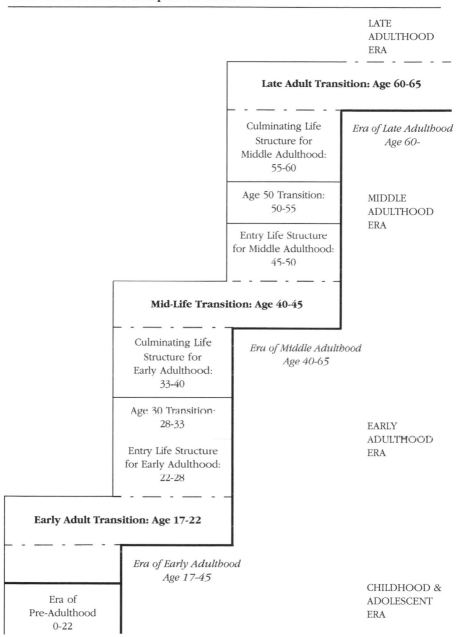

(Adapted from *The Seasons of a Man's Life,* [Knopf, 1978], and *The Seasons of a Woman's Life,* [Knopf, 1997].)

The primary components of life structure are *relationships* with others in the external world. A relationship must be described in terms of what is *done, its meaning, what is given and received, the context, the place* and *evolution over time.* There is an obvious correspondence between the elements of a relationship as defined by Levinson and our model of the reciprocating self. Life structures have central, peripheral and unfulfilled components. Life structures also include external and internal aspects. When the external realities, for example, become extremely distant from an internal vision, goal or dream, an individual needs to reformulate or re-vision the goal or dream. Too much dissonance between external and internal aspects of a life structure renders a person susceptible to unrealistic expectations at best, and sets him or her up for failure at worst. *Satisfactoriness* refers to a person's evaluation of the external and internal aspects of his or her life structures.

Within any era as assessment can be made of a person's investment of their self in life. While highly invested persons are intensely engaged in the process of living, lowly invested persons are disengaged from life. Investment in life can be both *positive* (excitement, enthusiasm or meaning) and *negative* (turmoil, suffering or fear).

Each era has development tasks that need to be mastered. A *developmental crisis* can be said to occur when a person is having great difficulty in meeting the tasks of the current period. One response to a developmental crisis may be to disinvest from life. Quitting a job, deserting the family or divorcing one's spouse are extreme examples of disinvesting.

Transitional periods consist of boundary regions that serve as bridges between eras or developmental periods. A glance at table 10.1 will indicate major transitions between one era and the next, and minor transitions between two periods within an era. Transitions include three tasks that are intertwined, and thus not necessarily done in sequence. *Termination* is more of a turning point than an end; it involves the transformation of a relationship. This might involve a person asking a question such as, What am I going to do about my life? *Individuation* is a process both within the self and with the external world. It might be the process, for instance, of establishing firm yet permeable boundary between the "me" and "not me." In so doing the individual is forming a more stabilized relationship with the external world. A healthy degree of individuation is necessary in order for a person to develop intimacy in a relationship with another. *Initiation* refers to the task of making choices to invest in new relationships or activities. When the reciprocating self is strong and secure, a person can better negotiate the many twists, turns and transitions that are a part of middle adulthood.

Crisis results when a person is having difficulty in mastering these tasks within the current period. An "adaptive" crisis involves an inappropriate response to a stressful situation. For instance, some men and women at midlife have a sexual affair because they are unsure of their attractiveness or sexuality.

While Levinson developed his theory based on data gathered from men, he argues that the evidence from the women's study in general supports the model developed for men.

He suggests that found gender differences in development can for the most part be understood in terms of *gender splitting*—the creation of a rigid division between males and females. (See the following section for a discussion of gender splitting among middle-aged adult women.) Men and women are both found to correspond to the suggested age sequencing of eras and developmental periods. Levinson is "embarrassed" by the order and eloquent simplicity of the sequence.

These three theories of adult development have several key findings in common. First, all three report a period of significant tension and transition between adolescence and early adulthood. Each confirmed that the period of struggle might continue well into the twenties as a young person strived to enter the adult world, in essence anticipating the need to establish emergent adulthood as a new developmental life stage. Second, all three theorists described a midlife crisis as occurring at roughly the same chronological age. Gould described the midlife crisis as occurring between thirty-five and forty-three, Vaillant at around forty but as early as thirty and as late as fifty, and Levinson at between forty and forty-five. Gould and Levinson found the crisis to be more severe than reported by Vaillant. A shared limitation of the three studies is that they represent a segment of the population that is significantly higher in education and income than the general population, a fact that should be kept in mind as we draw on them in gaining a picture of adult development.

The Stages of Middle Adulthood

Early middle adulthood. Middle adulthood begins with the age-thirty transition—roughly from ages twenty-eight to thirty-three. When people realize that they are moving out of the twenties, they begin to understand that there is little time left to change their life structure. Rather than trying to "keep options open," such a person begins to feel that "this is the last chance." For the person who is dissatisfied with his or her occupation, there may be the feeling that this is the last chance to "really do what I want to do." Early middle adulthood can also be a time of reevaluation, a time of considering new choices. After such considerations a person either concludes that he or she is satisfied with the life structure choices made or quickly plans to make changes while they are still possible.

The age-thirty transition is followed by the age-thirty-three to thirty-nine *settling down* period. In this second attempt at building adult life structure, individuals seek to invest themselves wholeheartedly in work, family, friendships, leisure, community—that which is most important in life. The tentativeness of the early life structure (the twenties) is gone. On the job they strive to prove that they can make it. They begin in earnest to climb the occupational ladder. In family life the demands of mothering and fathering call a person to spend time with their children—to play with them, to become a scout master, to coach a soccer team or take them camping over night. This is a period of time when both women and men are generally very busy and committed as reciprocating selves to building their life structure. Toward the end of the settling-down period a person may begin to assess the progress made in light of the goals he or she has set.

In traditional marriages this description of early middle adulthood may be more applicable for men than for women. Women who are homemakers have the luxury of investing themselves in the domestic life structure, settling into the role of being a wife and mother. For what has become a majority of middle-age adult women who are employed outside of the home, the above paragraph is applicable. As we move to an examination of the midlife crisis we will see that for these women an identity crisis at midlife can be responded to by *gender splitting.*

The midlife crisis. With the end of the settling-down period comes the age forty to forty-five *midlife transition.* The midlife transition is traditionally described as a crisis primarily for *men.* The issue of a female midlife crisis will be addressed following our focus on men. For most men the midlife transition is the "big one." It is the equivalent of an 8-point earthquake on the Richter scale. A number of factors contribute to the probability that this transition will produce the greatest crisis, the most important factor being the rapidity of social and technological change, which is described in the latter part of this chapter (see pp. 215-17).

In his study of career-oriented men, Daniel Levinson (1978, pp. 209-44) has identified four *polarities of midlife transition*. Although these polarities exist through the entire adult male life cycle, they are accentuated during transition periods. Men who have dealt with these polarities throughout their life, having met minor crises on a regular basis, do not experience the midlife transition as a crisis period. On the other hand, men who have not dealt with these polarities are candidates for a major midlife crisis. Men in midlife can occupy a marginal status because of the *young-old* polarity. These men feel older than young men, but they are not ready to join the rocking-chair set just yet. One sign of this concern is that these men will attempt to appear younger than they are. They may dress in a sporty style or put themselves on a rigorous weight lifting and running routine as ways of appearing young. The second polarity is *destruction-creation*. Having experienced conflict on the job and being battle-scared and hurt by others, men in midlife may resort to the same tactics. They also are aware of the heart attacks and even death of friends their age. At the same time they have a strong desire to be creative. Having accumulated the needed training and experience, professional men look to middle age and beyond as the time when they will reach their peak in creativity and productivity. The *masculinity-femininity* polarity points to middle-aged men's attempt to sustain their manly appearance of strength and toughness, while at the same time they come to have a desire to become more nurturing. Their masculine side pushes them to further achievement and ambition, while their feminine side calls them to be more relational and sensitive to the needs of others. Needless to say this masculine-feminine polarity is a struggle that seeks resolution within the structure of the reciprocating self. Finally, the *attachment-separateness* polarity points to the need to find a balance between being connected to others and being self-sufficient. Men have a high need for attachment during the early part of their career because they need to learn from others who are more experienced. There comes a point when these same men need to pull away, to be in charge, or at least to have the opportunity to try out their own ideas.

A major task that men must face during a transition is to confront a polarity as they become aware of it. Growth can come when a man finds a new way of being young, masculine, creative or attached. There is nothing wrong with a middle-aged man desiring to be young, for instance, but he must not allow himself to be stuck in a particular way of being young. For example, at the age of sixty-five I (Jack) still enjoyed playing intramural flag football with the students at Fuller Seminary. When I came to Fuller over twenty years ago, my body was still (barely) agile enough to play quarterback. Fifteen years ago I dislocated a knee but continued my attempt to play quarterback with a knee brace. After a few years of struggling I realized that I was stuck in my attempt to be young. Since I gave up my need to be quarterback, I learned to enjoy playing other positions—I learned to be young in a new way.

The more recent publication of *Seasons of a Women's Life* (Levinson, 1996) indicates that the midlife transition is less pronounced for most women. The major transition for women is the drawn-out process of moving from a traditional definition of femininity that largely limited them to a domestic roles to an expanded definition that allows them to pursue a career. In this transition Levinson found that women more than men engage in *gender splitting*—simultaneously holding dichotomous identities.

Four types of gender splitting are noted among women—*domestic-public, homemaker-provider, women's work-men's work* and *femininity-masculinity in individual psyche*. Most homemakers want to uphold a traditional view of marriage, while at the same time holding an antitraditional view that wants more independence, including equality with men, and to be in the public world. Many career women experience extreme conflict between an internal traditional view and an antitraditional view. The two groups have different resources and constraints as they move through life stages. Around midlife, homemakers may begin to experience a crisis in meaning and identity as their children move out of the home. Having invested so much of themselves in the mothering role, many midlife women respond by returning to school, continuing an interrupted career or beginning a new one. The crisis for career women is most likely from the tension of trying to balance marriage, motherhood and work. For these women leaving children (in daycare or preschool) might actually be a relief from the difficulty of trying to do it all. Given the dynamic changes that have taken place in gender roles, it should be no surprise to learn how profoundly these changes are affecting women's reciprocating selves at midlife.

Successful middle adulthood. The above descriptions of midlife tensions needs to be balanced by a recent study suggesting that middle age may be less stressful than previous writings have suggested. For ten years the MacArthur Foundation Research Network on Successful Mid-life studied over seven thousand midlife Americans. Its director, Orville Brim, said, "On balance, the sense we all have is that midlife is the best place to be" (Goode, 1999). The study revealed that in moving from age thirty-five to age sixty-five, persons report increased feelings of well-being and a greater sense of control over their lives. A majority of participants reported feeling better at present than they had during the previous ten years. Less than a quarter (23 percent) reported undergoing a midlife crisis, and of these only one-third attributed the crisis to the aging process. Seventy percent described their health as excellent and most were very optimistic about their health in the future. A majority described their marriages or relationships as stable and relatively happy. In regard to personal autonomy and effective management of their world, male and females alike scored higher from the beginning to the end of the midlife period. This evidence of increased psychological well-being was especially evident for women. Contrary to what Sheehy (1991) reported, menopause was not a major contributor to midlife stress among women.

At the later end of middle adulthood (the sixties), both women and men reported a loss in personal growth, a decrease in a continued sense of purpose and a declining optimism about continuing good health in the future.

Berman and Napier demystify the midlife crisis by reframing it in terms of a *narrative change*. The midlife transition occurs when "the narrative shifts to include the awareness of morality, and the understanding that one is in the middle of life and not the beginning" (Berman and Napier, 2000, p. 229). Thus midlife crisis is in reality "a period of life review in which the person reappraises his or her life, developing a coherent story about the past and present" (p. 229). Narrative change can involve revising life goals and aspiration, forgiving oneself for sins of omission and commission, making peace with a parent, reconnecting with an adolescent or redefining success or failure in life. The ability to construct a narrative that makes sense allows a person to look to the future with confidence and anticipation. A midlife crisis occurs when the reciprocating self cannot successfully negotiate a narrative change.

This emphasis on narrative change, combined with the Successful Mid-Life study serves as a corrective to a common emphasis on the stress of middle age. Persons in midlife generally see this as a good time of life, being satisfied with their lives and aware and thankful about their personal gains.

Midlife stress is centered more on worries about the future, especially around health and financial issues (Goode, 1999).

Erikson uses the term *generativity* to refer to the major developmental task persons must master during their middle adulthood years. Generativity is possible to the extent that polarities and gender splitting are confronted and dealt with creatively. To successfully combine all aspects of oneself into an integrated whole renders one a candidate for *ego integration* during Erikson's final age-sixty-plus developmental stage. The opposite of generativity is *stagnation,* the state of not growing, of being bogged down, of being static or of being stuck. When the polarities of *masculinity* and *femininity, young* and *old* or *attachment* and *separation* cannot be recognized and integrated into a whole self structure, the culmination of middle adulthood may lead to *ego despair* during the final stage of life.

Middle-aged persons are living out generativity when they invest themselves in other people and delight in seeing their work and ideas live on through younger persons. The sign of a generative person is that he or she is a person *for* others, or, in terms of our model, a reciprocating self who is an empowerer of others. Middle-aged persons have the knowledge and experience to influence others. Those who use their influence to control others are betraying a state of ego stagnation. Those who use their influence for others and to build others up are operating from a state of generativity, characterized by a mature reciprocating self.

Late middle adulthood. The amount of change brought about by the midlife transition may not be realized until it is over. For some, life is radically reoriented—a decision to prepare for the ministry, to begin a new career, to start a business, to take up a new hobby or even to quit work in support of one's spouse's career. For others middle age brings little change, which may reflect resignation to a boring job or a positive acceptance of the life structures already built. Others fail to listen to inner voices that question the meaning, value and direction of their current lives. For these the age-fifty transition can be crisis-filled. Persons who have seriously confronted and creatively dealt with the issues raised during their midlife transition seem to sail right through mature adulthood years.

The primary developmental task of mature adulthood, according to Erikson, is *ego integration*. Ego integration is the state in which the various parts of a person's life structure form a consistent and integrated whole, not a bad description of the ideal reciprocating self. Persons with high ego integration or strong reciprocating selfhood live with a confidence that their life has meaning, value and direction. Those who have shown mastery over the primary developmental task at each previous stage are candidates for high ego integration. For others, born into an atmosphere of distrust rather than trust, life has been experienced as a series of failures to master the primary task at each subsequent developmental stage. Lacking the needed inner resources, these persons experience mature adulthood with *ego despair,* in which life lacks meaning, purpose and a sense of direction. Due to accumulative strengths or deficiencies the lives of persons at the mature adulthood stage vary widely.

Beginning at about age sixty and continuing on until retirement, usually age sixty-five, is the *late adult transition.* In this transition an individual needs to conclude the efforts of middle adulthood and prepare for an anticipated retirement. He or she begins to *disengage* from the situations, relationships and commitments that were the driving force during the mature adulthood years. Signs of disengagement include a reluctance to make difficult or controversial decisions at work and a pulling away from group and relational involvements that will end at retirement. These individuals want to retire with a quiet dignity, having no desire to do anything that might rock the boat.

Family Life

Approximately 90 percent of humans marry, the vast majority before they reach age thirty. The typical couple who marry while in their twenties can expect to live two-thirds of their life married or in adjusting to a marriage terminated by divorce or death. During middle adulthood married individuals usually pass through two separate family-life stages—*launching* and *postlaunching*—before retirement and late adulthood.

The launching stage. The *launching stage* is that period of family life when children are in the process of leaving home. In chapter eight on adolescents, we identified some of the tensions and issues that arise in the family when parents reach middle age and children reach adolescence. The successful launching of children is directly related to the degree to which the tensions and issues of the previous stage were addressed and resolved before the children leave. A successful launch is characterized by children leaving home but continuing to orbit at a safe distance around the family. In a failed launch the child either continues to be physically or psychologi-

cally within the family, or is jettisoned so far that the family is no longer instrumental in the continued life development of the child.

One of the key developmental processes among adolescents is differentiation. When children reach the launching stage with unhealthy differentiation, they tend to either develop a pattern of *dependence on* or *independence from* their parents. Healthy differentiated children can assumed an
interdependent relationship with their parents as they learn to become truly
reciprocating selves. Unfortunately, the practice of adult children moving
back in with their parents has become such a common practice that the term
boomerang children has been coined to describe them. And middle-age parents can be greatly affected when their young adult children are unable to
assume adult responsibilities.

Differentiation issues are relational issues by nature. The overly dependent or independent needs within an adult child usually reflect unresolved
parental differentiation issues. When both parents have a mature reciprocating self, they can model a balanced relationship with each other and with
their children. In their chapter "Launching Children and Moving On," Mc-
Cullough and Rutenberg (1989) identify four things that parents can do to
assure a better transition through the launching stage. First, parents must *re-
focus on their marriage relationship* and not allow any carryover of the tensions and issues that might have been a part of their parenting of adolescent
and young adult aged children. If the marriage is strong, then it is easier for
their children to leave home. Second, parents and children need to learn to
relate to each other as adult to adult. Part of letting go for parents is accepting the adult status of their children. As long as their adult child remains a
child in their eyes, the parents' self-identity is that of a parent—a protector,
a caretaker and so forth. Accepting and allowing one's child to be an adult
calls for a reformulation of the reciprocating self. Parents must literally learn
to relate to their children in a new way—adult to adult.

Third, parents must *develop good relationships with the child's spouse and
his or her family.* The most conflictive relationship tends to be in the daughter-in-law to mother-in-law relationship. The major reason for this is that
mothers more than fathers involve themselves in their married children's
lives. Part of the conflict may emanate from a young husband comparing his
wife with his mother on such tasks as cooking, cleaning and parenting. This
puts the daughter-in-law in a no-win situation since what her husband defines as good cooking and what he experienced as parenting was shaped by

his mother. The next most frequent conflict is in the son-in-law to mother-in-law relationship. Although this may be due to the mother's involvement in her daughter's marriage, the stereotype of mothers-in-law an "interfering battle-ax" may work as a self-fulfilling prophecy. The next to least conflictive relationship is son-in-law to father-in-law, which tends to be absent of conflict if the father-in-law believes his son-in-law is adequately caring and providing for his daughter. Least conflictive is in the daughter-in-law to father-in-law relationship, which is frequently a good-natured teasing type relationship.

Fourth, so much of parents' time and energy is focused on their maturing children that issues with their own aging parents may need to be more fully addressed when children leave home. Thus *resolving issues with the older generation* can make for a smooth and successful launching. Such issues might include dealing with elderly parents' increased emotional and physical dependence, financial insecurities following retirement or emotional feeling following the death of a parent.

However, there may be some societal reasons why leaving home is not as easy a process as it once was. In a highly technological society the majority of well-paying jobs demand high education, training and skills. Most entry-level jobs require a college degree at a minimum. The cost of a college education today is $50,000 and upward. This means that more and more adult children find themselves economically dependent on their parents for longer and longer periods of time. Even those who have been "launched" may find it necessary to assume the status of "boomerang children" by returned to the launching pad.

The postlaunching stage. A major consequence of children leaving home is a greatly changed and often-reduced parental role for parents. Such "role loss" can be detrimental to either a parent or a marriage or both if parenting was what provided a sense of meaning and purpose to the individual or the marriage. This might explain a third peak in the divorce rate after twenty-five years of marriage (Shapiro, 1996). (The first two peaks being in the first two years and around fifteen to eighteen years of marriage.)

In a strong marriage, partners focus on each other, and the relationship is not dependent on the joint-parenting role. In general the decline in marital happiness that began with the arrival of children reaches its low point just before children leave home. Once children leave home marital adjustment increases, creating a U-shaped curve between length of marriage and marital happiness.

Increased life expectancy means that those in late middle adulthood may be "sandwiched" between their adult children and their aging parents. Since economic earning is generally the highest during late middle adulthood, this *sandwich generation* find themselves in the middle of two needy generations. They are called on to give emotional and economic support to their adult children and their elderly parents at the same time. By the time they anticipate retirement, this sandwich generation may be pleased to find that their adult children have finally gained a healthy degree of economic independence, but distressed to find that their aging parents have increased emotional and economic needs. Although the fact that people are living longer results in greater complexity in family relationships, it also allows for the possibility for greater cross-generational family intimacy and support.

Marital Issues

In their analysis of long-term marriages, Berman and Napier (2000) suggest that midlife marriages are under pressure in four ways. First, marital *commitment* may be tested when a common focus on the children declines and the couple finds they have more time for each other. For couples whose commitment has been on the marital relationship and each other, this can be a exciting time of joint participation in life. For couples whose primary focus has been on what they have together as parents, there may be a need to build common activities and interests. Middle adulthood can thus be a time when the focus of the marital commitment is tested.

At middle age a couple can have an accumulated history together that includes a backlog of unprocessed feelings and imbalances in the relationship that need a measure of grace if they are to be adequately addressed. Berman and Napier (2000, p. 223) suggest that some couples may have fought and not allowed themselves tenderness or softer emotions, while in other marriages there may have been an "underfunctioner and an overfunctioner—and both are tired of this sense of imbalance." There are also several boundary issues a midlife couple may need to negotiate. A boomerang child or an elderly parent, for instance, may need care and reenter the home. Needless to say it takes a considerable amount of grace on the part of both spouses to face one another's shortcomings and to agree to work on their relationship.

By early middle adulthood a couple usually develops a *balance of power* and a pattern of decision making. Middle age creates a more intense push in both partners to fulfill their dreams and incomplete identities. To the degree that the balance of power has served as a barrier to the self-fulfillment of one partner, difficulty may arise. In Gray-Little and Burk's (1983) review on the relationship between marital power and marital satisfaction, egalitarian marriages were found to be the most satisfying, followed by traditional marriages. Wife-dominated marriages were the least satisfying. Given changes in the balance of power, it is vital that midlife couples master the practice of mutual empowerment.

The final midlife marital pressure identified by Berman and Napier (2000) is the *desire and expectation for greater intimacy in their relationship*. Middle age jars a couple into evaluating the progress they have made toward greater intimacy. It is worth noting the similarity between the four midlife marital issues suggested by Berman and Napier and the centrality of unconditional commitment, gracing, empowering and intimacy to the biblically based model for relationships we presented in chapter three. In our biblical model of relationships we suggest that intimacy—to know and be known—is the goal of relationships. A number of barriers may retard the development of marital intimacy: inability or unwillingness to express feelings, over-involvement in work, focus on children's needs, lack of communication skills and so forth. When children leave home, a couple lacking intimacy may panic about what life will be like with just the two of them. Where intimacy has not been achieved, a spouse may be tempted to look elsewhere for emotional and sexual fulfillment. Insecurity about self-esteem or body image may also lead a spouse to seek affirmation of his or her attractiveness from another source. Inversely, when marriage is based on the interaction of two strong reciprocating selves, it will be characterized by both closeness and intimacy, as well as independence and separateness. Our model would suggest that true marital intimacy is possible only when both partners are highly differentiated individuals.

Mesosystem and Macrosystem Issues

We began this chapter by noting that persons in middle adulthood constitute the backbone of society because they are called on to provide much of the needed scaffolding in society. Participation and involvement in the major societal institutions beyond the family—religious, educational, political, economic—constitute the arena within which middle-aged persons play out major mesosystem issues. The degree of involvement in each of these social institutions varies greatly between persons. For persons with strong religious commitments involvement in church will be a high priority. Lee and Balswick (1989) have documented that mesosystem stress can be especially acute on clergy families when there are not appropriate boundaries between the family and congregational system. Mesosystem issues are not likely to emerge between the family and the political and educational institutions because involvement in the former is usually limited to voting, and in the latter to showing various forms of support to school-age children through participation in the PTA, serving as a homeroom parent or assisting in extra curricular activities.

The more serious mesosystem issues for middle-aged persons result from their participation in the economic institution. The competing demands of work and family life can be especially acute for younger middle-aged parents. The major issues are usually defined in terms of scarcity of *time* and *money*. Time is in short supply due to the dual demands of needing to prove oneself at work and the tremendous time it takes to parent young children. Money is obviously in short supply due to the fact that, while younger middle-aged couples desire and need to make large purchases such as a home, furniture and automobile, they have not had the time to accumulate much financially. As persons reach midlife, patterns may have been developed where much more time has been given to work than to family life. Those who have devoted long hours at their jobs realize when they reach midlife that they have *spent little time with their children*. Some find that when they attempt to reach out to their now nearly grown children, their children are not responsive, and the parents have had little actual influence over them.

At the macrosystem level the rapidity of social and technological change ushers in a variety of stressors for midlife persons. Personal and occupational crises develop when people are unprepared for the changes taking place in their world. Persons in the labor force today are especially vulnerable when the job they have been trained for can *become obsolete* due to the latest technological innovation. Automobile workers, for example, experience understandable anxiety when realizing that robots can do the type of work they were trained to do. A similar anxiety plagues white-collar workers when they witness a computer doing the work previously done by ten people. Persons at managerial levels fear being overtaken by younger, better-trained college graduates who have received specialized training that was not a part of the curriculum when they were in school. Changed social norms may cause some men to fear that this young college graduate may even be a woman.

Societal norms define success in terms of employment advancement to higher status and earning capabilities. Midlife can be a time of crisis for the individuals who realize that they will *not reach the lofty goal* that they have set for themselves. The crisis can be intense for those that believe reaching a particular goal is the criteria on which they are willing to accept themselves as worthy and valuable. Not reaching the goal in this case is a crisis in self-esteem. Other persons may feel that they accomplished their best work at an earlier age and that life is now downhill and boring. The term *career burnout* has been coined to refer to such situations. Other midlife persons compare the progress of their career with the progress of others of a similar age and become discouraged because they have not accomplished as much. Such persons experience a crisis because they feel that they are *not on schedule*. Still others have dedicated themselves to the hard work needed to climb the occupational ladder and find that they are unable to settle back and relax when they are off work or on vacation. The crisis in this case is that they have become a slave to work and career. They are *workaholics!*

Does Intelligence Change with Age?

Change in *intelligence* and *wisdom* are two developmental issues that arise during the middle to late adult life-span stages.

While it has long been assumed that intelligence declines with age, longitudinal research indicates that the decline is more gradual than previously assumed. Furthermore, decline is not even across all areas of intellectual functioning, occurs later than thought, actually increases in some respects and varies greatly from person to person. Evidence indicates that cognitive abilities related to daily living and work do not peak at young adulthood but continue into middle adulthood (Willis, 1989)

John Horn's (1982) distinction between *fluid intelligence* and *crystallized intelligence* is perhaps the most meaningful contribution to understand cognitive changes in middle and older adulthood. *Fluid intelligence* refers to the abilities used in new types of learning activities such as inductive reasoning, memorization and rapid perception of spatial relationships. The evidence points to this type of intelligence reaching its peak in late adolescence. *Crystallized intelligence* includes the abilities to analyze problems, make judgments and draw conclusion based on information and knowledge gained from past experience. There is evidence that crystallized intelligence continues to increase across the life span as long as a person is open to social, educational and cultural experiences.

Changes in cognitive skills also need to be understood within a cultural context. It is possible that middle-aged and older adults experience *obsolescence* as the rapid accumulation and application of knowledge renders the education they received as youth and young adults out of date. The ability to learn and use computer skills is a case in point. I (Jack) have more than once asked my sixteen-year-old grandson to bring me up to speed in utilizing my computer. It was also quite a shock to observe my three-year-old grandson using a computer-generated learning program. But can an old dog be taught new tricks? In actuality there seems to be an interaction between the effects of *obsolescence* and decreased *fluid intelligence.* Yes, middle and later adults are at a cognitive disadvantage because they did not learn today's knowledge in their formative years, but they also may have some declining capacities in memory and inductive reasoning. The interaction between these two factors may combine to yield what is perceived to be resistance to change or creativity among middle- and older-aged adults.

Believing that traditional ways of conceptualizing and testing for intelligence is inadequate, some have proposed new models for conceptualizing intelligence. Most suggestions point to the need for assessing a more *practical intelligence,* one that tests mental activity that successfully adapts to the environment. Birren (1985), for example, suggests that traditional intelligence tests might be limited because they fail to assess *competence.* Sternberg (1986) suggests that there are three kinds of intelligence. *Analytical* intelligence refers to the analytical abilities to evaluate, judge, compare and contrast. *Creative* intelligence involves the ability to originate, invent, design, create and imagine. *Practical* intelligence consists of the ability to implement, apply, use or put into practice. Sternberg (1999) claims to have identified a combination of strengths in intelligence: some people are high in each of these three types of intelligence, others are high in two and still others are high only in one.

Gardner (1983) has also proposed that intelligence is far more multidimensional than traditional intelligence tests would suggest. He argues that intelligence consists of the following "frames of mind": *logical-mathematical, linguistic, visual-spatial, musical, bodily-kinesthetic, interpersonal* and *intrapersonal* intelligence. Gardner believes that on any given task an individual is likely to draw on a number of these types of intelligence.

In a useful summary of the evidence on adult cognitive functioning, Lemme (1999) contrasts the *decrementalist view,* that cognitive development in adulthood follows a pattern of universal, inevitable decline, with the *continued-potential view.* While this latter view acknowledges that cognition declines in adulthood, it also recognizes that some cognitive skills may continue to improve with age, and that some new cognitive abilities may even increase. Since fluid intelligence is more biologically based, its decline corresponds with physiological decline. Crystallized intelligence, on the other hand, is more experientially based and thus tends to remain stable or even improve with age.

The above evidence may lead us to ask if cognitive development really does end with *formal operations* as suggested by Piaget. Although the evidence does not call for a new stage of cognitive developmental, it does suggest that "the capacities of formal thought may be applied in new contexts during adulthood" (Lemme, 1999, p. 149). Cognitive development in adulthood is *quantitative* (what one knows) rather than *qualitative* (how one knows it). The cognitive advantage that goes along with aging is experiential or practical knowledge.

Parenthetically, some researchers do believe evidence exists for *postformal thought.* Lemme defines postformal thought as "an increasing relativism, the realization that real-life problems do not always have absolute answers, that contradiction and uncertainty are realities of life, and that knowledge and reality are only true temporarily" (1999, p. 150). Much of the argument for a postformal stage among adults has the ring of postmodern relativism, in contrast to the certainty of modernity (formal thought). Arlin (1984) suggests that problem-solving operations may be replaced with *problem findings.* In naming the stage after formal operations Riegel (1973) even suggests that poor performance by adults on intelligence test might better be interpreted as their ability to see alternatives beyond formal thought and a reflection of a more advanced stage of development, *dialectical operations.*

Emotional Intelligence

Emotional intelligence (EI) has emerged as the more recent alternative to an exclusive cognitive conceptualization of intelligence. Although EI has been popularized by Daniel Goleman (1995, 2001), the formative model has been developed by Peter Salovey and John Mayer (1990). In essence, EI is the ability to process emotional information, particularly as it involves the perception, appraisal and expression of emotion, emotional facilitation of thinking, understanding and analyzing emotions, and the management of emotion to promote emotional and intellectual growth. In a practical sense, EI involves having the emotional sensitivity and mental ability to manage life in a way that will lead to emotional and relational stability, and thus happiness. This involves knowing how to identify healthy feelings and how to turn negative feelings into healthy feelings.

The emergent thinking on EI is especially relevant to our conceptualization of the reciprocating self as it changes over the life span. More than any other way of conceptualizing intelligence, EI is directly related to the process of developing and maintaining a healthy and strong reciprocating self. In fact, we suggest that EI and the reciprocating self are highly correlated. Note how the follow characteristics and abilities encompassed by emotional intelligence are also an integral part of a developed reciprocating self:

- the ability to identify emotions in one's self as they are related to feelings, thoughts and behaviors
- the ability to identify emotions in others, including the ability to read facial expressions, body language and tone of voice
- the ability to express emotions accurately, including wants, desires and needs
- the ability to discern between honest and dishonest expressions of feelings in oneself and in others
- the ability to stay open to all feelings, unpleasant as well as pleasant
- the ability to interpret the meanings that the emotions of self and others convey regarding relationships
- the ability to understand complex feelings, such as simultaneously feelings love and hate or surprise and fear
- the ability to recognize likely transitions among emotions in self and others
- an elaborated languaging ability that allows one not only recognize but to distinguish between feelings by labeling them

Each of the abilities in the above list directly contributes to the development and maintenance of reciprocating relationships and a healthy reciprocating self. It can be argued that these abilities might more accurately be conceptualized in terms of *wisdom* rather than intelligence. It might be best to respect the conventional way that intelligence is conceptualized, while arguing that there is a human quality beyond mere intelligence—wisdom—that is even more important than IQ in constructing meaningful relationships.

Does Wisdom Change with Age?

A recently added category in understanding human development is *wisdom* (Baltes and Staudinger, 2000; Baltes and Freund, 2003). Wisdom can be defined as "knowledge about fundamental pragmatics of life and implementation of that knowledge through the life management strategies of selection, optimization, and compensation" (Baltes and Freund, 2003, p. 23). Note that this definition contains two components. First, there must be a *knowledge* about what is good and right in life. Second, there must be a *practical ability* to use that knowledge.

Wisdom as knowledge is unfortunately not automatically translated into wisdom as wise behavior. The latter may in fact be the more problematic aspect of wisdom. It is perhaps for this reason that Baltes and Freund (2003, p. 29) elaborate on how wise behavior as "a specific strategy of effective life management" develops. Three fundamental processes of life-span development regulation are identified—*selection, optimization* and *compensation. Selection* refers to the life-management task of developing, elaborating and committing to goals, which serve to give direction to development and a focusing on resources needed to reach those goals. In a religious context, for example, if being rightly related to God is identified as a primary goal, then all of life's activity and involvement will be *selected* in terms of how they affect this goal. *Optimization* refers to the process of acquiring, refining, coordinating and applying the relevant means or resources to attain the goals selected. Being rightly related to God may call for any one of a number of optimizing resources—meditation, prayer, chanting or singing, worship, Bible reading (perhaps even learning the biblical languages), silent retreats and so on. *Compensation* refers to using alternative means to maintain a given level of functioning when existing means are lost. For example, with declining eyesight and impaired physical mobility, an elderly person may come to rely on listening to tapes, radio or television programs instead of Bible reading or church attendance as a means of maintaining and nourishing their relationship with God.

Parenthetically, this suggestion is a significant modification of cognitive-development theory in which development is conceptualized primarily in terms of rational functioning ability. Rather than being "the idea of a fixed and domain-specific end state as conceptualized by Piaget or Erikson," wisdom, it is suggested, is a desirable end state of development (Baltes and Freund, 2003, pp. 26-27). Introducing the concept of wisdom results in a more dynamic and fluid conceptualization of human development and human strengths. Baltes and Freund argue that the "development of a culture of old age has lagged behind," for although older people may not be genetically well-equipped for old age, "older people are expected to continue to actively participate in social life and to optimize their level of function" (2003, p. 24). These authors point to wisdom as the advantage elderly need in order to optimize their level of functioning in later life. A *culture of wisdom* is the optimal context in which elderly persons need to live. This wisdom culture consists of "an expert knowledge system about the fundamental pragmatics of life, including knowledge and judgment about the conduct, purpose, and meaning of life" (p. 27).

Baltes and Freund (2003, pp. 27-28) suggest that the core domain of wisdom addresses important and difficult questions and strategies about the conduct and meaning of life; includes knowledge about the limits of knowledge and the uncertainties of the world; represents a truly superior level of knowledge, judgment, and advice; constitutes knowledge with extraordinary scope, depth, measure, and balance; involves a perfect synergy of mind and character (an orchestration of knowledge and virtues); represents knowledge used for the good or well-being of oneself and that of others; and though difficult to achieve and to specify, is easily recognized when manifested. This list represents an attempt to describe the optimal, ideal or desirable state of human development.

We suggest that what is missing in the wisdom model presented is the acknowledgement of God or a divine Other to whom an individual can be personally related. A major corrective to the model is found in Proverbs 9:10: "The fear of the LORD is the beginning of wisdom." To fear, or to have awe or respect, of God is presented as the foundation upon which all other wisdom is based.

The subject of wisdom in the Bible is primarily dealt with in the Old Testament wisdom books (Proverbs, Job and Ecclesiastes) and in certain parts of the New Testament, most notably writing that centers on "Jesus Christ who is God's wisdom and who reveals it to us" (Goldsworthy, 1987, p. 16). As the fulfiller of the Old Testament, only Jesus Christ can provide an understanding of the full meaning of the wisdom books of the Old Testament.

The word *wisdom* (or *to be wise*) is used over four hundred times in the Bible. While many of these refer to *knowledge* of what is good and right, many also refer to how a person is to *practically live out* that knowledge. In Scripture, making the right decision and living the right way is linked with wisdom. Note, for example, Matthew's parable of the wise and foolish builders (Mt 7:24-29). While a wise man builds his house upon a rock, the foolish man builds his house upon the sand. The wise person "hears these words of mine and acts on them. . . . [But] everyone who hears these words of mine and does not act on them will be like a foolish man who built his house on sand" (vv. 24, 26). Although Matthew begins by associating wisdom as knowledge, he quickly adds that no one is wise unless they put that knowledge into practice. Thus Baltes and Freund's assertion that wisdom includes the two components of *knowledge* and *practical abilities* comports very well with a biblical perspective on wisdom.

Outside of the Gospels, 1 Corinthians 1—2 most directly addresses the issue of wisdom. The heart of the Corinthian passages can be summed up in 1 Corinthians 1:20: "Has not God made foolish the wisdom of the world?" We could wrongly conclude that Paul is discounting the value of any "worldly wisdom." In truth, all of us have absorbed and depend on much "worldly wisdom" in our daily living. The wisdom described in Baltes's model is valuable; those who have more of it are better off than those who have little. Goldsworthy (1987, p. 31) helps us understand the difference between such worldly wisdom and Godly wisdom by summarizing Paul's assertions on the two kinds of wisdom mentioned in 1 Corinthians 1—2:

> First, Paul says that the gospel would be emptied of its power if he were to preach it with eloquent worldly wisdom (1:17). This is because the wisdom of the world judges this gospel, the message of the cross, to be foolishness (1:18). Such wisdom is therefore doomed to perish (1:19). Worldly wisdom is actually foolishness because it cannot put man in touch with reality by bringing him to God (1:20-21a). God's way of salvation through the preaching of Christ crucified is an offense to the Jews and stupidity to the Greeks, yet it is both the power and wisdom of God (1:18-24). So, that which the unbelieving world calls foolishness is in fact wiser than the wisdom of the world (1:25). Paul avoids the wisdom which the world sees as superior and persuasive, and centers his whole message on Christ crucified (2:1-4). He does this in order that

faith might rest, not in man's wisdom, but in God's power (2:5). Paul's wisdom
is wisdom from God which is taught by the Spirit of God (2:6-13). He who
does not have the Spirit of God will never see this true wisdom for what it is
(2:14-16).

To Paul worldly wisdom has meaning in a *limited* sense, but it falls short
of God's wisdom, which has meaning in an *ultimate* sense. Paul is not saying
there is no value to worldly wisdom, only that it fails to answer the ultimate
questions of what the meaning and purpose is to life. The culmination of biblical wisdom is seen in the person and life of Jesus Christ, who was wholly
God and wholly human. Jesus Christ modeled wisdom as knowledge *and*
how to put it into practice in daily living and interaction with others. Even
though Baltes's model of wisdom is limited, it is valid to the extent that it is
modeled by the humanity of Jesus. Thus we find that the "worldly" model of
wisdom comports very well with a biblical view of wisdom.

While the development of wisdom comes with aging, it is a process that
goes on throughout the entire life span. Hopefully, the end of midlife is accompanied by the recognition of others that one is becoming wise. Where
there have been barriers to the development of wisdom, the mere passage
to the elderly years is no guarantee that a person will become wise. Where
the beginning of wisdom has emerged, the elderly years can be a time when
the more routine and material concerns of life can be put aside in favor of
a life in which the further development of wisdom can flourish.

Late Adulthood

THE SENESCING OF
THE RECIPROCATING SELF

DURING THE LAST HUNDRED YEARS THE average life expectancy has increased thirty years, in effect adding a new life cycle stage. This chapter focuses on the last stage of adult life, those years that usually begin at retirement and continue until death. During the early years of development, scaffolds are dismantled to correspond to a child's developing capabilities and maturity. During the elderly years the reverse needs to take place as *senescing* (development downward) outpaces *adolescing* (development upward) (Levinson, 1996). As physical, cognitive and socioemotional capacities decline, scaffolding needs to be correspondingly constructed to care for and meet the needs of the elderly. When deterioration is great, such as with dementia, there will be a corresponding decline in the capacity to reciprocate. In the declining years new types of scaffolding will need to be constructed, some within a familial context, some within the believing community and some within society at large. A variety of issues—adjustment to retirement, health, sense of worth, meaning in life, relational intimacy, independence versus dependence and so forth—are addressed in this chapter.

As in each of the life cycle stages, individuals vary in regard to the onset of their own developmental issues. Thus while we have addressed issues of launching children and becoming grandparents in the previous chapter on middle adulthood, for some these may continue to be central issues during the elderly years. For most, however, the late adult transition (age sixty to sixty-five) signals the end of middle adulthood and beginning of late adulthood. To Levinson this is a major transition that requires a profound reappraisal of the past and an entry into a new era.

The Retirement Years

There is no set age at which the elderly era begins; however, the age of sixty-five has conventionally been considered the age of retirement. While in the past this was a threshold primarily for men, the fact that two out of every three women are employed outside of the home means that retirement issues apply to them too. There is great variation in the degree of life satisfaction during the retirement years, with evidence suggesting a greater variation among men than women. For some men retirement is experienced as the pot of gold at the end of the rainbow. For others it is a difficult adjustment. The workaholic, for instance, is unable to relax and enjoy the fruit of his labor. Others may have tied their meaning and existence in life to busyness, activity and accomplishments. When they can no longer identify an objective accomplishment, they feel unfulfilled. In contrast, by their retirement age most women have developed a rich network of intimate relationships with family and friends. Thus the retirement years offer the opportunity to enjoy these relationships and spend more time with extended family, especially grandchildren. Many men, on the other hand, can claim to be intimate only with their wife, meaning they must learn to cultivate relationships beyond the world of work.

Retirement can produce stress at both the individual and marital levels. At the individual level Atchley (1982) suggests that retirement is a five-stage process beginning with the *honeymoon,* in which anticipated leisure time becomes a reality. This is especially true of those who have worked hard all their life and were spurred on by the dream of financial security and leisure that they believed would be the fruit of their labor. For men this is often experienced as a time to "be a boy again," to pursue hobbies, tennis or golf, and to engage in leisurely travel that was not possible while working. For women leisurely pursuits are combined with the opportunity to be with family, especially grandchildren.

The *disenchantment stage* emerges when all play and leisure fails to yield a sense of purpose and meaning. Now the stimulation offered by a job might even seem appealing. To the workaholic who has few interests outside of work or who defines self-worth purely in terms of work, disenchantment can be extreme. Some retirees get stuck at the disenchantment stage, experiencing later life as void of meaningful fulfillment.

The fortunate majority moves to the *reorientation stage,* characterized by the retiree seeking to engage in new, more fulfilling and meaningful activities. This is a transition stage that can be very brief for persons who quickly settle into retirement pattern. If retirees do not successfully navigate this transitional stage, they may continue to be disenchanted with retirement. The retiree who reaches the *retirement routine stage* has learned to come to grips with the realities of retirement by finding activities that provide meaning and a sense of purpose. This is most possible for persons who have mastered their developmental tasks throughout life and who have created a strong and supportive life structure of family and friends. We suggest that a strong reciprocating self is vital to successfully navigating through these stages, and that, in turn, successful navigation serves to maintain a healthy reciprocating self, or what Erikson refers to as ego integration.

This view of maturity, characterized by ego integration and a network of supportive family and friends, is consonant with a biblical view of spiritual maturity. The spiritually mature individual will be an empowerer of others, seeking to invest him- or herself in others rather than needing to be served by others. The mature elderly person is able to combine the strengths of separateness and independence with an interdependence and connectedness within a network of reciprocally caring others. Such a balance between separateness and connectedness can be seen in the life of the apostle Paul. As Paul was nearing the end of his life, he prepared to pass the torch on to Timothy by writing, "The time of my departure has come. I have fought the good fight, I have finished the race, I have kept the faith" (2 Tim 4:6-7). For some there is a further stage—*termination*—the ending of retirement as an identifiable period, which can come when a person decides to return to work or when physical or mental capacities are so diminished that it eliminates retirement as an identifiable phase. We could do worst than to hold up Paul as a model of maturity during the retirement years, so when we look to the end of life we can affirm we have finished well.

Family Life

Retirement provides the time needed to reconnect with family in a way that may not have been possible during the preretirement years. The majority of retirees will be married and will have children and grandchildren. Each of these types of family relationships represents a potentially rich source of meaning and fulfillment for the retiree.

Retirement can have a positive or adverse effect on the marriage relationship. Most couples report postretirement as the most satisfying stage of marriage. Couples who are most satisfied maintain control of their time so they can engage in rewarding activities. These couples also tend to report a healthy sexual relationship with satisfactory expressions of affection and open communication, which allows then to confidently resolve marital conflicts. Other characteristics of highly satisfied couples include good health, financial security and involvement with church and friends. Attitudinally such couples view retirement positively and do not view their mates as moody, stubborn, jealous or possessive (Bradbury, Fincham and Beach, 2000; Swensen, 1994).

In a less-than-satisfying marriage, involvement in work may have served to keep the focus off of the relationship. With increased time together the retired couple needs to confront marital issues that have been avoided in the past. Wives who enjoyed a certain degree of autonomy and privacy while their husbands were employed may experience his continual presence in the home as a bother. This is especially true in marriages where the retired husband fails to develop a network of male friends to pal around with. Retirement can increase marital control issues, a development that might be related to the finding that in the postretired marriage wives become more assertive and the marriage relationship becomes more equal (Long and Mancini, 1990).

A major transition takes place in retirement marriages when one of the spouses becomes chronically ill, making it necessary for the other spouse to assume the role of caregiver. Given that husbands are usually older than their wives and that women have a longer life expectancy, wives more often assume the caretaking role in marriage. As time and energy is focused more and more on the illness, the couple decreases involvement with other couples and friends. This is the time when an elderly couple most needs the assistance of their adult children and other family members. When this does not happen, the caretaking spouse becomes overburdened and overstressed.

One of the greatest potential joys in late adulthood is in *grandparenting*. Spry and active elders dressed in jeans and tennis shoes are replacing the popular image of grandparents as part of the graying, frail, rocking-chair set. In nonindustrial societies most grandparents are highly involved in the lives of their grandchildren. With parents needing to devote much time to work, the care of children and the inculcation of morals, beliefs and values are most likely to be passed down from grandparents to grandchildren. The only biblical reference to grandparenting points to the wisdom of this, as Paul writes to Timothy, "I have been reminded of your sincere faith, a faith that lived first in your grandmother Lois and your mother Eunice and now, I am sure, lives in you" (2 Tim 1:5). Due to the decline of the extended family and the new mobility of modern life, few grandparents have the day-to-day involvement with their grandchildren that will allow them to effectively pass on their faith. They are not present to assume the place they have had in the past in their grandchildren's lives.

Involvement by grandparents in the lives of their grandchildren varies greatly in contemporary societies. Neugarten and Weinstein (1964) identified five grandparenting styles—*formal, fun-seeking, parent surrogates, reservoirs of family wisdom* and *distant figures.* The alternative styles reflect the differing circumstance in which grandparents find themselves in relationship to their grandchildren. For those who live a great distance from grandchildren, much must be packed into brief visits once or twice a year, meaning that they might be fun-seeking when present but distant figures the rest of the time. At the other extreme some grandparents become parent surrogates due to an inability of their grown children to parent. Regardless of grandparenting style, most grandparents can be counted on to become much more involved in their own children's and grandchildren's lives during times of stress and crisis. This is especially true when children divorce. Most grandparents give a significant amount of support to their divorcing adult children and grandchildren (Johnson, 1988). Given the amount of financial and emotional support grandparents give to married children and grandchildren, it is probably more accurate to describe the North American family as a modified-extended rather than as a nuclear family form.

Research has generated insights into the changing nature of what grandparents contribute to their grandchildren as they mature. Infant and toddler grandchildren benefit most, in the form of secure bonding, from grandmothers who provided physical and emotional care. During their early school-age years (five to ten), grandchildren most value what grandparents do for them and with them, such as showing love, giving presents and doing fun things. As grandchildren enter preadolescence they continue to value indulgent grandparents but also stress the importance of connectedness with them, and in so doing deriving a sense of family pride from their relationship with them (Ponzetti and Folkrod, 1989).

Given the often-strained nature of parent-teenage child relations, a grand-parent can serve as a sensitive nonjudgmental listener to teenage grandchildren's problems and self-esteem issues, and give affirming attention to their performances and achievements. The existence of an intimate and meaningful relationship between grandparents and teenage grandchildren can be mutually beneficial, contributing to the grandparent's mental health (Kivnick, 1982), and grandchildren's successful resolution of adolescent identity issues (Baranowski, 1982). In relationships between sixty-five- to ninety-one-year-old grandparents and their adult grandchildren, grandparents most benefited from their grandchildren's emotional support (Langer, 1990).

A reoccurring issue among grandparents who are highly involved with their grandchildren centers on boundaries. Grandparents might observe ineffective parenting methods in their grown children and think "been there, done that." Their dilemma is in deciding whether they should attempt to share their knowledge and in so doing risk being accused by their own children of interfering.

Aging Well

Before the advent of modern medicine, most people died of illnesses for which there is now effective intervention. As people are living longer, the question increasingly being raised is, What does it mean to age well? Gerontologists have traditionally focused on the negative aspects of aging, being content with "counting the wrinkles of aging" (Carstensen and Charles, 2003, p. 76). More attention has been given to elderly decline in personal functioning, psychological and social structures, and how this decline impairs the behavior of the elderly.

Gerontologists began a new perspective called "successful aging" or "aging well" in the 1990s. The result has began a more positive view of aging in later life (Aspinwall and Staudinger, 2003). The main components of successful aging have been identified as "low probability of disease and disease-related disability, high cognitive and physical capacity, and active engagement in life" (Rowe and Kahn, 1997, p. 143). Rocio Fernandez-Ballesteros (2003) added environmental or external variables to this list, such as access to health and social services.

With the increased life span, attention was initially given to the biological factors associated with aging. As it has become evident that chronic illness is "strongly associated with behavior factors such as lifestyle (e.g., diet, exercise), coping mechanisms, social networks, and social support" (Fernandez-Ballesteros, 2003, p. 142), more attention is now given to the study of social and psychological factors. A result of this redirected focus has been the discovery of a variety of positive aging experiences among the elderly. In one longitudinal study most participants reported aging to be a generally positive experience (Fernandez-Ballesteros, 2003, p. 143). Cognitively, elderly persons reported having a broader capacity for analyzing problems both intellectually and socially. Emotionally, the elderly reported feeling much more serene and relaxed than they were at previous life-span stages. Another very fulfilling social dimension of the elderly life is relationships with grandchildren. Up until the age of eighty the elderly perceive that their gains outrun their perceived loses (Heckhausen, Dixon and Baltes, 1989).

That social interaction decreases with age is an accepted finding in social gerontology; it has been explained by a variety of theoretical models—withdrawal due to increased depression, the feeling by the aged that they have little to offer in social relationships, the death of friends, friendships impaired by sickness or cognitive decline, and social disengagement in preparation for death (Carstensen and Charles, 2003, p. 77). Laura Carstensen and Susan Charles (2003) report recent evidence revealing that each of these theoretical models has in fact little empirical support. Carstensen suggests that older adults are much more proactive in managing their social lives than is suggested in these theories. She finds evidence that older adults "pruned" relationships "so that only most important people remained" (p. 77).

The culmination of Carstensen's research was the development of a model called *socioemotional selectivity theory,* which "argues that under time constraints, emotional aspects of life are illuminated . . . [as goals] . . . shift from the search for novelty or information to the quest for emotional meaning." Thus "older people are not suffering from limited opportunities to pursue social relations with others . . . [but] . . . are investing carefully and strategically in the people who matter most" (p. 78).

Needless to say, Carstensen's theory helpfully informs us of what is taking place in the reciprocation selves of elderly persons. We can view older people as having diminished reciprocating selves. But in so doing, we should not assume that the elderly have necessarily lost personal agency. The capacity for being in interpersonal relationships with others remains, but given the decreased time left in life, the elderly become more selective and judicious in assessing which relationships are worthy of time and investment.

Granted, a proportion of the elderly are limited in their personal agency due to dementia and other conditions, but many elderly continue to assertively act in ways that will assure maximum control over their own lives in the time they have left. What is typically defined as "stubbornness" on the part of the elderly might sometimes better be reframed in terms of selectively maintaining only that which is worth keeping in life.

Caring for the Elderly

In traditional nonurban societies the elderly are primarily cared for within an extended family unit. In modern societies the elderly are more likely to be placed in professional retirement care communities. This change has strengths and weaknesses. On the positive side, retirement communities provide a ready-made community in which to participate and needed social and medical attention when a senior becomes less self-sufficient. On the negative side, the security that an intimate, caring family provides may be hard to duplicate in the context of larger impersonal elderly care communities. Family life has truly come full circle when a mature bilateral commitment of unconditional love between parents and their dependent children is reciprocated when the parents themselves age and become socially, emotionally and physically more dependent on their adult children.

Scripture gives some general guidance on elderly care. In 1 Timothy 5:16 Paul writes, "If any believing woman has relatives who are really widows, let her assist; let the church not be burdened." This advice needs to be understood in the context of Paul calling the church to care for dependent elderly who have no family. Members of the early church were called on to care for any widow who had no one to care for her, as if she were one's own mother (1 Tim 5:2-3). If the way elderly parents were cared for during biblical times is to be taken as an ideal for all times, then the inclusion of elderly dependent parents within the adult child's household is the ideal. When desired by both elderly parents and adult children, this would seem to be as close to the biblical ideal of cross-generational nurturing care as a family could achieve.

However, it seems that God could honor alternative forms of elderly care systems. Given the strong emphasis on community in the Old Testament, a case could be made that the entire tribe or community rather than merely the adult children are responsible for care of the elderly. Some religious groups and denominations have established elaborate networks of retirement homes to care for the elderly, both their own and, in some cases, those who have no other source of care. Some interpret *tribe* in its broadest sense to argue that a society is morally obligated to make sure no elderly are uncared for. The overarching biblical principle seems to be that elder care should begin with family members as they are able. Given a lack of family, the responsibility then seems to fall on the believing community to care for their elderly as they are able. Only as a last resort should the elderly be placed in large institutions that are not embedded within the believing community. On a practical basis, a variety of social, psychological and economic circumstances need to be taken into account in deciding the best way to care for an elderly person. Along with a variety of circumstances and needs, we believe that God will honor alternative structures of care. At the very least, however, it seems to us that societies that build "safety nets" for the weak, homeless and uncared for are reflecting the biblical ideal most closely.

Demographers warn that modern societies in the future will be characterized by an "inverse pyramid" in which a greater proportion of the population are elderly. It is estimated that by the year 2040, over 20 percent of all people in the United States will be sixty-five or over (Hargrave and Hanna, 1997, p. 42). Some believe that due to the lengthening life expectancy, over half of the population will eventually be affected by such diseases as Parkinson's, Alzheimer's and other forms of dementia. The cost of maintaining this cohort of nonworking elderly, many of whom will live into their eighties and nineties, may exceed the combined funds available through Social Security and retirement accounts. Not only can medical expenses during the final years of life be enormous, but placement in a convalescent home can average between $30,000 and $50,000 a year. People who have worked hard and saved money over a lifetime can see their nest egg vanish in a very short time due to medical expenses.

Creating zones of proximal capabilities. Pruyser (1975, pp. 107-18) has suggested that the elderly person is a mirror image of the child, only in reverse. The elderly must cope with three potential stress-producing transitions: *physical decline and disability, mental decline and dementia,* and *death.* While the child begins helpless and moves toward self-sufficiency, the elderly person is self-sufficient but devolves toward helplessness. While the child gains increasing mastery over objects in the environment, the elderly person has decreasing capacities over the objective world. While the child increases in security and self-respect, the senior becomes more insecure and loses self-respect. While the child has the security of dependency and moves toward independence, the elderly begins with security but experiences the insecurity of moving toward dependency.

Vygotsky's *zone of proximal development* refers to the range of skills that a child can accomplish only with the assistance of another (see p. 117). The task of parenting, caretaking or teaching is to build scaffolds that enable a child to perform a task just beyond their present capability, but the scaffolding needs to change as the child begins to accomplish the task without assistance. Given the mirror image of childhood and the aging person, we suggest adapting Vygotsky's model to include the concept *zones of proximal capabilities*. By identifying such zones among the elderly, help—scaffolds—can be provided that will allow elderly persons to continue to accomplish tasks.

Elderly persons who experience a decrease in skill-oriented capacities have a increased need for scaffolding. Although it may appear that the caretaking of the elderly is the same as the caretaking of children, there is one significant difference. While children are on a trajectory toward increased task and skill development, the elderly are on a trajectory toward decreased task and skill capability. We suggest zones of proximal capability as a useful way of conceptualizing the range of tasks and skills that the elderly are capable of with the assistance of others.

Numerous examples of zones of proximal capability can be found within "assisted living" programs. Seen through the lens of the zone of proximal capability, the legitimate goal of assessed living is to allow the elderly to continue to do as much on their own as they are capable of doing. As they are able, the elderly must be allowed to be responsible for daily tasks such as personal grooming, dressing, preparing and eating a simple meal, driving to the store for groceries and so on. With decreasing capabilities, the elderly may be able to continue living independently with assistance with some of these tasks. Delivery of a hot meal through Meals On Wheels is a good example of an assistance program that allows the elderly to continue to live in their own homes. Door to door shuttle transportation likewise allow the elderly who can no longer drive a car to continue to participate in a wide range of community activities while still living on their own.

Recognition of zones of proximal capability encourages caretakers to assess the present capabilities of the elderly and in the process anticipate their future needs. If the minimum amount of assistance needed is given, then the maximum amount of elderly independence is likely to be kept intact. Elder care can err in two directions—by either *under* building or *over* building scaffolds. An elder whose need for assistance is underestimated may become frustrated, fearful and hopeless. But if the assistance is overestimated, the elder may experience helplessness, worthlessness or overdependence. Due to their size and impersonalness, institutional care may not provide elaborate enough scaffolding. On the other hand, family caretakers, because of their emotional involvement, are most likely to construct excessive scaffolding.

The best examples of institutional care are those with gradated comprehensive-care communities. At one level of these institutions, the living units for the most self-sufficient elderly merely serve as a convenient place to participate with similarly aged, self-sufficient people. With decreasing capabilities and increasing needs, residents can move to more intentional care units where they can draw on a wide range of services—meals, laundry, household clearing, transportation, daily physical assistance and so forth. The emergence of dementia or severe physical limitations usually means moving to a care unit that provides even more intense personal care. Finally, a hospital care unit is provided for the most needy. Such gradated comprehensive-care communities may come the closest to providing appropriate scaffolding for the elderly. The best of these have ongoing built-in assessment programs capable of anticipating the increased needs of the elderly.

Parenthetically, it is easiest to illustrate a zone of proximal capability by using physical- and motor-skill-oriented examples, as we have done, but the elderly's need for relational scaffolding might be even more important. Research reveals that loneliness and lack of meaningful interpersonal relationships are among the greatest reported difficulties among the elderly. Although elder persons residing within caretaking communities need interpersonal scaffolding, those elders outside of such communities need it even more. Scripture has much to say about including the elderly as family. In the case of those who have no family the church needs be the family of God for them.

The relationship between coping and health is cyclical. It is not only true that healthier persons are better able to cope but also that the act of coping contributes to the health of the individual (Whitbourne, 1996, p. 91). When caretakers offer a helping hand too quickly, they may be inadvertently hindering the elderly from maintaining health. Caretaker intervention might be most needed when the elderly resort to the unhelpful coping strategies of denial or withdrawal. In such cases, caretakers who do nothing may actually be enabling nonresponsiveness because they fail to encourage the elderly to confront a stressful situation.

The Diminishing Reciprocating Self

Physical, psychological and *social* capabilities in the aging process reflect self-identity of the elderly. Although we might expect these three sources of identity to be interrelated, there is evidence that elderly persons are capable of drawing on their one source of greatest strength (Whitbourne, 1996). In a study on how the story of aging is told, it was found that in the narratives of elderly persons the body is often split from the mind. In the narratives that our elders create, the body ages, but the self remains ageless. The self seems to be disassociated from the body, able to have a younger identity than the aging body would suggest (Oberg, as reported in Ruth and Vilkko, 1996). Jan-Erik Ruth and Anni Vilkko suggest that hope may occasionally be maintained in later life by repressing awareness of the present and instead remembering a younger, more active and well-functioning self (p. 177). Included in this, we suggest, is the ability to maintain a strong reciprocating self in the face of physical deterioration.

Now that I (Jack) and my wife are in our mid-sixties, we sometimes kid each other about having a "senior moment" when we temporarily cannot remember the name of an acquaintance. This is a normal (we hope) part of the aging process and is not to be confused with more serious forms of dementia such as Alzheimer's disease. It is estimated that, assuming current trends continue, by 2050 over fourteen million people will be victims of Alzheimer's (Frishman, 1997). Although there is much we could say about dementia among the elderly, we will focus our remarks on the theological questions posed by this condition, which seriously erodes the reciprocating self.

In chapter one we rejected a material body-nonmaterial soul dualism in favor of a nonreductive physicalism in which there is no soul but rather a human being having soulishness. Forms of dementia, such as Alzheimer's, are capable of seriously robbing a person not only of memory but also of other mental processes. It seems obvious that the effect of these diseases is to diminish the capacities of being a reciprocal self. Given the emergent functions model summarized in chapter one (see p. 20), it might be legitimate to say serious dementia effects one's soulishness. It would be wrong, however, to not view such a person, regardless of the effect of dementia, as a soul to be nurtured and cared for. The medical ethicist Stephen Post states, "The moral task is always to enhance the person with dementia" (Brown, Murphy and Malony, 1998, p. 201). Our commitment to a Christian ethic of agape means that regardless of an individual's emotional or intellectual capacities we will have utmost concern and compassion for every human being. It might even be argued that the soulishness of a person, regardless of the severity of the mentally incapacitating disease, is maintained by the love and care showed by a human community.

Death and Dying

Although death may come at any age, dying as a self-conscious drawn-out event is most common in the last phase of elderly life. Since dying elicits all sorts of emotions and reactions, it is worth considering what it means to die well. The most widely known model for understanding a person's reaction to death is that proposed by Elizabeth Kübler-Ross (1970). In her five-stage model, Kübler-Ross posits an initial stage of *denial,* where a person rejects the reality that they are going to die. This is followed by *anger,* which can be directed at anyone or everyone—spouse, children, God or people in good health. In the third stage, *bargaining,* the dying person may try to negotiate a way out of death—resolving to stop smoking or to eat healthier foods or by promising God to live a better life. *Depression,* the fourth stage, can be both a reaction to the sadness associated with the losses already experienced and an anticipation of future losses, such as not being able to see one's grandchildren grow up. When a person has worked through this depression, which can be a quick or slow process, the stage of *acceptance* is reached. This model, which is based on firsthand observation of how people die, has greatly influenced how we think about the process of dying.

In his attempt to develop a theology of death Ray Anderson builds on three relevant scriptural truths:

> that the body and soul alike are subject to death; that there is no dualism between the immortal soul and the temporal body; and that the individual's hope for redemption from death lies in God alone, who is the Lord of both life and death, rather than in personal immortality as an essential aspect of human existence. (1986, p. 45)

As a ministerial application of these truths, Anderson argues for a "human ecology of death and dying"—for a network of caring human beings to surround the dying person. We see this as consistent with what we have suggested about the maintenance of the reciprocating self. It is essential for the living to remain in community with the dying, for it is in the context of community that the self of the dying remains reciprocal.

Before his own untimely death in an automobile accident, Mansell Pattison was one of the leading Christian psychiatrists in the world. Several years before his death Pattison (1977) proposed an insightful theory of the dying process that is consistent with a biblical view of death and dying. Pattison suggested that all people project a trajectory of their life that includes an anticipated life span within which their lives and activities are arranged. This trajectory is suddenly challenged when the *probability* of a premature death is known. The person cannot continue to live according to the constructed trajectory but must revision the trajectory. The period between the *crisis created by the knowledge of death* and the *point of death* is referred to as the *living-dying interval.* Pattison divides this interval into three phases, the *acute crisis phase,* the *chronic living-dying phase* and the *terminal phase.*

Pattison's key contribution is the importance of the reaction of the caring community to the dying person. He emphasized that it is crucial that the family or support system help the dying person respond positively during the acute crisis. A positive response will result in *integrated dying;* a negative response will result in *disintegrated dying* during the chronic living-dying phase. The end result, *termination,* ranges from being peaceful on the one hand to isolation, loneliness or terror on the other.

I (Jack) have recently witnessed events leading to integrated dying in my own Christian community. Several years ago the wife of a Fuller Seminary professor was told that she had terminal cancer and would die within several months. On learning this the couple planned to return to Australia where both of their extended families resided. During their ten years of living in Pasadena, California, the couple had developed a rich network of caring friends. Before leaving for Australia, small groups of their friends were invited into Julie's bedroom for a time of farewell goodbyes and prayer. After Rob and Julie moved back Australia, their families were able to give the support and comfort she needed to move into the inevitable terminal phase. Through much grieving and many tears, Julie's entire network of friends and relatives, both in the United States and in Australia, joined with her in the *integrated dying* process.

In a disintegrated dying process the dying either shut off family and friends or the family and friends shut themselves off from the dying. Either way, the result is to not die well.

Pattison also provided helpful insights into understanding differing paths or patterns of death. This he does by suggesting that one might distinguish between *sociological death* (people withdrawn from the dying), *psychic death* (the patient acquiesces), *clinical death* (the brain ceases to function), and *physiological death* (the body dies). One path of dying involves first sociological death, followed by psychic death, then clinical death and finally physiological death. Another path involves first giving up (psychic death), followed by sociological death, both occurring long before clinical and physiological death. Another path of dying is for the patient and family to refuse to accept the probability of death, resulting in severe shock when physiological death does occur. In other cases the dying may reject life (psychic death), but family and friends tenaciously try to rally around the dying to motivate the person to live. A final path entails the family's refusal to accept the fact of both psychic and clinical death, resulting in the patient being kept alive physiologically by artificial means.

Although death can be a relief in the case of a severe illness, it usually comes as a numbing shock to a surviving partner. Free from responsibility with children and work, the lives of elderly partners usually revolve around each other, often resulting in mutual emotional dependency. Grief from the loss of a spouse can take the form of crying, anxiety, depression, sadness, loss of appetite, weight loss, sleep disturbances, tiredness and declining health or interest in life. When compared with married women of the same age and life circumstances, it takes from two to eleven years for the psychological effect of a husband's death to disappear among widows (Heinemann and Evans, 1990)

The Old Shall Dream Dreams

In a multitude of ways the rate of diminishment speeds up during the elderly years. However, it would be a mistake to end this chapter by only documenting the diminishing capacities of the elderly. In the previous chapter we suggested that wisdom increases with age and is the desired end state of human development. This is a welcome counterexample to thinking of the elderly years only in terms of diminishment. Growing old can literally be a *growing* process in which a human rises above temporal concerns by growing closer to God. Quoting the prophet Joel, Acts 2:17 says that "old men shall dream dreams." In commenting on this, James Loder states:

> To say the elderly will dream dreams is not a description of dementia setting
> in, as if they were drifting further from reality. Actually, the tone of the pas-
> sage is thoroughly positive, triumphant, and focused on God's version of the
> future; their dreams occur because they are drifting closer to reality. This part
> of the passage refers to the privilege of the aging person to allow dreams,
> often God's language to his people, to speak beyond the organic condition
> and the present perceptions of circumstances about the time to come. (1998,
> p. 316)

Loder (1998, pp. 323-26) suggests that by focusing on elderly loses, it is
possible to fail to recognize their gains in competence. One of these gains
can take the form of *simplification,* as the elderly have less material and
ego needs. In *Towards a Theology of Dying* Paul Pruyser suggests nine ways
simplification can be realized in aging. The first is to give up stubborn insistence on independence and accept some assistance as wholesome. The
second is to let go of the tendency to maintain one's status in society
through more meaningful definitions of what it means to "make it" in life.
Third, ego individuation becomes more possible since one's self-esteem is
less dependent on what others think. Fourth, an acceptance of failures and
ambiguities in life allows relaxation of one's defenses. Loder suggests that
as defenses relax, "the human spirit can be released into the assurance of
forgiveness and God's providential care" (p. 324). Fifth, work can be integrated into life instead of held separate from life and used to definite self-
worth. Sixth, the aged also have the privilege of living in the present without being anxious about the future. Seventh, having given up responsibility
for the future, the elderly can invest themselves in the dreams of the
younger generation without self-interest. Finally, the aged have the freedom to disclose their inner thoughts.

Taken together the above points can be understood as tasks of the elderly
as they work toward ego integration. Within Erikson's perspective, an elder
who does not develop these tasks risks ego despair. From a biblical perspective a person gains life by losing it—by dying to self and all of the symbols
associated with self-importance. In dying to self, one finds oneself, a particular self that is anchored and maintained in a relationship with God. In old
age people need no longer attempt self-validation through deeds and actions but can claim self-worth and identity that is derived from their relationship with God.

It is not necessary, of course, for a person to reach his or her elderly years before developing the tasks that will contribute toward ego integration. Hopefully, these processes are part of life-span development during the middle years. Old age merely brings with it the type of psychosocial conditions that may make it more possible.

From a Christian perspective true ego integration means that our self-identity is centered in the person of Jesus Christ. This is the developmental teleology of the model we have presented. The goal of development is to be a reciprocating self in relationship with God and others.

A self that is truly centered in Christ can even embrace death, not in a morbid way but in the assurance that when death comes he or she will be in the presence of Christ. The Christian's identity is found in being raised in Christ. As Paul writes in 1 Corinthians:

This perishable body must put on imperishability, and this mortal body must put on immortality. When this perishable body puts on imperishability, and this mortal body puts on immortality, then the saying that is written will be fulfilled:

"Death has been swallowed up in victory."
"Where, O death, is your victory?"
"Where, O death, is your sting?" . . .

But thanks be to God, who gives us the victory through our Lord Jesus Christ. (15:53-55, 57)

PART THREE

Building the Scaffold

APPLICATIONS FOR MINISTRY

Special Issues in Human Development

MORALITY

AS WITH RELIGIOUSNESS AND SPIRITUALITY, morality is a uniquely human phenomenon that defies simple psychological explanations. The reciprocating self is unquestionably a moral self, capable of making both mundane and complex moral decisions leading to specific actions or consequences. Yet despite best intentions, human behavior will always reveal an earthy mixture of failures and successes. Consequently, it is essential to remember that the reciprocating self as *imago Dei* is a self under construction, already beloved by God in the present but not yet transformed into eschatological perfection. Barth underlined the source of this transformation with clarity when he observed that in Christ we are presently bound to the person of God (Barth, 1961). This reciprocating vision of *sanctification* includes moral transformation and renewal. In a Christian sense the psychology of moral development should be premised on an understanding of reciprocity as sanctification.

With this theological provision we will turn to the problem of moral functioning in the development of a reciprocating self. Because our interest in sanctification reflects a concern for the integrity of Christian witness, we want to find out what motivates and sustains exceptional moral behavior. For the theologian this task requires further work on doctrines of reconciliation, sanctification and justification. For us the task relates to moral judgment and processes associated with the reciprocating self. One way to explore these processes is to consider those individuals who demonstrate outstanding moral functioning capable of making a difference in the lives of others.

Lawrence J. Walker, a leading moral psychologist, notes that outstanding moral functioning might differ depending on context (Walker and Hennig, 2004). A college undergraduate worker with World Vision might function morally on behalf of marginalized indigenous peoples in Chiapas, Mexico, by seeking *justice* for fair treatment. A middle-aged man might function morally by diving into a fast-moving river to save a drowning child, an act of spontaneous *bravery*. Or an emerging adult woman might forfeit a lucrative career as a lawyer to live in community with the developmentally disabled, *caring* deeply for their needs. Whereas moral reasoning is important to each of these scenarios, it is likely that sustained behaviors in each area reference a deeper point where moral goals, values and spiritual commitment are known in terms of personal identity or reciprocating self. What then is the role of the reciprocating self in moral functioning?

In order to better understand moral functioning and the reciprocating self, we will take a brief tour of the moral psychology field. Our tour will cover three sections. First, we will consider the work of Lawrence Kohlberg. Kohlberg's emphasis on justice, reasoning and moral judgment in human development is influential but limited in helping us to understand how the reciprocating self is related to moral functioning. Second, we will examine moral identity as a theory and then in the lives of morally outstanding individuals reported in the work of Anne Colby and William Damon (1992). Moral identity is implicated as a subset of the reciprocating self, and is typically preceded by experiences of transformation. Finally, we will conclude with a discussion of recent research with caregivers in L'Arche communities for the developmentally disabled. This research suggests that for many who demonstrate moral functioning it is their reciprocity with God as well as other people that motivates and sustains moral commitment.

Morality in Stages: Lawrence Kohlberg

The roots of Lawrence Kohlberg's theory of moral development are clearly found in Piaget. This lineage makes it necessary for us to briefly review Piaget's ideas of moral development. Piaget interpreted ethical action in terms of *moral judgment*. Moral judgment represents the application of human reason in order to obtain the best (moral) solution to any situation. Piaget's thinking reflects the strong rationalism of the Enlightenment, including thinkers such as Immanuel Kant and René Descartes. For Piaget all humans are capable of reason and therefore of moral judgment. Consequently, the best means to understanding moral development include the use of *di-lemmas* or hypothetical problems that require the application of moral judgment through problem-solving.

Based on his work with children in the 1930s, Piaget observed two general stages of moral development. Piaget's observations were premised on the means by which children deal with dilemmas. For children under the age of ten, dilemmas were resolved by rigid and unbending application of rules. Rules provide a framework for understanding the consequences of any action for the younger child. Kela is a six-year-old girl who lives in New York City. Kela hears two stories that together represent a dilemma. In the first story a boy is helping his mother to make cookies. During their activity he accidentally bumps a shelf loaded with porcelain cups. The shelf is up-ended and the cups slide off, hit the floor and shatter into pieces. Twelve cups are broken. In the second story another boy knocks a single cup off the same shelf while trying to steal a few cookies. Kela is asked which of these two boys behaved the worst. She immediately concludes that the child who broke the most cups misbehaved the most. Kela makes this moral conclusion on the basis of raw consequences (broken cups) rather than referencing motivation relative to the boys and their behavior (Piaget, 1932).

After a transition around the age of eleven, Piaget observed that children apply their growing sense of abstract thinking to moral dilemmas with altered effect. With the advent of formal thought, older children and adolescents reach different conclusions about the same dilemmas. If Kela happens to be thirteen years old, she might view rules not as fixed benchmarks but as general guidelines to help human beings get along together. Thus rules are capable of bending where motivation becomes a higher or more abstract basis for moral standards. In the above scenario Kela might judge the boy who was stealing cookies to have misbehaved the most. Kela explains that the broken cups are accidental in both instances. However, the first boy is motivated to help his mother. This caring posture carries more moral currency than the thieving boy of the second story. Whereas the first boy accidentally causes more damage than the second, this issue is peripheral to his good intentions.

Some thirty years after Piaget's initial observations of children, Lawrence Kohlberg worked to establish a stagelike framework for morality in human development. Kohlberg began by interviewing adolescent and preadolescent boys from urban Chicago. Like Piaget before him, Kohlberg presented participants with a hypothetical dilemma designed to access the child's moral processing. In the now famous "Heinz dilemma," participants were asked to respond to an awful conundrum. Heinz's wife is near death from cancer. A new drug is capable of fighting the cancer, but it costs a small fortune. Heinz cannot afford the drug, and fruitlessly attempts to borrow the money from local townsfolk. Heinz pleads to the pharmacist to purchase the drug at a lower rate, but the pharmacist wants to make a profit and is unrelenting. Heinz ends up breaking into the pharmacy and stealing the drug for his wife.

Obviously, the Heinz dilemma has no simple right or wrong answer. This is by design; Kohlberg sought to use the dilemma as a means for understanding how children and adolescents apply reasoning through moral judgment. Kohlberg and his team noted a range of participant responses to the Heinz dilemma. He organized the responses into a taxonomy or classification framework for moral judgment. To provide a check and balance against his own subjectivity, Kohlberg asked other psychologists to organize the same response data. The result was a six-stage framework for moral development that is widely known in psychological, educational and theological circles. As with Piaget before him, Kohlberg's stagelike framework assumes incremental change across the life span, although it is not expected that everyone will reach the highest levels of moral development (Kohlberg, 1984; Kohlberg and Diessner, 1991). Kohlberg's scheme builds on the justice ethic of Kant, emphasizing more and more abstract solutions to hypothetical dilemmas as evidence of moral maturity.

Stage 1. Preconventional (obedience and punishment). This is the moral-judgment orientation of early childhood. Like Piaget before him, Kohlberg noted that the child makes moral judgments with rules foremost in mind, particularly when immediate consequences are evident. A stage-one response to the Heinz dilemma might include the child's insistence that stealing is against the law and therefore wrong. Despite the motivational issues behind Heinz's action, the child is unwilling to justify the man's behavior. Because Heinz failed to obey the law, he should be punished.

Stage 2. Preconventional (individualism and exchange). Stage two represents a more finely nuanced understanding of moral judgment than in Piaget. For this stage Kohlberg noticed that older children are able to make sense of the fact that different people have different viewpoints. A child's response might focus on the fact that the pharmacist perceived Heinz's action as wrong, but Heinz did not see his theft as wrong. Preconventional moral judgment at stage two emphasizes the individualistic needs and self-interests of other people. In this case the child understands that Heinz badly needs the drug. The drive for fairness makes its presence felt in the moral judgment of the child. Heinz made a fair offer for the drug, but the pharmacist was unwilling to make an exchange. Heinz's offer justifies his decision to break the law.

Stage 3. Conventional (interpersonal relationships). Kohlberg noted that children in early adolescence demonstrate more abstract moral judgment, following the pattern outlined in Piaget. Now Heinz's motivations are clearly a basis in forming moral judgments. Participant responses at stage three emphasized Heinz's good intentions to save his wife. Responses also noted that the pharmacist had poor intentions, namely, to profit on the new cancer drug at the expense of human life. Some respondents became visibly angry at the pharmacist's refusal to cut a deal with Heinz, a result of their ability to take on the perspectives of others. Participants were well aware of character traits in all of the dilemma personalities and formed abstract conclusions that were conventional by virtue of the fact that anyone would have a right to do what Heinz did. Kohlberg found that stage-three moral judgment is often found in adults as well as adolescents (Kohlberg, 1984).

Stage 4. Conventional (maintaining social order). Kohlberg argued that more advanced conventional thinkers (typically adults) made moral judgments about society as a whole. Heinz is recognized for his good motives in a no-win situation, but this knowledge is balanced with a greater appreciation for maintaining social order through the maintenance of laws and societal responsibility. These thinkers are fairly sophisticated in their ability to hold the many tensions of the Heinz dilemma in balance, but they tend to favor social order against a single exception such as Heinz. Thus these respondents tend to reason through the issues in a manner resembling stage-one conclusions that Heinz's actions are still against the law. Unlike the young child, however, these people understand the more abstract reasons that laws exist and the social order that they serve.

Stage 5. Postconventional (social contract and individual rights). Beyond stage four, Kohlberg noticed that some individuals use the Heinz dilemma as a way of considering what constitutes a good society. For this respondent (almost always an adult), moral judgment is applied on the basis of societal goodness, recognizing that social order does not necessarily mean that a society is a decent place to live. Respondents cited fascist and communist societies as examples. Usually this line of thinking includes some consideration of individual rights and the means by which democratic principles can be enlisted to ensure maximum respect for everyone. These respondents pointed to the wife's right to live as a moral imperative. Thus Heinz's actions were strongly justified in this view.

Stage 6. Postconventional (universal principles). Kohlberg identified stage six as a "dilemma-busting" perspective similar to great moral philosophers such as Immanuel Kant (Walker and Pitts, 1998). Like Kant, respondents articulate their own philosophical principles that define justice, not only for Heinz and his wife but for society as a whole. Moral judgment results in universal conceptions of what is just for everyone. This perspective recognizes that all people have value and should be treated accordingly. These respondents argued that the wife's life is the higher good above the values of commerce and financial transaction.

The elegance of Kohlberg's moral-judgment scheme quickly influenced a generation of thinkers. Many scholars and educators immediately found real-world application for the six stages, which turned up in curricula for moral education, assessment instruments and even theories of spiritual development (Fowler, 1995). However, the magnitude of Kohlberg's influence also made his scheme the object of criticism. Gilligan (1982) noted that Kohlberg focused primarily on boys in his early studies. Gilligan (1982) argued that morality took a different developmental course in girls, who emphasized caring principles over the stark justice of Kohlberg's moral judgment paradigm. Turiel (1983) contended that moral judgment in fact arose through different domains of thinking. *Moral justice* represented societal interactions whereas *convention* represented cultural rules that may not apply in all situations or cases. Finally, Shweder (Shweder, Mahapatra and Miller, 1987) argued that morality was culturally bound, making the universal claims of Kohlberg untenable and potentially dangerous when applied in other societies.

Kohlberg's scheme explicitly identifies justice through moral reasoning as the basis for moral functioning. Shortcomings in this approach were evident early, particularly through the critique of Augusto Blasi. Blasi argued that moral reasoning is only obliquely related to moral functioning. Blasi (1980, 1983) proposed a "self model" of moral functioning emphasizing the importance of *responsibility* in mediating between reason and behavior. In the model an individual's fidelity to responsible courses of action must be consistent with personal goals, values and beliefs. Blasi argued that being moral in the end is an extension of one's self as expressed in identity. Blasi (1984) suggested that *moral identity,* or those features of a reciprocating self that support the flourishing of others in a manner consistent with one's personal goals, values, and beliefs, constituted a stronger basis for understanding moral functioning.

James Rest sought to find some middle ground in between Kohlberg and Blasi by offering a four-factor model of moral functioning. Rest (1983) believed that four components are involved in moral functioning, including (1) moral sensitivity (or the ability to interpret situations in moral terms), (2) moral judgment (basic moral reasoning), (3) moral motivation (impetus to incorporate moral issues into possible options for response) and (4) implementation of moral action (follow-through with moral motivation). Rest's model received good acceptance in the field but required further qualification given its narrow articulation of justice in moral reasoning borrowed from Kohlberg.

Blasi's argument for moral identity became increasingly compelling, given a growing body of empirical evidence suggesting that justice-oriented moral reasoning was only a small component in moral functioning. One of Kohlberg's students, Daniel Hart, tested the importance of reasoning and judgment with morally outstanding adolescents in the early 1990s. Hart decided to study youth from Camden, New Jersey, one of the poorest urban zones in America. Hart reasoned that moral features of a reciprocating self would clearly stand out where adolescents demonstrated high moral functioning despite difficult personal circumstances. Using criteria established by local Camden social workers and youth leaders, Hart and colleague Suzanne Fegley located fifteen adolescents in Camden that demonstrated outstanding moral and caring commitments (Hart and Fegley, 1995). These remarkable youth took leadership in caring for infirm parents and family members, and volunteered service to the poor in their neighborhoods. Hart and Fegley matched these exemplar youth to fifteen everyday kids from the same urban locations. All youth were given lengthy face-to-face interviews along with Kohlberg's moral judgment interview (Kohlberg, 1984).

The Camden study surprised everyone, even its authors. Exemplar adolescents from Camden were clearly different from others in the manner by which they thought about the self, others and relationships. Their moral functioning was nothing short of exceptional. Yet these exemplars scored

no differently than others on Kohlberg's six-stage scheme of moral development. Both exemplars and comparisons were mostly at the stage three (conventional) level of moral judgment and reasoning. This meant that Kohlberg's assumptions regarding moral judgment in general and justice in
particular may have less to do with the developmental processes that coin-
cide with moral functioning. Even more important, moral judgment is only
moderately able to sustain individuals in their caring commitments over time
(Hart and Fegley, 1995; Reimer, 2003; Walker and Reimer, forthcoming).

The Camden study serves as a reminder that the development of moral
functioning is highly complex, reflecting varied contexts of influence significant to a reciprocating self. Moral identity might be understood as a domain
of the reciprocating self forged in the context of relationships with others
who are capable of providing moral influence. Whereas the self and its reciprocating processes are more difficult to study than moral judgment, it may
be that the moral-identity perspective is a logical next step beyond Kohlberg, particularly in an interest to avoid "losing the person at the center of
morality" (Blasi, 1984, p. 138).

The Development of Moral Identity

Moral functioning might be understood as a universal human phenomenon,
yet the details of how it is formed in a reciprocating self are likely based on
context. Developing moral commitments appears to defy any single formula
or combination of religious, cultural and educational influence. What developmental similarities can we identify that might indicate the origins of moral
identity? In response to this question, we will suggest that exemplars typically become extraordinarily moral because of experiences of transformation. Additionally, we will argue that social influences help to sustain moral
functioning over time.

Moral transformation. Early theoretical work on moral identity implied
a reciprocating self behind moral commitment. Moral identity was thought
to arise on the basis of social influences (Blasi, 1984). These influential relationships were somehow able to change an individual's personal goals
around explicitly moral concerns. In a famous American study, Anne Colby
and William Damon (1992) conducted detailed interviews with individuals
nominated on the basis of outstanding moral functioning. Individuals noted
experiences of personal *transformation* when social influences altered their
personal goals and commitments. Generally, these experiences of transfor-

mation were gradual, where social influences caused exemplars to reevaluate their capacities and define new strategies to achieve goals. The most potent social influences came from relationships where exemplars were challenged to grow and change. Over time, exemplars experienced successes in their work on behalf of others, learning to integrate their reciprocating selves with moral functioning.

Colby and Damon (1995) give an example of this process. In an exemplar interview a woman known for her care for the developmentally disabled told of how she began her career as an elementary school teacher. A mentor at this stage of her life encouraged her to take a job with dyslexic children because she needed work. In the context of the job the mentor helped the woman develop new skills and interests centered on the needs of the disabled. This gradual experience of moral transformation led to a complete restructuring of her personal goals around the care of those with profound disabilities.

The astute reader might ask whether the process of transformation leading to moral identity simply reflects a developmental transition up the "ladder" of Kohlberg's six-stage scheme. As in the Camden youth study Colby and Damon (1992) gave exemplars Kohlberg's moral judgment interview. Despite the remarkable achievements of the exemplar group, half scored at the conventional level (stages three and four). This is exactly the same finding made by Kohlberg himself when he randomly interviewed adults from the general populace over a twenty-year period (Colby et al., 1983). Essentially, exemplars did not score differently from the general populace in moral judgment level. It seems that the transformational processes leading to moral functioning are integrated on the basis of reciprocating self-related processes rather than the ability to reason effectively about moral dilemmas.

It is likely that processes of transformation leading to moral-identity formation are cued by emotions that accompany the individual's experience of influential relationships. Eliana is a fifteen-year-old girl who lives with her mother and brother in a four-hundred-square-foot room in a very poor neighborhood of a large American city. Almost single-handedly Eliana began a neighborhood program to care for the elderly in a convalescent hospital about three blocks away. A year after its inception her program involves many people in relationships with infirm seniors. Eliana was interviewed in her tiny apartment while cockroaches climbed the walls and music blared from the apartment next door. In response to a question regarding how she came to identify herself as a caring person, Eliana's eyes grew misty:

> I would like to be a person like my mom. She doesn't let herself go by what people think of her. She lets herself go by what she thinks of herself and she doesn't do like most people and judge people by what she sees. She judges them by what they think and the way they are. This is how I learned to care. (Reimer, 2003, p. 131)

Eliana's relationship with her mother is deeply influential. It is also clear that Eliana's representations of self are framed in terms of her mother and that these are linked to emotion. In the justice-oriented thinking of Kohlberg and Piaget, emotion may be an unwanted distraction to the application of moral reasoning and judgment in the face of dilemmas. Yet Eliana's reciprocating self is evidently able to make excellent decisions that lead to moral functioning in spite of, or perhaps because of, intense emotion related to representations of her mother. This paradox should give us pause with regard to the place of emotion in moral reasoning and, potentially, transformation anticipating the development of moral identity in the reciprocating self.

Recent work in the field of cognitive neuroscience suggests that emotion is a critical factor in the development of moral functioning. The renowned neurologist Antonio Damasio (1994) retells the unfortunate story of Phineas Gage, a twenty-six-year-old railroad foreman in mid-nineteenth-century New England. Leading work crews in New Hampshire, Gage won a reputation as a diligent, conscientious boss who took a personal interest in his men. Gage was an expert in tamping blast powder for controlled explosions to dislodge rock impeding the progress of the rail line. Using a meter-long iron rod, Gage would carefully tamp powder into small holes bored around the perimeter of large rocks. One day Gage accidentally struck flint with the side of his tamping rod, resulting in a premature explosion. The force of the blast drove the rod completely through Gage's skull, entering at a point beneath the left cheekbone and exiting through a quarter-sized hole in the top of his head. Incredibly, Gage survived his wound and recovered from the incident. However, it soon became evident that he had been altered by the injury. Gage was no longer able to make positive decisions about matters of relational and financial significance. His previously cherished moral standards and work ethic evaporated. Gage was not able to hold a job, could not execute the most basic plans, was insolent and uncaring toward his fellow workers, squandered his money, and left his wife for a life of promiscuity. After a brief career as a circus show freak, he died penniless and in obscurity some seventeen years later.

Damasio (1994) observed that Gage's injury was to the prefrontal cortex of the brain. A close comparison of Gage's skull to other similarly injured patients revealed that the brain's central processor for emotion, the limbic system, had been badly damaged. Damasio's patients evidenced many of Gage's symptoms. After their injuries, prefrontal-damaged individuals failed to work conscientiously, were impaired in their ability to realize goals through planning and effort, had poor social skills, and were dramatically affected in their moral functioning. Damasio and his wife, Hanna, gave several of these patients Kohlberg's moral judgment interview, asking for responses to the Heinz dilemma (H. Damasio, 2002). Patient responses to the moral judgment interview were entirely normal, demonstrating conventional-level (stages three and four) reasoning when matched to a comparison population without prefrontal injury. Yet despite this performance, patients continued to struggle greatly in attempts to achieve personal goals, living an uncaring and immoral existence.

From these findings Antonio Damasio (1994, 2002) proposed that mental representations of self and others are stored in episodic memory on the basis of emotions. These *somatic markers* of emotional memory help individuals confronted by morally significant circumstances to consider a range of facts, personal goals and options toward a positive response. Anticipated consequences are evaluated on the basis of emotion labeled representations that recall similar situations, dilemmas and outcomes from the past. Moral reasoning pertinent to Kohlberg's dilemmas is for the most part unaffected by the absence of somatic marker representations. However, *this deficit makes the regulation and motivation of caring behavior extraordinarily difficult.* Thus it would seem that the process of transforming personal goals into moral ones might require a considerable degree of emotional regulation.

In Eliana's case transformation of goals might happen where she is able to recall past situations experienced with a particular emotion or set of emotions. Cognitively, Eliana weighs the goals that were significant to her in the past with her present circumstances. This process of goal evaluation is emotion-cued and may result in the alteration of her present goals based on past experience, her present situation and her ability to anticipate future outcomes. Somatic markers of emotion provide Eliana with cognitive guideposts that outline the similarity of her present circumstances to past situations and the possible options that best incorporate her goals and priorities consistent with a caring, reciprocating self. These emotion representations become Eliana's gut instinct that motivates her to care even when circumstances might suggest otherwise.

Antonio Damasio's findings (1994, 2002) raise the possibility that individuals with high moral functioning undergo transformation of personal goals through a cognitive process that links past, present and future with emotion-cued mental representations. Transformation may reflect cognition of broad dimensions, where moral judgment is augmented by emotional connections of social influences and experiences significant to the caring self. Thus moral development might at one level be aligned with the onset of autobiographical memory in middle childhood, leading to an increasingly sophisticated reciprocating self.

Ecology of moral identity. Given the importance of context and relationship in the formation of moral identity, are some relationships more important than others in helping to establish moral functioning? Kevin Reimer and David Wade-Stein (2004) used the rationale behind Hart and Fegley's (1995) Camden study to help address this question. Fifteen morally outstanding adolescents were nominated from poor urban neighborhoods in Central and Southern California. As with the Hart and Fegley (1995) study, exemplar adolescents were matched to everyday youth from the same neighborhoods. All youths were given lengthy interviews. Questions were asked about the adolescent's reciprocating self, namely, in terms of who the individual understood him- or herself to be at that moment, but also in the past and in the future (temporality). Youth were additionally asked questions regarding mother, father, best friend and an admired adult such as coach or teacher. These questions were designed to find out how close or distant these others were relative to the participant's self as an index of relational influence on moral concerns. Representations of self and others were then mapped using a computational language program and advanced statistics.

Not surprisingly, the two sample groups revealed radically different moral identity ecologies. The actual self of exemplar adolescents was nested within a web of significant reciprocating relationships with others. Because of the remarkable moral functioning present in this group, the map implied that exemplar youth understood themselves as distinct individuals but also as closely related to significant others. These relationships helped them to maintain continuity between personal goals and moral-identity processes resulting in moral functioning. Moreover, exemplar youth knew themselves well on the basis of past experiences and could clearly anticipate who they would be in the future. By contrast the actual self of comparison youth was isolated from other people. This implied that everyday adolescents are still establishing their identities in their own minds. Given that the reciprocating self emerges from experience in relationship with others, it is little surprise that everyday youth have yet to learn how to sustain relationships, much less glean moral influence and wisdom from others. Comparison youth demonstrated little knowledge of the self of the past and had difficulty envisioning who they would be in the future.

It seems that relationships are a significant means by which moral identity is transformed and indicated for moral functioning. Rather than frame moral behavior on the basis of rationalistic function around moral dilemmas, it is probably better to think about emotional and social influences that conspire to help form moral identity in development, particularly through a reciprocating self. We have emphasized the importance of human relationships in the process of moral development. Returning to the theological provision given at the outset of this chapter, it is time to consider how divine relationship might additionally influence moral functioning.

Moral identity in L'Arche. In their 1992 study of American exemplars, Colby and Damon (1992) made an unexpected finding that sent ripples throughout the field of moral psychology. The vast majority of the exemplars in the study reported faith in God. It turned out that faith proved a major inspiration to care and a general support for moral functioning. Many exemplars in the Colby and Damon (1992) study were detailed and explicit in accounts of how God's influence was the basis for their moral identity. Most devout Christians would find this to be an intuitive if blatantly obvious connection. But for a secular psychological community the Colby and Damon (1992) discovery was something of a surprise. In one account a woman known as the "Queen of the Dump" spoke revealingly about her remarkable outreach to children living on top of a Mexican landfill:

> I used to get away from the house and away from my kids and I used to ask the Lord "Am I in the right place? Is this where you send me?" Because if I didn't have that vision I would have gone back because of what I was going through. But now my faith is stronger. See, at that time when I started it was weak. I was just going by that vision. (Colby and Damon, 1992, pp. 44-45)

With a generous grant from the Fetzer Institute, Kevin Reimer and Lawrence J. Walker (2004) explored the relationship between faith commitment and moral functioning in a unique setting. L'Arche communities for the developmentally disabled are probably best known through the writings of Henri Nouwen. These Christian communities provide a unique opportunity to explore the relationship between spirituality and moral functioning. As it turned out, for L'Arche assistants who work with the developmentally disabled, God is directly implicated in moral functioning related to a reciprocating self.

L'Arche (French for "the ark") is an international federation of more than one hundred communities in twenty-nine countries that cares for persons with developmental disabilities. Although officially multidenominational, L'Arche is predominantly Christian in ethos and Roman Catholic in practice. L'Arche is the genius of Jean Vanier, Canadian philosopher, religious leader, statesman and activist. In 1962 Vanier established a residential community for the disabled that was marked by relational commitments of altruistic love, not simply from caregiver assistants to the *core member,* as the disabled are known, but in mutual exchange between assistants and core members. Vanier's mission with the developmentally disabled led to a philosophy of agape love as the redemptive element in L'Arche communities where

> everyone is of unique and sacred value, and everyone has the same dignity and the same rights. People with a mental handicap often possess qualities of welcome, wonderment, spontaneity, and directness . . . able to touch hearts and call others to unity through their simplicity and vulnerability. In this way they are a reminder to the wider world of the essential values of the heart without which knowledge, power, and action lose their meaning and purpose. (charter of L'Arche Internationale, 1993)

In L'Arche communities, assistants and core members live peacefully together, sharing faith and everyday experience. L'Arche assistants are widely considered to be living altruists, given the scope of their moral commitment (Post, 2002). In the United States most L'Arche assistants live on a tiny monthly stipend of around $500. Some leave lucrative careers to serve in L'Arche. Assistants are invited to participate in community on the basis of theological commitments. Individuals are asked to carefully weigh their commitment in terms of a *calling,* which is typically ratified in year-long increments that require periods of spiritual *discernment* prior to renewal. In his many books outlining the philosophy and spirituality of L'Arche, Vanier describes a *downward mobility* of care and compassionate commitment:

> We live in a world of competition, where importance is given to success, a good salary, efficiency, distractions, and stimulations. Our world, however, needs to rediscover what is essential: Committed relationships, openness and the acceptance of weakness, a life of friendship and solidarity in and through the little things we can do. It is not a question of doing extraordinary things, but rather of doing ordinary things with love. (Vanier, 1999)

The grant-funded study of moral identity in L'Arche focused on assistants. What motivates individuals to give up so much in order to serve others in this way? As before, what sustains these individuals in their moral commitments? Not surprisingly, these questions were of interest to the leadership of L'Arche. In the United States, L'Arche had discovered that many assistants burn out in their first year of service, sometimes leaving communities abruptly. However, some assistants seem to overcome initial costs associated with their moral commitment to become long-term assistants of five, ten or even fifteen years. To find out what was happening, two study groups of L'Arche assistants were selected.

The first group represented those assistants who had served in L'Arche for a year or less. These were dubbed *novice* assistants. In the United States, novice assistants tend to be young, mostly under the age of thirty. Many novice assistants come to L'Arche through Americorps, a government-funded service program that allows individuals to volunteer while gaining experience and tuition subsidy against college or university costs. The majority of novice assistants have little religious background. The second group represented *experienced* assistants who had served in L'Arche for three years or more. These individuals tend to be older and more religiously oriented. Both groups are well-educated, with at least a bachelor's degree in hand.

Both groups were interviewed with questions similar to the Camden study of adolescent exemplars. This time, however, God was included as an "other" along with parents, best friend and romantic partner. Actual selves of both assistant groups were compared to various others. For the novice assistants the actual self is fairly isolated, reminiscent of the comparison adolescents in the Reimer and Wade-Stein (2004) study. But for experienced assistants God is the closest and most significant other relationship relative to the self. Clearly, experienced assistants understand their moral commitments around a relationship with God. This suggests that the longevity of caring in L'Arche is related to the "kind of person God expects me to be."

These expectations become a significant motivator in experienced assistants.

How might God's expectations become incorporated into moral identity? This is a golden question of enormous significance to pastors, parents and educators alike. Specifics of identity formation in L'Arche assistants were a primary concern for Ursula Moore, a doctoral student in psychology at Fuller Seminary. Her work on the L'Arche project revealed that experienced and novice assistants spoke differently about their life experiences relative to their moral commitment to care for core members. Experienced assistants tended to speak of their lives in terms of community and a sense of belonging. It was rare for them to speak of individual achievement or friendship with specific individuals. These unique people described their work with the disabled in terms of care giving but typically spoke of their relationships with core members in terms of mutuality where they learn from and were nurtured by the disabled. Many experienced assistants spoke of a crisis or transformational event while in L'Arche, where they considered leaving but prevailed in the end. In a number of instances, these transformational events included spiritual references to God. This is beautifully illustrated in the following narrative:

> When I tell my story this is the story I tell. So this is an easy one to share. It really was the turning point in terms of my understanding of God and L'Arche. I was really seeing the gifts of the core members [disabled] and how I was beginning to receive a lot more than I was giving. I was on retreat with Jean Vanier, and things were coming together. I thought I'd already had transformative experience; I'd quit my job to live in L'Arche and do things differently. When I got to Grandview, things were rough and I had to live in the house because we were so short of assistants. It was very difficult. I was living in one of the houses and this was about six months into it. Alan, one of the core members, he's blind and he has a mental disorder so he's on psychotropic medication. He was in an institution all his life, since a year old. They didn't think that he could ever be deinstitutionalized because he was so violent. Of course, he comes to L'Arche. And he definitely had some bad moments at times, but every night he slept with his radio on. My guess would be that in the institution he couldn't. I had this real compassion for Alan and a real connection with him. I could calm him down, I enjoyed him. He was very clever. I'd play with him for hours and I'd say, what's this? And he'd feel it, and he has a singsong voice and he'd say, "that's a telephone." Amazing things, things you wouldn't think he knew. He was so institutionalized that he put his underwear and his shirt on his bed perfectly. Just amazing. One night I was giving him his bath and I was drying off his back. He says, "you're my friend,

right?" I stopped for a minute. What occurred to me is how many people had bathed this man, strangers. How many people didn't see this sacred life in front of them, just wanted to get the job done. How many times he had to put up with that. What he was saying to me—I get upset about it, he's so *vulnerable*—what he's really saying is, Can I trust you? Are you safe? It occurred to me that this man has probably lived through hell. Abuse. People being incredibly insensitive to him. And yet he still can trust. I realized that I was in a transformative moment, knowing that I'm more broken than Alan. I realized he was teaching me something that I hadn't learned. God was really present in that moment. That is when I could say that I didn't choose L'Arche, but L'Arche has chosen me. That's our spirituality.

Did it change you?

I think it did, fundamentally, absolutely. I really can have a voice with the core members. And I think I can really touch the assistants when I talk to them and share a story like that. To get them to think about what our people do. L'Arche is founded upon pain. That doesn't mean that we have to be miserable, unhappy people. We spend a lot of time celebrating. But L'Arche is founded on incredible suffering. If we forget that, we don't walk in that; if we try to bury that, there is something that is lost. Vanier says that we come to serve the poor and find out that we are the poor. L'Arche is not therapy. It's liberating to be in a place where you can say this is how I'm broken and vulnerable. Not get written up for it. Really get rewarded for being real. The core members teach us that over and over and over again. They are our prophets. (unpublished data)

By contrast, novice assistants thought of their commitment in terms of a specific role, as caregiver. Their identities were forged on the basis of worth and value they received from competently meeting the needs of the disabled. Responses for this group were more individualistic and achievement-oriented in nature. Few of the novice group identified a crisis or transformational event as part of their time in L'Arche.

It seems clear from Moore's dissertation work that transformation is a key player in the longevity of moral commitment. Moreover, God is in most cases an acknowledged participant in such transformational events. Many Christians might respond to this finding with the conclusion that we should intentionally orchestrate crisis events in development in order to spur on the formation of moral identity. But there is no theological justification for the view that God actually *caused* the crisis events that precipitated moral transformation. The cause of these events remains a mystery for L'Arche caregivers, and should also be for us. The point is that God is present as an active participant in the assistant's life through the experience. It is through this divine participation that the assistant grew deeper in his or her relationship with God, learning to more significantly incorporate God's expectations into moral functioning. Significantly, these experiences are linked to the developmentally disabled, who functioned as teachers to the assistant. Clearly, God's presence in human communities is a vital if mysterious force in the development of extraordinary moral commitment.

Concluding Thoughts

We have considered the importance of moral functioning in a Christian psychological project, reviewing the developmental argument for moral judgment in Lawrence Kohlberg. Recognizing the limitations of Kohlberg's paradigm, we considered moral identity as a way of thinking about the reciprocating self through relationship with others. For adolescent and adult exemplars alike, moral identity unfolds in the context of transformation and social influence. These contextual factors are experienced, recorded in memory and are cued by emotion. Perhaps most significant of all, in many instances moral identity is related to our knowledge of God in relationship. With this in mind, we turn now to consider the developmental significance of God's influence in human affairs.

Differentiated Faith

SPIRITUAL AND RELIGIOUS DEVELOPMENT

ALTHOUGH SPIRITUALITY AND RELIGION have been a central part of people's lives for thousands of years, the study of spiritual and religious development remains significantly underexplored within psychology. The paucity of research on a central element of human functioning within the developmental sciences is surprising considering that youth and adults alike report high levels of religious beliefs and participation (Gallup and Bezilla, 1992). A Gallup International Association (1999) poll of fifty thousand adults in sixty countries found that 87 percent of respondents report being a part of a religious denomination, 63 percent indicate that God is highly important in their lives, and 75 percent believe in either a personal God or "some sort of spirit or life force." In addition, Gallup poll data on adolescent religious beliefs and practices report that 95 percent of youth age thirteen to seventeen believe in God and 75 percent "very much" or "somewhat" agree with the statement "I try to follow the teachings of my religion." Forty-two percent of American youth report praying alone frequently, while 36 percent report participating in a church youth group. Twenty-three percent report participating in faith-based service projects (Gallup and Bezilla, 1992).

What little research exists primarily focuses on adulthood, despite the mounting evidence that the first two decades of life are particularly vital in how spirituality is developed, thwarted or misdirected. Issues of beliefs, meaning, purpose, identity and relationships are particularly salient during adolescence. Many scholars note that major spiritual or religious transformation and conversion occur during these years. Furthermore, many scholars (e.g., see Roehlkepartain et al., 2005) recognize adolescence as a particularly fertile time in the life cycle for examining issues of spirituality and religion. Despite the predominant and important role they play in development, spirituality and religion in childhood and adolescence have been underrepresented in the mainstream developmental sciences. A recent analysis of major databases, PsychINFO and Social Science Abstracts found that about 1 percent of the articles on children and adolescents cataloged in these comprehensive social-science databases addressed issues of spirituality or religion (Benson, Roehlkepartain and Rude, 2003). Spiritual and religious development are addressed much less frequently than all the other forms of development examined, including cognitive, psychosocial, moral, emotional and behavioral.

These recent realities reflect a long and complex history of the place of spirituality and religion in the social sciences. In fact, psychology of religion predates the official founding of the American Psychological Association (1892). Early psychologists were committed to establishing psychology of religion as a scientific enterprise. At the turn of the century William James and G. Stanley Hall and their students pioneered theoretical and empirical studies in psychology of religion. However, as the twentieth century progressed, social scientists such as Thorndike and Watson rejected spirituality and religion as a viable field of scientific study. The new behavioristic thinking of the day suggested that religion (and spirituality) belonged to the past and was not a part of the modern scientific world. Thus the academic field of developmental psychology as well as other social sciences emerged without a central concern for spirituality and religion (Kerestes and Youniss, 2002). As noted in the recent *Handbook of Applied Developmental Science,* "According to the new behavioristic thinking of that day, religion belonged to the past and was unnecessary in the modern scientific world. Thus, the field of academic developmental psychology and the formal study of adolescence grew up without interest in religion, fully committed to secular culture, and dependent on the canons of modern science" (Kerestes and Youniss, 2002).

Throughout this time the subfields of psychology and sociology of religion remained alive (though marginalized), producing significant theoretical and empirical advances. Toward the end of the twentieth century developmental psychologists began to heed the overwhelming evidence that spirituality and religion were a significant part of the life for young people and adults globally. The increased evidence in the scientific literature established a positive relation between spirituality/religion and health, well-being and positive mental health as well as decreased risk factors. This data, coupled with the mass media's coverage of youth violence in the 1990s, propelled further research exploring factors that promote positive development in youth. Currently, the social sciences are experiencing a revival of interest in spirituality and religiousness. As noted, polls demonstrate that spirituality and religion are important to a significant number of adults and youth in America. Sociologists are documenting new and growing trends in American spirituality and religiosity (see Smith and Denton, 2005). Although mainline denomination attendance is down, figures for newer religious traditions and nonreligious forms of spirituality are up. For example, more people re- port being engaged with Eastern religions, yoga, Pentecostalism and nondenominational churches (in particular mega-churches and house churches). Religious institutions are being recognized for playing an important civic role in society (Berndt and Miller, 2000; Orr et al., 1995; Putnam, 2000). Finally, the current literature demonstrates a positive association between religion and positive developmental outcomes (Donahue and Benson, 1995; Resnick et al., 1997; Wagener et al., 2003).

The purpose of this chapter is to address the current psychological understanding of religious and spiritual development in light of the reciprocating self. If we recognize God's intention for us to become reciprocating selves, what does that mean in terms of our spirituality or our religious experience? Do we have a reciprocating relationship with God? How might psychologists understand this? How do other aspects of human development (e.g., cognitive, social, moral) relate to religious or spiritual development? What is the difference between religious and spiritual development?

Now for a mental experiment. Think of a person who is spiritual. Who comes to mind? Perhaps someone who is into meditation, yoga, and finding the light within themselves. Perhaps an environmentalist who is rejuvenated by spending time in and is dedicated to preserving creation. Perhaps yourself or a friend at church who has a deep relationship with God, who always seems to be able to discern the presence of the Holy Spirit in his or her life. Now, think of a person who is religious. Who comes to mind? Is this a rule-bound person, who religiously goes to church on Sunday? Is he or she moralistic? Judgmental? Often these are stereotypes about spiritual and religious people within our culture. What does it look like to be spiritual and religious?

How would you describe yourself? I (Pam) would like to note that I do not find these stereotypes helpful but overly simplistic. However, they are important to acknowledge because they exist. As we think about our own faith development or attempt to nurture faith in others, it is important to acknowledge the complexity and richness of spiritual and religious development.

What is the difference between spirituality and religion? In general, *spirituality* is often described in personal or experiential terms; *religion,* on the other hand, generally includes personal beliefs, institutional beliefs and practices, and a specific community of believers. Current research suggests that for the most part Americans understand "being religious" and "being spiritual" as distinct but overlapping constructs. In other words, people can be spiritual without being religious and vice versa, or they can be both. Research also documents that most American adults would describe themselves as both (Marler and Hadaway, 2002).

Within the social sciences the *spiritual* refers to that which is considered divine, holy or beyond the material. *Spirituality* can be understood as a universal human capacity or a quality of a person's character, personality or disposition. This quality is that which is aware of something beyond the self—whether God, absolute truth, all of humanity, or creation. As such, spiritual development has been defined as "the process of growing the intrinsic human capacity for self-transcendence, in which the self is embedded in something greater than the self, including the sacred. It propels the search for connectedness, meaning, purpose, and contribution. It is shaped both within and outside of religious traditions, beliefs, and practices" (Benson, Roehlkepartain and Rude, 2003, p. 207).

Central to this understanding of spirituality is *transcendence,* the notion that an individual has an acute awareness of something or some other greater than him- or herself. In this regard, spirituality as an attribute of personhood usually relates to a manner of living that is carried out with the deep awareness of self, others and the divine. For some, spiritual development entails the ability to be connected in a meaningful way to God, to fellow believers, to all of humanity or even to nature. Contemporary understandings of spirituality distinguish between religious spirituality, humanistic spirituality and natural spirituality (Emmons and Paloutzian, 2003).

Generally, spirituality calls people beyond themselves to have concern and compassion for others (Fetzer, 1999). It has an emotional orientation that moves the self to commit to contributing to others and institutions (Lerner,

2004; Lerner, Dowling and Anderson, 2003). Spirituality calls forth devotion and thus exerts ordering power on the rest of our lives and provides a sense of meaning and purpose in life. Dietrich Bonhoeffer wrote, "The individual personal spirit lives solely by virtue of sociality. Only in interaction with one another is the spirit of human beings ever revealed; this is the essence of spirit, to be oneself through being in the other" (1963, p. 48). According to Bonhoeffer, not only does a person's self-identity take shape in relationship with others, but spiritual identity also develops in the context of relationship with other. Spirituality is dependent on sociality. Spirituality is thus contingent on social being as prior to and the foundation for religious instincts and experiences.

Within the social sciences religion is understood to be an institutional phenomenon and is related to a specific faith tradition. Religion is socially constructed and defined by their boundaries of belief, practices and polity. Religion has been defined as "an organized system of beliefs, practices, rituals, and symbols designed (a) to facilitate closeness to the sacred or transcendent (God, higher power, or ultimate truth/reality) and (b) to foster an understanding of one's relationship and responsibility to others in living together in community" (Koenig, McCullough and Larson, 2001, p. 18). Miller and Thoreson (2003) point out that religion is a fundamentally social or societal phenomenon, whereas spirituality is usually understood at the level of the individual.

Religious development refers to a relationship with a particular doctrine about a divine Other or supernatural power, a relationship that occurs through affiliation with an organized faith and participation in its prescribed rituals. Specifically, religious development involves the growing capacity to engage with a faith tradition. Given that religions generally incorporate specific beliefs, moral standards, practices, communities of believers and the acknowledgement of a divine or supernatural Other, religious development involves many aspects of human functioning, including cognitive, emotional, moral, spiritual and social development.

How does the capacity to be spiritual or religious develop? Although this question has been neglected within the social sciences, there are a few existing and emerging theoretical explanations. In the next section of the chapter we will look at a biblical and theological perspective of such development, review existing theories in light of our understanding of the reciprocating self and then discuss how other aspects of human development affect spiritual and religious development.

> I thank my God every time I remember you, constantly praying with joy in every one of my prayers for all of you, because of your sharing in the gospel from the first day until now. I am confident of this, that the one who began a good work among you will bring it to completion by the day of Jesus Christ. . . . And this is my prayer, that your love may overflow more and more in knowledge and full insight to help you determine what is best, so that in the day of Christ you may be pure and blameless, having produced the harvest of righteousness that comes through Jesus Christ for the glory and praise of God. (Phil 1:3-6, 9-11)

These are some of Paul's opening words to the church at Philippi. There are several theological truths relevant to religious and spiritual development embedded within this text. First, Paul reminds us, "the one [God] who began a good work among you will bring it to completion by the day of Jesus Christ." The Reformed tradition firmly believes that God initiates faith in us. We believe that humans are not able to initiate faith, but faith is a gift from God. Second, Paul states that this good work of faith that God began in us is a process. Our experience of religion and faith is a developmental journey that will be completed only when Christ comes again.

Paul prays that the Philippians' love may "overflow more and more in knowledge and full insight." He suggests that our love for God (and others) is to grow in understanding. It is not an ignorant, blind love, but a love informed by knowledge and wisdom that makes a difference in our lives—this increased understanding will enable us to "determine what is best" and to be "pure and blameless." This statement teaches that religious development involves growing in the capacity to love God (and others), to grow in knowledge and understanding so that we may live rightly (according to God's will), suggesting that religious development involves socioemotional and cognitive development.

Paul reminds us that we are to be "filled with the fruit of righteousness that comes through Jesus Christ" (NIV). Paul clearly states that righteousness does not come on our own but through Christ. Theologians use the term *imputed righteousness* to refer to the mysterious act of Christ exchanging our sin for his righteousness. In a sense he makes a trade with us. He takes our sins and gives us his righteousness. Calvin referred to this as the *mirifica communitatio,* or wonderful exchange. Christ takes what is ours and makes it his, and he takes what is his and makes it our own. Consequently, Paul is suggesting that there is a supernatural or divine aspect to religious development. No matter how sophisticated our moral development or our sense of ego identity might be, this kind of development is beyond our control. Finally, Paul reminds us that the faith initiated in us and the love, knowledge, and righteousness all happen for the glory and praise of God. Ultimately our religious development relates to God and is not solely about us.

James Fowler's Stages of Faith

James Fowler (1981) proposed a theory of faith development that emphasizes the motivation to discover meaning in life, either within or outside of an organized religion. Fowler identified six stages of faith development that explain how religious and spiritual development occur from infancy through the latter years in life. For Fowler, faith is a universal, dynamic quality of human life that involves trust in and loyalty to centers of value (e.g., religion, family), images of power (e.g., God, government), and master stories (e.g., the biblical narrative). Trust in these sources provides meaning and guidance for our lives and acts to sustain and encourage us in our life's journey.

Fowler's stage theory will sound familiar in many ways because it is rooted in other developmental theories such as those of Erikson, Piaget and Kohlberg. Although Fowler and his colleagues have spent two decades researching this stage theory among diverse populations in age and religious tradition, Fowler bases much of his understanding of faith development on the emergence of other developmental capacities (e.g., identity, cognition and moral reasoning). Specifically, Erikson's understanding of crisis, psychosocial development and the eight stages of ego development strongly inform Fowler's understanding of faith development. Piaget's explanation of cognitive development also play a strong hand in Fowler's articulation of the role of religious beliefs in faith. Similarly, Fowler draws on Kohlberg's theory of moral development to explain the moral aspect of religious development.

Primal faith (infancy). Primal faith is derived from an infant's experience of mutual interaction with parents and caregivers, being formed in the basic rituals of care and interchange. This earliest form of faith is what enables infants to endure the anxiety resulting from separations from care providers. While it does not determine later faith, it lays the foundation on which faith is built.

Stage 1. Intuitive-projective faith (early childhood). The first stage of faith takes place in early childhood. Acquisition of language and imagination and emotional development play an important role. Stories, gestures and symbols stir the imagination that is not yet controlled by logical thinking. When fused with children's own feelings, they invent their own intuitive images of what good and evil are. Reality and fantasy are undistinguishable. The stage involves the awakening of moral emotions and standards that corresponds with a struggle for autonomy and will. Right and wrong are understood in terms of consequences to the self. During this stage children form conscious images of God.

Stage 2. Mythical-literal faith (middle and late childhood). As elementary children move into Piaget's concrete operational stage, they begin to reason in a more logical and concrete, but not abstract, manner. They now can order the world with categories of time, space, number and causality, which allows them to differentiate between reality and fantasy. Also at this stage children can begin to take the perspective of others as well as begin to capture meanings from stories. They interpret stories and symbols literally. Their perception of God is anthropomorphic, based on humans they know—often their parents or characters from other stories. Their understanding of right is often perceived of as fair exchange. People get what they deserve.

Stage 3. Synthetic-conventional (adolescence). The onset of formal operational thinking enables adolescents to wrestle with abstract ideas and concepts. Youth begin to integrate what they have learned about religion into a coherent belief system and sense of identity. These new cognitive abilities also make possible mutual, interpersonal perspective-taking. Consequently, intimacy and friendships are a powerful force in the lives of adolescents. The desire for personal relations with significant others is often associated with a hunger for a personal relationship with God in which a young person feels known and loved. God takes on great depth.

Adolescents' understanding of self takes on new depths as well. They become concerned with their identity, vocation and future. When an adolescent faces the identity crisis, often this sense of knowing God leads to a deep integration of God into identity. As youth integrate sets of images of themselves into their identity, they simultaneously form a set of beliefs, values and commitments that provide direction and guidance for living. Although these beliefs are not settled without some abstract thinking, people at the synthetic-conventional stage may still conform to the religious beliefs of others (as in Kohlberg's conventional level of moral reasoning) and have not fully analyzed alternative religious ideologies. They have a tacit system of religious beliefs and values, which they know but they cannot necessarily explain because of their unquestioning allegiance to an external authority. Right and wrong are determined by whether relationships are harmed or what others might say.

Stage 4. Individuative-reflexive faith (emerging-young adulthood). This stage generally occurs in the transition between adolescence and adulthood. To reach this stage the young adult must question and examine the values and beliefs that they have accepted in life thus far. Consequently, their commitments become explicit, are consciously chosen and can be critically supported, unlike the tacit commitments of the synthetic-conventional faith where commitments are unexamined and uncritically approved. At this stage authority is relocated to the self, where it, not the greater community, assumes the burden and responsibility for faith and belief. Symbols are questioned and not taken literally. However, they often have a cognitive rather than mystical meaning. Fowler parallels this stage to the Enlightenment, proposing that individuals use their intellect to explain and rationalize their religious beliefs and experiences.

At this stage an identity emerges that is not merely defined by a person's relationships to others but is consciously chosen. Fowler argues that emerging adults take full responsibility for their lives and their religious beliefs at this time. For example, during the college years individuals often intellectually challenge their personal values and religious ideologies. Formal operational thought enables this individual self-reflection that is characteristic of the individuative-reflexive faith stage.

Stage 5. Conjunctive faith (middle-late adulthood). During middle adulthood only a small number of adults move into conjunctive faith. At this stage individuals no longer need to be able to explain or rationalize all aspects of their beliefs and values. They begin to embrace paradox and integrate polarities in their lives. For example, they begin to recognize that they are simultaneously a constructive and a destructive person. Paul captured this well when he wrote, "For I do not do the good I want, but the evil I do not want is what I do" (Rom 7:19).

Individuals at this stage do not need things to be black and white, rather they grow comfortable with the gray areas—the ambiguities and mysteries—of life. For example, they can live with the tension that God is all powerful and loving, yet great suffering and pain remain in this world. Symbols, narrative and myth become very important. After having looked critically at traditions and having analyzed their meanings in the pervious stage, adults in this stage hunger for a deeper relationship with the reality that the symbols mediate. Spiritual disciplines such as meditation, silence and *lectio divina* (a method of meditative Bible reading) serve to draw believers into that reality of the presence of God, allowing Scripture and the Holy Spirit to reform and shape them rather than studying Scripture and analyzing the text for meaning. Fowler suggests that it requires a second naiveté in order to enter into the symbols and narratives.

Stage 6: Universalizing faith (middle to late adulthood). Very few individuals ever achieve universalizing faith, according to Fowler. Two things that characterize people at this stage are (1) their ability to transcend specific belief systems and experience a sense of connection with all beings, and (2) their commitment to overcoming division, oppression and violence. Mohandas Gandhi, Martin Luther King Jr. and Mother Teresa are examples of individuals at this stage. They were able to move beyond self-interest and their own religious ideologies in order to bring about love and justice. At this stage individuals begin to see value in others and injustices in the world from God's perspective rather than through their own perspective. Fowler refers to this as decentralization from self. For Fowler this leads to a transformation from personal values to a universalization of the capacity for love, compassion and justice. Persons at this stage lead lives marked by a sustained commitment to love and justice.

Beyond Fowler

Although Fowler's theory has been enthusiastically received (especially in the 1980s and 1990s) as a helpful means for understanding the emergence of religious faith and for creating and evaluating religious education and ministry programs, it has come under scrutiny, as have many of the linear, modern developmental theories. Scholars today recognize that development is not always straightforward and does not always proceed according to stages (Lerner, 2002). Postmodern sensibilities have highlighted the need for more complex and less reductionistic theories that emphasize the influence of systems, person-context interaction and nonlinear development.

One such author is James Loder, the late practical theologian from Princeton Theological Seminary, who proposed that faith development is not a linear continuum. Loder wrote about the development of the *human spirit,* which he distinguishes from the ego. The human spirit most closely approximates what might be referred to as our *soul*—it is in the deepest sense the "self," yet it has a spiritual component that seeks out unity with God. Loder articulates three important points about the development of the human spirit: (1) spiritual growth is separate and distinct from other developmental competencies; (2) spiritual development involves radical, nonlinear transformation, such is the case often with conversion; and (3) faith is relational rather than rational.

Loder proposes that spiritual development may occur independently of other aspects of psychological development. For example, although spiritual development may be influenced by our cognitive, identity and moral development, it is not dependent on the emergence of these other psychological characteristics. He states that spiritual growth has its own unique axis of development:

> The development of the ego and all its various competencies (for example, language, intelligence, moral judgment) unfolds along a different axis from that of spiritual development. The two axes of development may intersect and complement each other, but they diverge preeminently as to primary aim. The ego's aim is adaptation to its physical, social, and cultural environment so as to maximize satisfaction and ensure survival. (1998, p. 72)

He explains that these two axes have different trajectories, based on their goals. The goal of ego development is to successfully adapt to its context in order to increase personal satisfaction and survival. On the other hand, the goal of the human spirit is personal union with the presence and purpose of God. These two distinct purposes direct independent patterns of growth. Thus the human spirit does not follow according to other developmental trajectories.

Loder acknowledges that spiritual development often involves a radical reordering in our lives brought on by the Holy Spirit. He writes about the significance of the transforming moment when the Holy Spirit brings about fundamental change in our lives. "It is not one's own initiative but the initiative of the Holy, working deeper than consciousness and well beyond it, that brings forth the inside-outside reversal in the transformed person" (Loder, 1989, p. 103). Although such a transformation recenters the whole person around a spiritual center—the person of Christ—ego functioning is preserved.

For example, he writes about the conversion experience of Martin Luther. He explains that while in seminary the young Luther had an epiphany, while of all things, on the toilet. Originally, Luther went to seminary out of a sense of obligation, but after this "experience on the privy" he had a profound sense of calling that reordered his sense of self. Loder explained that Luther was transformed by "the pattern set by the Creator Spirit, not the pattern set by any stages of human development" (p. 246). Luther was still fundamentally the same person, but his identity, purpose and goals had been altered. Because of the Holy Spirit moving in him, he became defined by his awareness and relationship to God. Loder uses Erikson's psychosocial stages of development to explain that the development that occurred for Luther was not linear. Loder explains that Luther jumped instantaneously from identity (stage of adolescent development) to integrity (the final stage) in a moment on the privy.

Loder argues that faith is not about reason, insight or meaning, but it is relational. Fowler's stages emphasize the significance of cognition—beliefs, meanings and perspectives. Fowler's stages are determined by an individual's ability to reason critically about religious beliefs and values as well as the ability to take others' or God's perspectives, which in turn ultimately propels a person to lead a life in a universally loving manner. Loder takes the emphasis off the rational and puts it on the relational. Faith is about knowing God and God's love for us, and responding to it. Our deepest longing or our developmental goal is "to behold the face of God" (p. 272). From a teleological perspective the purpose of human life is to deepen intimacy with God, which occurs directly through encounters with the spiritual presence of Christ and also through the family of God. For Loder spiritual development does not occur through increased understanding of religious beliefs or universal truths, but rather it is through the deepening of our intimacy of God that the Spirit is released more fully in our lives. Through this spiritual presence of Christ we are given meaning, guidance, hope and motivation to act.

For Fowler spiritual transformation is embedded in human development, but for Loder human development is shaped by spiritual transformation. Fowler argues that faith development is dependent on an individual's level of cognitive, moral and psychosocial growth. Loder believes that these aspects of psychological development can be determined by the spiritual transformation brought about through the divine intervention of the Holy Spirit, which brings about radical change in a person's life. In this way the spiritual growth axis acts independently from the rest of human development.

Differentiated Faith

We acknowledge that approaches like Fowler's and Loder's contribute to an understanding of spiritual and religious development. At the time this book went to press, there was little other theoretical or empirical work beyond Fowler that contributes to a psychological understanding of the development of these transcendent capacities. Consequently, we will put forth our best understanding of spiritual development based on our teleological assumption of the reciprocating self.

From a trinitarian theological perspective the purpose in life is to be in a reciprocating relationship with God and others. As such it is our understanding that the goal of spiritual and religious development is very consistent with Loder's: to experience intimacy with God that allows for communion with the Godhead and does not sacrifice the particularity of the individual. We refer to this as *differentiated faith*. Differentiated faith incorporates both spiritual and religious expression that allows for a reciprocating relationship with God that emphasizes both unity and uniqueness. Although differentiated faith is nonreductionistic and allows for the presence and action of God in the process of formation, it can be influenced by other aspects of human functioning. Finally, differentiated faith is not only characterized by intimacy with God but also a life that responds in action to the mutual love of the Creator and created.

Based on the discussion of the *imago Dei* in chapter two (see pp. 29-32), differentiated faith is lived out in communion with God in a way that facilitates a deeper knowledge of God and self. In this way a relationship with God is characterized by a differentiated believer and a differentiated deity. As figure 13.1 illustrates, differentiated faith occurs when an individual's relationship with God is balanced by unity and uniqueness. Such faith does not lead to enmeshment with or detachment from God. This is important. Some faith traditions emphasize unity with God to the extent that the unique will, gifts and interests of an individual are subjugated to the perceived will of God. The Bible is very clear that we are uniquely gifted and that our uniqueness enables the body of believers to function effectively. In our relationship with God, we do not lose our unique selves. At the same time, neither are we to emphasize uniqueness to the extent of losing our intimacy with God or God's family.

Consequently, from the perspective of the reciprocating self, spiritual development is understood as growing the basic human capacity to transcend

Figure 13.1. Differentiated faith

the self and deepen awareness and relatedness to God (as Father, Son and Holy Spirit) and God's created order—both human and nonhuman—in such a way that provides meaning and guidance for life according to a Christian ethic. Religious development is then understood as the emergence of the ability to engage and participate in the doctrines, practices and community associated with a religious tradition that facilitates intimacy with God and fellow believers. Differentiated faith, then, incorporates both the spiritual and religious, recognizing that (1) spiritual development emphasizes the experience of transcendence and that (2) religious development emphasizes the institution and traditions of a particular religion—both resulting in greater intimacy with God (and others) and motivating individuals to respond with God's love for the world. Differentiated faith is not solely about being spiritual and being in touch or having a profound relationship with God. Nor is it merely about being religious and believing all the correct doctrines or performing the right religious practices or being a part of the right congregation. Both spiritual and religious development are necessary for differentiated faith. Both draw us into intimacy with God and the church and move us to serve as a response to a loving encounter with God.

Differentiated faith also recognizes the possible supernatural, biological and psychological influences that might in theory operate within spiritual and religious development. Like Loder, we acknowledge the life-altering power of God's presence and acknowledge that psychology does not provide us with the language or tools to explain how the Holy Spirit might bring about transformation, whether conversion, growth or healing, in the life of an individual. Similar to Fowler we also accept that the emergence of differentiated faith is affected, but not exclusively, by other aspects of human development. For example, identity, cognitive abilities, emotions and social skills can play a significant role in spiritual and religious development.

Finally, differentiated faith manifests itself in a life lived in response to knowing God and God's love. Such a life is marked by living in covenant with other believers or participating in a worship community as well as serving and reaching out to the greater community. Differentiated faith, spiritual development and religious development at their best result in an individual that contributes to society in a manner of love and justice.

How does differentiated faith develop? Because differentiated faith is constituted of both spiritual and religious development, we must turn to an examination of both of these. We have taken an ecological perspective of development, recognizing that development takes place in the interactions between the person and their multiple contexts. After discussing the dynamics of an ecological approach to spiritual and religious development, we will consider how specific aspects of human functioning may contribute to the growth of spiritual and religious development.

Context and differentiated faith. From an ecological perspective, we are interested in how characteristics of the individual and the context interact over time to influence differentiated faith. We see the individual as a dynamic entity at the center of a network of biological, psychological, sociohistorical, cultural and supernatural contexts. The bidirectional influences between person and context provide the basis for the high levels of variability in religious and spiritual development that exist among individuals. Such a view acknowledges both the core domains (e.g., relationships with family, peers) and processes (e.g., cognitive capacities) that religious and spiritual development involves. In addition to these core processes, those uniquely religious and spiritual elements (e.g., relations with the divine) and religious and spiritual contexts (e.g., worship) that contribute to differentiated faith must be considered.

Consequently, spiritual and religious development are not simply a process of "unfolding of an entity" but is the interaction of biological, social, cultural and spiritual factors in which multiple domains and functions develop to promote differentiated faith. Recognition of multiple contexts and their interactive relationship with variables of the self necessitates much more than a singular conception of religious or spiritual development. Consequently, development is not linear but is multidimensional and multidirectional. As a result, we do not talk about the development of undifferentiated faith in stages but rather in terms of the interactions of a person and context over time. It is these interactions that help or hinder the development of the reciprocating self in relationship to God. Consequently, there is not one path to religious or spiritual maturation.

This approach to spiritual and religious development allows for appreciating the role of different aspects of human functioning and the social, historical and divine influences. For example, this view acknowledges that because of an individual's cognitive capacities, religious knowledge can show growth at different time throughout the life span. In addition, it can account for the influence of historical events in shaping religious beliefs or spiritual experiences that might contribute to a deepening intimacy with God. Furthermore, such a systems view recognizes divine influence bringing about change in the lives of individuals.

When thinking about the development of differentiated faith, we are less concerned with what stage a person is at and more interested to know how an individual's interaction with his or her environment spurs on growth of the reciprocating self. This view acknowledges the richness and complexity of spiritual and religious development. It does not seek homogeneity in development but allows for heterogeneity. For example, it allows for a mentally challenged adult to have a profound sense of faith based on an experience of a loving relationship with God, whereas using Fowler's stages of faith the mentally challenged adult would be judged as having lower level of faith because of the cognitive challenges faced.

Contexts such as family, peer relationships, schools, congregations and culture may all play potentially rich roles in the development of differentiated faith. Although it is beyond the scope of this chapter to cover in depth these areas of potential influence, we will consider the unique role of the religious influence. Because religion is very complex—including a belief system, people and an acknowledgment of a transcendent other (e.g., God, a higher power, absolute truth)—there are many ways that religious environments shape an individual's religious development. In particular, religion has the potential to provide opportunities for religious development and commitment through ideological, social and spiritual contexts (King, 2003).

Religions have a rich ideological context in that they actively promote a coherent worldview that offers prosocial values and behavioral norms grounded in a belief system. Especially in a culture where people are bombarded with many different values and beliefs, religion's ability to provide a clear and consistent set of beliefs and values enables people to grow in their ability to make sense of the world, find meaning and have faith. Religion offers ultimate answers and perspective about the larger issues in life, enabling individuals to become more clear and committed about their religious beliefs and religious identity.

From a social perspective, religious institutions intentionally teach these values, and members may embody these ideals and values and serve as role models. In addition, the faith community provides an intergenerational network of enduring, caring relationships through which youth may wrestle with issues pertinent to identity exploration as well as offer experiences in which they can explore personal gifts.

Finally, such institutions offer a spiritual environment that enables youth to transcend their daily concerns and encounter a supernatural Other and a faith community in a meaningful way that nurtures their religious growth. Often spiritual experiences (e.g., answered prayer, corporate worship) call individuals' attention beyond themselves, inspiring them to commit to something greater than themselves (Lerner, Dowling and Anderson, 2003; Youniss et al., 1999).

As such, religion is recognized as an important environment for the development of differentiated faith. Although an ecological perspective recognizes the important contribution of context, such a perspective also acknowledges the potential influence of individual factors. Next we will explore how different aspects of human functioning may contribute to spiritual and religious development.

Areas of human functioning and spiritual and religious development. We have recognized spirituality to be the human capacity for self-transcendence and connecting with God and others. Therefore it is contingent on social being and is foundational for religious instincts and experiences. Thus we will consider spiritual development prior to religious development. Spiritual development is the nonlinear process of increasing the capacity for self-transcendence, care for others and devotion to and intimacy with God. According to our understanding of the reciprocating self, for the self to become more aware of or giving toward another, the self must itself grow. As the self develops, some of the elements of human functioning will also grow. This recognizes that with spiritual development, the development of certain human functions, such as identity and moral, civic and cognitive development, will grow in a nonlinear manner based on interactions with a person's context.

Lerner and colleagues (Lerner, 2004; Lerner, Dowling and Anderson, 2003; Lerner et al., forthcoming) argue that spiritual development is predicated on the emergence of fidelity that results from the resolution of the identity crisis during adolescence. Fidelity, the unflagging commitment to an ideology that transcends the self, allows young people to integrate their moral and civic identities during adolescence, giving them a spiritual sensibility. As youth commit to an ideological framework and gain a sense of fidelity, they are able to transcend individuality and engage in a more noble purpose (Damon, Menon and Bronk, 2003). In this sense, "Ideology provides the social glue that allows identity to transcend individuality and become synthesized with the collective" (Youniss and Yates, 1997, p. 23). Youth, within a moral and value-laden framework, develop not only integrated civic and moral identities and a commitment to an ideology but also a transcendent or spiritual sensibility that propels them to contribute to the common good (Lerner, Dowling and Anderson, 2003). For example, a young woman may be involved in serving lunch to the homeless, where she has the opportunity to get know an elderly homeless woman. This encounter with the homeless woman may motivate her toward further service and a deeper commitment in her faith.

Just as aspects of human development may influence spiritual development, the same may be true for religious development. An individual's cognitive abilities greatly influence his or her engagement with religion. Some scholars explain religious development occurring as a function of cognitive stages of development (Elkind, 1997; Fowler, 1981). From this perspective religious development is thought to begin during the elementary school years, when children can begin to use logic and can discern reality from fantasy. Although young children are limited to concrete thinking and are not able to reason abstractly about the religious rituals and traditions to which they are introduced, they still have an ability to think about their religious beliefs and the object of their belief. These scholars suggest that with the increasing ability to understand complex and abstract thought (such as why a loving God might allow evil and suffering to occur in the world), an individual's religious development increases. An increased capacity to understand and accept religious beliefs, doctrines or traditions enables a person to engage more fully with the religion. This abstract-reasoning skill is typically apparent in the cognitive capacities of the adolescent.

Despite the attempt to describe and explain religious development as a consequence of cognitive development, there are very young children who think abstractly about issues related to the divine and experience a profound sense of faith, and there are adults who think quite concretely about issues related to the divine (see Reimer and Furrow, 2001). There exists a great diversity in trajectories of religious development both between individuals and between communities and cultures. Consequently, religious development cannot be understood solely by cognitive development, nor can the assumption be made that the brighter an individual is the more religiously developed he or she is.

Emotions are also an important part of religious development. Emotions such as love, awe and joy often are a motivating factor that propels individuals toward religious conversion, commitment and ongoing devotion (Keltner and Haidt, 2003). Looking again at the examples mentioned, it becomes evident that emotion, along with reason, influences religious devotion and commitment. Profound doctrinal understanding does not often predicate a religious conversion, but experiencing a profound sense of love or gratitude often does (James, 1902). Such emotions may stir or initiate commitment as well as serve to motivate a sustained commitment to a religious tradition.

Social development also affects an individual's religious development. An individual's ability to be in relationships with other human beings shapes the way people develop religiously. Some scholars believe that religious development begins in infancy, as the young child becomes involved in relationships with caregivers. For example, the relationship between a baby and its mother is thought to influence the way an infant can distinguish between itself and others, whether God or another person. The amount of trust experienced in these early relationships might also affect the degree to which the individual will experience relationships with God or other people. Thus if a young girl experiences a warm, close relationship with her mother, she is more likely to experience God as a warm and caring being.

Other scholars (e.g., Youniss, McClellan and Yates, 1999) discuss the value of service to others. Active participation within a religious community (e.g., through worship or community service) places the individual within the sphere of other religious adherents. For example, when youth volunteer to serve at a homeless shelter affiliated with their church, they identify themselves as active members and contributors to their specific religious tradition and community. Shared social relationships with others therefore motivate individuals to question, affirm, doubt and wonder about their own understandings and beliefs and their own place within the religious family.

An individual's ability to interact with fellow believers may influence his or her religious growth by facilitating closeness to the sacred (or transcendent) and by fostering an understanding of the individual's relationship and responsibility to others. For example, many religious traditions acknowledge that a believer can experience the sacred through relationships with fellow human beings (e.g., through service or worship; Youniss et al., 1999). Consequently, social competencies can be helpful in developing spiritually.

Religious development also includes moral development. As religions prescribe moral standards and practices, an individual's ability to follow his or her religious tradition is dependent on the ability to carry out the moral code of the religion. For example, in many cases research has demonstrated that religious people are often extremely moral people (Colby and Damon, 1995; Walker and Pitts, 1998). People who have been recognized for their extraordinarily moral behavior (e.g., Mother Teresa, Gandhi) are often very religious people as well. Religious development therefore involves different aspects of moral development: moral identity, moral emotions, moral sensitivity and moral reasoning (see Walker and Reimer, 2005).

An individual's sense of spirituality must also be considered. Although not as frequently studied as other areas of human functioning (e.g., cognitive, emotional and moral development), spiritual development is a central part of being human and is central to religious development. When understood as the capacity for self-transcendence that results in caring for others and devotion to and intimacy with God, spirituality is recognized as an important component of religious development. Spirituality is that which fosters an individual's relationship with the sacred Other, connection with fellow human beings or appreciation for nature in such a way that inspires meaning, purpose and a commitment to contributing to something greater than the self. Spiritual experiences motivate individuals to internalize religious beliefs and moral principles as well as inspire devotion and commitment. For example, people do not usually make a lifetime commitment to a set of rules by memorizing them. However, if they have an experience of answered prayer or a meaningful encounter with God, they may be more apt to follow a set of religious beliefs and feel a deep sense of commitment to them (Smith, 2003).

A Proposed Model of the Development of Differentiated Faith

Differentiated faith comprises both spiritual and religious development. As young people interact with the many contexts of development a differentiated faith promotes (1) transcendence, caring of others, and intimacy with God (i.e., spiritual development) and (2) the capacity to participate in the doctrine, beliefs, and traditions of one's faith (i.e., religious development) in a way that enhances a reciprocating relationship with God and others. Hopefully, this approach borrows from the best of scholars like Fowler, Loder and Lerner. With Fowler, we acknowledge that differentiated faith may be influenced by psychological development in many ways—but not exclusively. With Loder, we recognize that the divine may intervene in supernatural ways beyond the scope of scientific explanation. Also consistent with Loder, we recognize that differentiated faith is relational, not just rational. With Lerner, we acknowledge the significance of the developmental context and the role of fidelity and identity in the emergence of spirituality during adolescence.

Figure 13.2 illustrates the development of differentiated faith. The various trajectories are depicted by a Wernerian spiral made of several strands. The spiral indicates that development is not linear. Each strand represents different aspects of human development. The spiral ascends through the nested spheres, representing adaptive interactions with different contexts of development. Potential divine intervention (e.g., conversion, healing) is indicated by the thunderbolt, suggesting that the Holy Spirit may interrupt and reorder the development of the human spirit at any point.

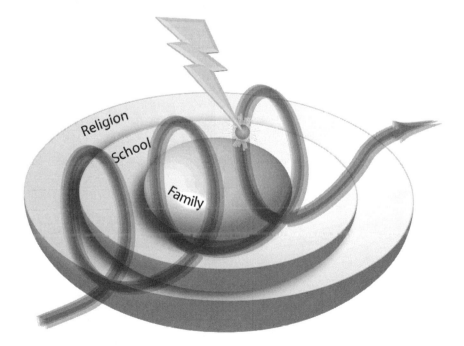

Figure 13.2. The development of differentiated faith

Conclusion

We are created to live in reciprocating relationships with God and others (see chap. 2). As Christians this is the goal of all of human development, and it guides our understanding of spiritual and religious development. Thus *spiritual development* involves the emergence of the human capacity to relate to God (as the Father, Son and Holy Spirit) and fellow believers in such a way that provides meaning and guidance for life and that yields a life lived according to the Christian ethic. *Religious development* then refers to growing in the capacity to participate in the doctrine, beliefs and traditions of one's faith in a way that promotes a reciprocating relationship with God and human others. Differentiated faith calls us into a loving relationship with God our Creator—to be more who we were created to be, and to live as God's beloved servants in this world.

Turning Steeples into Scaffolds

THE RECIPROCATING
RELIGIOUS COMMUNITY

IN THE LAST CHAPTER WE CONCLUDED that a differentiated faith is the spiritual and religious side of the reciprocating self. In this concluding chapter we examine the wider religious and social context within which a differentiated faith might be best developed, nurtured and maintained. In doing so we will look at some implications for ministering to persons as they move and develop through each stage of the life span. Just as trinitarian theology has been foundational for our model of the reciprocating self, so we will utilize it in understanding the biblical ideal for the religious community.

Nurturing Differentiated Faith

How is differentiated faith nurtured? Although there is a growing distinction between spiritual and religious development in the field of psychology, since differentiated faith is dependent on both we will examination the two together. Within this book, we have taken an ecological/systemic perspective of development, recognizing that development takes place in the interactions between people and their multiple contexts. Consequently, we are interested in how characteristics of the individual and characteristics of the context interact over time to influence differentiated faith. In considering development as systematic change, we see the individual as a dynamic entity at the center of a network of biological, psychological, sociohistorical, cultural and divine/supernatural factors. An ecological/systemic approach recognizes that individual differences between and among people expressed by nature, nurture and the timing of interrelations between nature and nurture provide the bases of the high levels of variability in religious and spiritual development.

Such a view identifies the core elements and processes of human development that are involved in religious and spiritual development by describing the various behavior domains (e.g., relational experiences between self and other) and processes (e.g., cognitive capacities) that religious development involves. In addition to these core processes, those *uniquely* religious and spiritual elements and contexts that contribute to differentiated faith must be considered.

Consequently, spiritual and religious development are not simply processes of "unfolding of an entity" but are the interactions of biological, social, cultural and spiritual factors in which multiple domains and functions promote differentiated faith. Recognition of multiple contexts and their interactive relationship with variables of the self necessitates much more than a singular conception of religious or spiritual development. This is true both in terms of quantitatively measured growth (e.g., in amount of religious knowledge) and qualitative growth (e.g., change in subjective experience of the sacred). Consequently, development is not linear, but is multidimensional and multidirectional. We must avoid a dualism that views religion and spirituality as separate from the person as a whole.

It is best to not conceptualize the development of undifferentiated faith in stages, but rather in terms of the interactions of a person and context over time that help or hinder the development of the reciprocating self in relationship to God. Consequently, there is not one sequential order of development along the path to religious or spiritual maturation. This view emphasizes the change that occurs through time based on the interaction between the person and the multiple levels of context.

This approach to spiritual and religious development allows for appreciating the role of different aspects of human functioning and social, historical and divine influences. For example, such a view acknowledges that because of an individual's cognitive capacities, religious knowledge can show growth at different times throughout the life span. In addition, it can account for the influence of historical events in shaping religious beliefs or spiritual experiences that might contribute to a deepening intimacy with God. Furthermore, such an ecological/systems approach recognizes the possibility for divine influence in bringing about change in the lives of individuals.

The thesis of this book—that human beings are created to live in reciprocating relationships with God and others—points to the general goal of all of human development and guides our understanding of spiritual and religious development specifically. Thus spiritual development involves utilizing our human capacities as persons created to bear the image of Christ. This will be manifested as we relate to God and fellow believers in a way that provides meaning and guidance for life and a consistently lived Christian ethic.

Following a section on how the reciprocating self may be adversely effected by the *saturated self,* we will examine the most important ecological niche for the development and maintaining of the reciprocal self, the reciprocal faith community.

The Issue of Identity in Contemporary Society

In *The Saturated Self: Dilemmas of Identity in Contemporary Life* (1991) Kenneth Gergen suggests the emergence of three types of selves corresponding to societal change in the last two hundred years. Prior to 1900 a *romantic self* with a fixed inner core that was passionate and volatile was the norm. Based on "deeply committed relations, dedicated friendships, and life purposes" (p. 6), the core of the romantic self was thought to be a moral character responsible for personal actions and willing to accept the consequences for them. Gergen believes that during the 1900s the *modern self* gradually replaced the romantic self. The modern self is viewed as being machinelike and governed by reason. Within modernity volatility is treated as a mental problem and passions are harnessed by way of involvement in rationally based educational, religious and familial institutions.

At present the modern self is becoming *saturated* by technologies that dominate life. Thus the modern self is beginning to be replaced by the *postmodern self.* Lacking a stable inner core or a reason-governed personality, the postmodern self is a *relational self* in which relationships with others are mediated by various technologies. Gergen predicts that forms of mediating technologies such as the Internet, cell phones and computer-based mate selection will increasingly dominate the formation of relationships in the future. Lacking an inner core, the identity within the postmodern self will exist only as a collection of external images.

In modern consumer-oriented society each individual develops relationships based on a social exchange model in which the goal is to maximize profit within each social relationship. Investing in relationships with an expectation that they will result in a handsome return becomes the bottom line for relationship formation. Lacking a socioemotional dimension, relationships become increasingly instrumental, measured in terms of what can be gained from the relationship. Through the marvel of electronic technology the sheer number of relationships multiply, while at the same time they become superficial, lacking any sense of commitment or depth.

At the risk of yielding to the language of the *relational self,* we suggest that it may be profitable to view Gergen's assessment of the modern self through the lens of our reciprocating self model. If Gergen is right, the significance of our model becomes even more timely. Relationships are dependent on well-formed personal identities. Where personal identities are shallow, the ability to enter into deep, caring and intimate relationships are limited, thus contributing to a shallow, less secure or even vacuous self.

The Reciprocal Self Embedded in the Reciprocal Community

Our model for understanding human develop—the reciprocating self—is based on a trinitarian analogy of being and becoming. In *After Our Likeness* Miroslav Volf (1998) develops a model of the church based on the image of the Trinity. Volf's stated purpose is to find a "theologically appropriate ecclesiological response to the challenge of modern societies" (p. 16). Structural elements of modern societies have affected the church and community life in a way similar to how they have affected the self. Thus we draw on Volf's model as an appropriate bridge to move from a focus on the reciprocal self to the reciprocating community.

Volf suggests that members of the church are to indwell each other in the same way that the Father, Son and Holy Spirit mutually indwell each other in a *trinitarian fellowship.* This is humanly possible to the extent that that the Holy Spirit dwells in the hearts of a people living in a community of the Spirit. Volf uses the concept of *mutual interpenetration* to describe the nature of the relationships between the Father, Son and Spirit. This mutual interpenetration involves a "mutual giving and receiving" wherein "Trinitarian persons are not only interdependent, but also *mutually internal*" (p. 208). This can be seen in the words of Jesus: "so that you may know and understand that the Father is in me and I am in the Father" (Jn 10:38). This is read by Volf as pointing to the *mutually exteriorization (perichoresis)* of the Father and the Son, a reciprocal *interiority* of trinitarian persons. Within every divine person as a subject, the other persons also dwell; all members of the Trinity mutually permeate one another. While together being the one God, in their mutual indwelling the Father, Son and Holy Spirit do not cease to be distinct persons. Since persons who have dissolved into one another cannot exist in one another, the distinctions between the three persons of the Trinity are precisely the presupposition that makes interiority possible. *Perichoresis* is "co-inherence in one another without any coalescence or commixture" (p. 209).

Just as the reciprocal interiority of the Father, Son and Spirit determine the character of their unity, so the reciprocal interiority of members of the body of Christ determine the unity of the local church or fellowship. "Like the divine persons, so also ecclesial persons cannot live in isolation from one another; Christians are constituted as independently believing persons through their relations to other Christians, and they manifest and affirm their own ecclesial personhood in mutual giving and receiving" (p. 206). Each person in the church is to *give* to each other member as God has gifted them. In a reciprocal sense however, each member is to freely *receive* from each other member as God has gifted them. This last point is important, for it points to the need for persons to receive from others without any sense of inadequacy. To be empowered by another is how God intends for the body of Christ to function in a normal sense. This may mean that the hyperindividualistic Western cultural influence on the church needs to be tempered by the communal emphasis of New Testament Christianity.

Christ himself is acting in the endowment of the gifts of the Spirit to the church. Endowment of spiritual gifts are universally distributed; they are given to all members of the body of Christ and to all local fellowships. Universal distribution implies common responsibility for the life of the church. This in turn implies mutual subordination (Eph 5:21), which means that members of the body are interdependent in regard to their giftedness (1 Cor 12:7-11). Finally, gifts of the Spirit are not to be thought of as irrevocable, but can change over the life of an individual's life span and within the body over the life of a church. Gifts of the Spirit are endowed to members of the body of Christ as a dynamic whole, within which members of the body are to reciprocally use their gifts for one another.

In our human frailness the issue of power is likely to interfere with God's ideal for mutual empowerment within the body of Christ. Drawing on Jürgen Moltmann, Volf suggests the principle that "the more a church is characterized by symmetrical and decentralized distribution of power and freely affirms interaction, the more will it correspond to the Trinitarian communion" (p. 236). If the church is truly reflecting the trinitarian model, relationships will be reciprocal and symmetrical, with all members expressing their gifts for the good of all others. God's ideal for human community is that each member will want to be and to do what God wants them to be and do in relationship to each other—to participate together as a community of love. Objectively, Paul states that those outside of the church will know Christians by their love for one another.

The Christian community can love perfectly to the extent that they are participating in God's own love. In *Life Together,* Dietrich Bonhoeffer (1954) details his concept of a reciprocating community, developing both spiritually and psychologically. In his chapter "Confession and Community," he suggests that mutual confession is the final breakthrough to fellowship and community.

Since no community this side of Christ's return will love perfectly, there is a place for rules and regulations in the body. A measure of both developmental and spiritual maturity, however, is the degree to which external rules and regulations become internalized—an interior part of each members self-structure. Just as Jesus prayed to the Father in anticipation of his death— "Not my will but yours be done"—so members of the church are to give up self-will, loving each other enough to give their lives for the other.

Congregational Differentiation

In the trinitarian model the Father, Son and Holy Spirit consist of a *differentiated unity.* Although each indwells the other, each maintains a distinct personhood. What would differentiated unity look like at the congregational level? Drawing on family-systems theory, differentiation can be conceptualized along a continuum leading from *enmeshment* at one extreme to *disengagement* at the other. Each extreme represents the lack of differentiation. Enmeshment is the state of fusion between persons, sometimes referred to as *undifferentiated ego mass.* Here unity is so complete that individual members have no separate identity of their own. In its most extreme form, persons cease functioning as individuals related to God. Instead, they have given over their identity to the group. Congregational enmeshment can be accompanied by collusion between an authoritarian leader who needs to dominate and followers who need domination. Less extreme forms of congregation enmeshment can be seen in high-demand or abusive congregations, where blind obedience is given to a leader by followers.

There is little interdependence in the enmeshed church since all members are dependent on the leader. A constant barrage of authoritarian commands and demands maintains dependence. There is little empowerment taking place in enmeshed churches. There are few personal boundaries. One fixed boundary around the entire congregation functions to keep congregation members from being influenced by anyone or anything outside of the church. Full allegiance and attention must be given to the leader.

The disengaged church is the opposite of the enmeshed church. Rather than too much unity, church members in a disengaged church hardly interact with each other. Membership consists of being on the church roll, but active participation together as the body of Christ is rare. Whereas sufficient personal boundaries may exist for individual members, there is practically no boundary around the congregation as a body. Energy and enthusiasm for life is found outside rather than from within the church. Identification with the body of Christ is minimal. Dietrich Bonhoeffer offer this appropriate warning: "Let him who cannot be alone beware of community. Let him who is not in community beware of being alone" (1954, p. 78).

The church that reflects the trinitarian model encourages a differentiated unity that is maintained by members finding their primary identity in Jesus Christ. Differentiated unity in the church body goes hand in hand with each member's differentiation in Christ. This can be seen in Paul's writing to the Galatian church, "I have been crucified with Christ; and it is no longer I who live, but it is Christ who lives in me. And the life I now live in the flesh I live by faith in the Son of God, who loved me and gave himself for me" (Gal 2:19-20). In a similar way we find in Romans 6 that Paul contrasts his old self, which has been crucified with Christ, with his new self, which is alive in Christ. The apostle John writes of the believers' new identity in terms of an exchanged life where "I am in him and he is in me" (see Jn 17:21).

With members of the family of God finding their identity in Christ, relationships are characterized by a mutual reinforcing and supporting of each other. At the organizational level, healthy differentiation is characterized by members experiencing unity in their connectedness with the congregation and their separation from the congregation as a whole. While personal boundaries exist around each individual, they are permeable, open to mutual interpenetration. Each member creates a place in his or her self for the other while not losing his or her own self. While the congregation needs strong boundaries to provide support and accountability for each member, these boundaries are also permeable. Based on a secure identity in Jesus Christ, members are free, and they are encouraged to live fruitful lives outside of the community.

Intergenerational Reciprocity

At the structural level the church must be a community in which relational interdependence is allowed and even fostered. The church must be structured so that it can respond to the developmental needs of persons at all life-span stages—infants, toddlers, teens, young and middle adults, and the elderly. It is imperative that those working in the church and in parachurch organizations have a good understanding of age-specific developmental issues. This includes knowledge of age appropriateness in such areas as faith and moral development, so there will no be unrealistic expectations of persons of a certain age. Thus Christian ministry has rightly used developmental psychology in emphasizing age-appropriate religious learning and worship activities.

The rate of change in popular culture—dress and fashion, music, the popular arts, communication style and the like—makes it necessary to focus Christian ministry (outreach, evangelism, worship) on specific age cohorts, igniting what has come to be know as *worship wars*. I (Jack) recently witnessed a multigenerational worship service in a church that has tenaciously resisted change to a multiservice, generation-specific format. I found congregants' reactions to the wide variety of worship styles both a bit humorous and a bit tragic. Older members of the church sang the old hymns fervently. The dominant response by the younger generation to the hymns ranged from mild tolerance to boredom. When the lyrics of an upbeat praise song were projected onto a screen, accompanied by a worship band, the younger folks clapped their hands and sang with great gusto. But most older congregants stood in confused bewilderment. The end result for many churches has been the creation of separate generational worship services for the different age groups.

However, an unintended negative consequence of such generational age grading is the potential construction of barriers across the groups, hindering the development of caring cross-generational relationships. Such churches are in danger of becoming isolated, age-specific, homogeneous subcommunities. Why is this not good, or what is being lost in the process? The answer can be seen in the complementary nature of the body of Christ (1 Cor 12).

In a profound way both the gifts and the needs of church members correspond to the ages of its members. Simply put, to a large extent the needs of younger persons correspond to the gifts and resources of older persons, while the needs of older persons correspond to the gifts and resources of younger persons.

Some may argue that such intergenerational needs can best be met between members within the same extended family and that the church should not be burdened with the responsibility of fostering intergenerational relationships. However, this ignores the weakening effect on contemporary family life caused by high geographical mobility. A strength in the extended family of the past was the rich interchange between families members of different generations. Crosscultural research suggests that traditionally the main socializers of children have been grandparents. In the past children learned morality and values at the knees of their grandparent. The majority of children growing up in modern societies are deprived of the benefits of an everyday relationship with their grandparents. Today's children often grow up with their nearest grandparent hundreds or even thousands of miles away. Correspondingly, many grandparents are living out their elderly years void of regular face to face contact with their children and grandchildren.

We suggest that the best way to foster intergenerational relationships in modern society is for the church to become what it was designed to be. The primary Greek word used in the New Testament in describing the church is *koinonia,* a word referring to a community in which Christians are united in purpose and identity. Robert Banks (1980) points out that in the economy of the New Testament society, *koinonia* was meant to represent a new type of community between the all-inclusive, impersonal state *(politeia)* and the excusive, blood-based household *(oikonomia)*. He suggests that the size of the first Christian churches were limited to between twenty and thirty persons since this is the number that could meet in a home of New Testament times. Research suggests that most persons are able to maintain intimate relationships with twenty-five to thirty persons at most (Pattison, 1984). Putting this together, we suggest the early church functioned much like an extended family. All believers cared for and support each other as family.

Banks (1980) observes that of the many metaphors used in the New Testament for church, none are used as extensively or as adequately as the family metaphor. The New Testament describes church members as the *family of God* who are the *children of God* and who are *brothers* and *sisters* in Christ. Although Jesus did not dissolve the natural order of the family, his desire for the church is that care and support transcend the family to the Christian community. In response to the message that his mother and brother had arrived, Jesus rhetorically replied, "Who are my mother and brothers?" We are told that he then looked at those sitting around him and said, "Here are my mother and my brothers. Whoever does the will of God is my brother and sister and mother" (Mk 3:33-34). John 19:26-27 records that "when Jesus saw his mother and the disciple whom he loved standing beside her, he said to his mother, 'Woman, here is your son.' Then he said to the disciple, 'Here is your mother' and from that hour the disciple took her into his own home." By his words and actions Jesus radically redefined the meaning of family. The church needs to be a community characterized by family-type relationships.

The focal point of references for the New Testament church was "neither a book nor a rite but *a set of relationships,* and that God communicated himself to them . . . *through one another*" (Banks, 1980, p. 111).

Perhaps what is most needed in the local church today is a radical redefinition of *family* (Clapp, 1993). The term *fictive kin* has been coined to refer to the development of familylike relationships between persons whose biological families are not available. During my (Jack's) children's formative years, we lived over one thousand miles away from both my and my wife's parents. Across the street from us, however, lived Hank and Mimi, an elderly couple whose own children and grandchildren lived far away. Our family became as *fictive kin* to Hank and Mimi, celebrating birthdays, anniversaries and special occasions together. Hank and Mimi became grandfather and grandmother to our children, and Jacque and Jeff became granddaughter and grandson to them. Many a meal, milestone and ritual were shared together as an extended family.

Young parents and their young children who are deprived of grandparents can benefit from the attention and nurture given by nearby elderly persons. At the same time elderly persons who are without family nearby can benefit from their involvement with these younger children and families. Young parents are overloaded and have little time, but time is the one commodity that elderly persons have plenty of. The elderly are often lonely, but in sharing life with younger parents and their children, their loneliness may yield to intimate belonging.

Principles of Cross-generational Fellowship and Ministry

The above is just one example of cross-generational complementarity that might be fulfilled within a religious community. We suggest several principles that might be helpful in facilitating cross-generational reciprocity in fellowship and ministry. First, *worship and ministry need to be conceptualized as normative activities to be engaged in by members of all ages.* God gifts all members of the body to minister to other members of the body. Even without self-awareness, God uses little children to minister to other members of the body.

Second, *ministry is to reflect the combination of giftedness and spiritual maturity.* In *Life Passages for Men* (1993) James Wilder observes that Scripture distinguishes between giftedness and maturity. Whereas gifting is God's domain, spiritual maturity is a human domain. Maturity is a relatively independent dimension of human life God gives us that unfolds through time and involves interaction with Christian community. The combination of giftedness and spiritual maturity brings about a fruit-bearing stage that Scripture describes as *fruitfulness.* Whereas fruitfulness is a characteristic found among all members, God allows for seasons of spiritual development that can correspond to chronological age. The Christian community needs to be sensitive to the specific developmental needs of members at every age. The point made earlier in this book—that human development involves both *adolescing* (growth) and *senescing* (decline)—may be worth noting in this regard. As persons age, they become less self-sufficient, less able to met the needs of others, and they become more needy of others.

Third, *while ministry is to be to reciprocal, it need not be a symmetrical exchange.* This gets at our earlier point about a covenant relationship with God and each other. *Mutuality* does not quite convey the idea since *mutuality* so strongly suggests equal and identical give-and-take. In relationships the give-and-take (reciprocity) may not be equal. A person may receive from another what he or she cannot give in return. Inversely, a person may give to another what the other may not be able to give in return. This lack of symmetry is, however, no defect or detriment to a covenantal relationship—it may in fact be its essence. God does for us what we cannot do for ourselves!

Scripture has much to say about a more mature member discipling or caring for the less mature or less self-sufficient member. It is obvious that the very young and immature and the very old and dependent will need to be supported and cared for more than what can be expected of them. Unconditional love means rejecting any "score-keeping" of how much one member of the body is getting from another.

Fourth, *ministry is to be an empowering process where one person uses his or her personal resources for the other with the purpose of building up and serving the other in Christ.* Developmentally, members within the family of God will be at different level of maturity—cognitively, socially, emotionally, intellectually and spiritually. The teleology of development in a community context is that members of the body of Christ have the capacity to give from their own giftedness and receive on the basis of their needs. Acts 4:32, 34 describes the early church this way:

> The whole group of those who believed were of one heart and soul, and no one claimed private ownership of any possessions, but everything they owned was held in common. . . . There was not a needy person among them, for as many as owned lands or houses sold them and brought the proceeds of what was sold. . . . [A]nd it was distributed to each as any had need.

The principle here is equally true for all types of needs and resources within the Christian community. In more than just material needs, members of the body are to emotionally and socially care for one another. There is no place in Christian ministry for a dualism that separates out physical, emotional and social needs from spiritual needs; ministry must be to the whole person.

Conclusion

Let us revisit how the reciprocating self as a developmental teleology helps us with the predicament of the developmental dilemma raised at the beginning of this book. First, the reciprocating self provides a theological lens through which to view development. We find that, in general, developmental theories are not strong in providing any sort of teleology. That is, they are tentative in addressing or defining the goal of development. Existing theories generally define processes inherent in development, but without directly discussing the goal of development.

Second, our model of the reciprocating self takes the focus off of pathology by emphasizing positive development. The psychological community has built much theory and practice on the repair and healing of persons. This emphasis has resulted in a deficient model of human development, lacking a clear understanding of positive or optimal development. We suggest that our model of the reciprocating self provides a theological perspective of optimal development.

The study of life-span development largely consists of a number of separate theories. The understanding of life-span development has been hindered by the lack of an overall metatheory, which would help us understand the many different existing theories and approaches to the different stages and aspects of development. We suggest that our reciprocating-self model might provide a general framework through which to understand and even evaluate these theories.

The journey that takes a newborn infant from total dependency to human maturity is a long and complex process. Along the way there are a number of biological and sociocultural factors that contribute to individuals becoming all that God intended them to be.

God's intention for humans is to develop as distinct individuals in mutual and authentic relationships with divine and human others—for God's glory. Although infants are born human, potential for maximum human development is contingent on being nested in caring and supportive relationships with others. Progress toward becoming a mature reciprocating self is fostered best within a network of relationships characterized by unconditional love, grace, empowering and intimacy. The goal of the maturation process is to become a person with the capacity and inclination to reciprocate each of these characteristics: to love and be loved, to forgive and be forgiven, to empower and be empowered, and to know and to be known. Our model for this is not found in human wisdom but in the very nature of our triune God and the relationship God seeks to establish with us.

Appendix

Chapter 1. The Developmental Dilemma

1. Does every theory of human development have an implicit and explicit teleology?
2. Where does soul fit in to an understanding of human development?
3. Distinguish between the concepts reciprocating self, soul and human spirit.

Chapter 2. The Reciprocating Self

1. Describe your reciprocating self.
2. How do you experience the image of God within yourself?
3. Share struggles you may have in coordinating your own needs for particularity and relationality.

Chapter 3. Reciprocating Relationships

1. On a scale of 1 to 10, where would you place your parents or caretakers in providing you with unconditional love, grace, empowering and intimacy?
2. Do you see any limitations in basing a human model of relationship on the way God relates to human beings?
3. Is it always possible to distinguish between behavior that empowers, controls or enables?

Chapter 4. The Reciprocating Self and Developmental Theory

1. Which developmental theory do you find comports most closely with the reciprocating-self model?

2. How might a theology of sin best be integrated with theories of human development?

3. Do you find the concepts of original sin, inherited sin or social sin helpful in working toward an integrated view of human development?

4. Compare and contrast development theories in terms of their capacity to view individuals as possessing human agency.

Chapter 5. The Reciprocating Self in Social Context

1. Identify the most important exosystem and macrosystem factors that were or are important in affecting your own development.

2. Is there a common consciousness that formed your own age group into a generational unit?

Chapter 6. Infancy

1. How would you respond to the statement that infants are not born human?

2. Drawing on your constructed memory, describe the ecology of your own infancy.

Chapter 7. Childhood

1. From memory, describe the ecology of your own childhood.

2. Give examples from your childhood of good scaffolding on your behalf.

3. Give examples from your own childhood where you might have benefited had others understood your zone of proximal development.

4. Give examples from your own childhood of risk and resilience.

Chapter 8. Adolescence

1. Evaluate the view that adolescence is a condition produced in urban-industrial-type societies.

2. Share the types of risks you took during your adolescence period. Which of these would you identify as healthy or unhealthy risks?

Chapter 9. Emerging Adulthood and Young Adulthood

1. Share your dream during your emerging adulthood (if you are beyond emerging adulthood, share the dream as you remember it). What might be problematic about this dream?

2. To what extent is emerging adulthood a life-span stage limited to more

affluent urban societies? Do you believe there is enough evidence available to add it to the list of life-span stages found in more traditional models of development?

Chapter 10. Middle Adulthood

1. Based on either personal experience or your observation of what your friends or parents have experienced, is there such a thing as a midlife crisis?
2. Is there a relationship between the state of a reciprocating self and the likelihood of a person experiencing a midlife crisis?
3. What is your emotional intelligence? How might the theological model of the reciprocating self proposed in this book point to the importance of paying more attention to emotional intelligence?
4. As a woman or a man, compare with each other your own fears, worries or concerns about reaching your middle adulthood years (or share them if your currently are there).
5. Is there such a thing as wisdom that is beyond intelligence? Does *wisdom* come with age?

Chapter 11. Late Adulthood

1. Describe the relationship between you and your grandparents. What is most meaningful to you and your grandparents about this relationship? Where do or did your grandparents find the most meaning in life during their elderly years?
2. Share examples of people you have observed who have retired well and not so well. What factors contribute to the difference?
3. Is there a biblical perspective on caring for the aged? Share how your understanding of Scripture informs your view on this issue.
4. Give examples you have observed where the principle of the zone of proximal capability has been either used or abused.
5. Share examples of people you have observed who have died well or not so well. What factors contribute to the difference?

Chapter 12. Special Issues in Human Development

1. How well does Kohlberg's model of morality in stages fit your own experience?
2. Do you find that the moral identity model allows for moral development to be freed from a cognitive bias?

3. Describe the ecology of your own moral identity.
4. What insights about moral development do you find from the discussion of moral identity in L'Arche?

Chapter 13. Differentiated Faith

1. Distinguish between spiritual and religious development in your own life. In what way are they interrelated?
2. How interrelated or independent do you find moral, spiritual and religious development to be in your own life?
3. Do you find Fowler's stages of faith model to comport with your own personal faithing experience?
4. Describe what a differentiated faith would look like in your own life.
5. What does it mean to be differentiated in Christ?

Chapter 14. Turning Steeples into Scaffolds

1. Describe how unconditional love, gracing, empowering and intimacy were or are expressed in your primary religious community.
2. In your experience, how possible is trinitarian fellowship?
3. Identify some of the obstacles that prevent, or conditions that facilitate, the development of a reciprocating community
4. Reflect on the concept of congregational differentiation. In your experience what are the barriers against a church achieving healthy differentiation?
5. Writings on worship wars would suggest that intergenerational reciprocity is very difficult in the church in contemporary society. How can a church facilitate intergenerational reciprocity?

Bibliography

Adams, G. R., Montemayor, R., and Gullota, T. P. (1989). *Biology of adolescent behavior and development*. Newbury Park, CA: Sage.

Ahammer, I., and Baltes, P. (1972). Objective vs. perceived age differences in personality: How do adolescents, adults, and older people view themselves and each other? *Journal of Gerontology, 27,* 46-51.

Ainsworth, M. (1979). Infant-mother attachment. *American Psychologist, 34,* 932-37.

Amato, P. (1993). Children's adjustment to divorce: Theories, hypotheses, and empirical support. *Journal of Marriage and Family, 55,* 23-38.

Amato, P., and Booth, A. (2000). *A generation at risk: Growing up in an era of family upheaval*. Cambridge, MA: Harvard University Press.

Amato, P., and Keith, B. (1991). Parental divorce and the well being of children: A meta-analysis. *Psychological Bulletin, 110,* 26-46.

Anderson, R. (1985). *The gospel of the family*. Unpublished manuscript. Fuller Theological Seminary, Pasadena, CA.

Anderson, R. (1986). *Theology, death and dying*. Oxford: Basil Blackwell.

Anderson, R. (1990). *Christians who counsel: The vocation of holistic therapy*. Grand Rapids: Zondervan.

Anderson, R. (1995). *Self care: A theology of personal empowerment and spiritual healing*. Wheaton, IL: Bridgepoint.

Anderson, R. (1998). On being human: The spiritual saga of a creaturely soul. In   W. Brown, N. Murphy and H. Malony (Eds.), *Whatever happened to the soul? Scientifc and theological portraits of human nature* (pp. 175-84). Philadelphia: Fortress.

Anderson, R. S. (1982). *On being human: Essays in theological anthropology*. Grand Rapids: Eerdmans. (Reprinted in 1991, Fuller Seminary Press)

Anderson, R., and Guernsey, D. (1985). *On being family: Essays on a social theology of the family*. Grand Rapids: Eerdmans.

Antonovosky, A. (1987). *Unraveling the mystery of health: How people manage stress and stay well.* San Francisco: Jossey-Bass.

Arlin, P. K. (1984). Adolescent and adult thought: A structural interpretation. In M. L. Commons, F. A. Richards and C. Armon (Eds.), *Beyond formal operations: Vol. 1. Late adolescent and adult cognitive development* (pp. 258-71). New York: Praeger.

Arnett, J. J. (2000). Emerging adulthood: A theory of development from the late teens through the twenties. *American Psychologist, 55*(5), 469-80.

Arnett. J. J. (2000b). High hopes in a grim world: Emerging adults' view of their futures and of "Generation X." *Youth and Society, 31,* 267-68.

Aspinwall, L. G., and Staudinger, U. M. (Eds.). (2003). *A psychology of human strengths: Fundamental questions and future directions for a positive psychology.* Washington, DC: American Psychological Association.

Astley, J. (1996). The role of the family in the formation and criticism of faith. In S. Barton (Ed.), *The family in theological perspective* (pp. 187-202). Edinburgh: T & T Ltd.

Atchley, R. (1982). Leaving the world of work. *Annals of the American Academy of Political Social Science, 464,* 120-31.

Atwood, G. E., and Stolorow, R. D. (1993). *Faces in a cloud: Intersubjectivity in personality theory.* Northvale, NJ: Jason Aronson.

Bachman, J. G., Johnston, L. D., and O'Malley, P. M. (1996). Transitions in drug use during late adolescence and young adulthood. In J. A. Graber, J. Brooks-Gunn and A. C. Petersen (Eds.), *Transitions through adolescence: Interpersonal domains and context* (pp. 111-40). Mahwah, NJ: Erlbaum.

Balswick, J. K., and Piper, B. (1995). *Life ties: Cultivating relationships that make life worth living.* Downers Grove, IL: InterVarsity Press.

Balswick, J. O. (1975). The function of the dowry system in a rapidly modernizing society: The case of Cyprus. *International Journal of Sociology of the Family, 5,* 158-67.

Balswick, J. O. (1988). *The inexpressive male: A study of men who express love too little.* Lexington, MA: Lexington Books.

Balswick, J. O. (1974). The Jesus people movement: A generation interpretation. In V. L. Bengston and R. S. Laufer (Eds.), *Youth, Generations, and Social Change: Part II, Journal of Social Issues, 30*(3), 23-42.

Balswick, J. O. (1992). *Men at the crossroads: Beyond traditional roles and modern options.* Downers Grove, IL: InterVarsity Press.

Balswick, J. O., and Balswick, J. K. (1987). A theological basis for family relationships. *Journal of Psychology and Christianity, 6*(3), 37-49.

Balswick, J. O., and Balswick, J. K. (1995). *The dual earner marriage: Coping with stress when it's hard to do it all.* Grand Rapids: Revell.

Balswick, J. O., and Balswick, J. K. (1997). *Family pain: Getting through the hurts of family life.* Grand Rapids: Revell.

Balswick, J. O., and Balswick, J. K. (1999). *Authentic sexuality*. Downers Grove, IL: InterVarsity Press.

Balswick, J. O., and Balswick, J. K. (1999). *The family: A Christian perspective on the contemporary home* (2nd ed.). Grand Rapids: Baker.

Balswick, J. O., Balswick, J. K., Piper, B., and Piper, D. (2003). *Relationship-empowerment parenting*. Grand Rapids: Baker.

Balswick, J. O., and Macrides, C. (1975). Parental stimulus for adolescent rebellion. *Adolescence, 10,* 253-66.

Balswick, J. O., and Morland, K. (1990). *Social problems: A Christian perspective*. Grand Rapids: Baker.

Balswick, J. O., and Ward, D. (1984). *The church, the family, and issues of modernity. Consultation on a theology of the* family. Seminar at Fuller Theological Seminary, Pasadena, CA.

Baltes, P., and Freund, A. (2003). Human strengths as the orchestration of wisdom and selective optimization with compensation. In L. Aspinwall and U. Staudinger (Eds.), *A psychology of human strengths: Perspectives on an emerging field*. Washington, DC: American Psychological Association.

Baltes, P., and Staudinger, U. (2000). Wisdom: A metaheuristic (pragmatic) to orchestrate mid and virtue toward excellence. *American Psychologist, 55,* 122-36.

Bandura, A. (1974). Behavior theory and the models of man. *American Psychologist, 29,* 859-69.

Bandura, A. (1977). *Social learning theory*. Englewood Cliffs, NJ: Prentice-Hall.

Bandura, A. (1978). The self system in reciprocal determinism. *American Psychologist, 33*(4), 344-58.

Bandura, A. (1998). Exercise of agency in personal and social change. In E. Sanavic (Ed.), *Behavior and cognitive therapy today: Essays in honor of Hans J. Eysenck*. Oxford: Anonima Romana.

Bandura, A., and Walters, R. (1959). *Adolescent aggression*. New York: Ronald Publishing.

Banks, R. (1980). *Paul's idea of community*. Grand Rapids: Eerdmans.

Baranowski, M. (1982). Grandparent-adolescent relations: Beyond the nuclear family. *Adolescence, 17,* 575-84.

Barrett, C. K. (1978). *The Gospel according to St. John*. Philadelphia: Westminster Press.

Bartchy, S. (1978). Power, submission, and sexual identity among the early Christians. In C. Wetzel (Ed.), *Essays on New Testament Christianity* (pp. 50-80). Cincinnati: Standard.

Bartchy, S. (1984). *Issues of power and a theology of the family. Consultation on a theology of the family*. Seminar at Fuller Theological Seminary, Pasadena, CA.

Barth, K. (1918/1963). *Epistle to the Romans* (E. C. Hoskyns, Trans.). New York: Oxford University Press.

Barth, K. (1975). *Church Dogmatics. Vol. 1/1* (G. W. Bromiley and T. F. Torrance, Trans.). Edinburgh: T & T Clark.

Barton, S. (1996). Biblical hermeneutics and the family. In S. Barton (Ed.), *The family in theological perspective* (pp. 3-23). Edinburgh: T & T Ltd.

Baumrind, D. (1971). Current patterns of parental authority. *Developmental Psychology, 4,* 1-103.

Baumrind, D. (1996). The discipline controversy revisited. *Family Relations, 45,* 405-14.

Baumrind, D. (1991). Effective parenting during the early adolescent transition. In P. Cowan and E. Hetherington (Eds.), *Advances in family research*. Hillsdale, NJ: Erlbaum.

Baumrind, D. (1978). Parental disciplinary patterns and social competence in children. *Youth and Society, 9,* 239-76.

Baumrind, D. (1972). Socialization and instrumental competence. In W. Hartup (Ed.), *Research on Young Children*. Washington, DC: National Association for the Education of Young Children.

Baumrind, D. (1996). The parenting controversy revisited. *Family Relations, 45,* 405-15.

Baumrind, D. (1972). Socialization and instrumental competence in young children. In W. Hartup (Ed.), *Research on young children* (pp. 202-24). Washington: National Association for the Education of Young Children.

Baumrind, D., and Black, A. (1967). Socialization practices associated with dimensions of competence in preschool boys and girls. *Child Development, 38,* 291-327.

Begley, S. (2000, February 28). Getting inside a teen brain: Hormones aren't the only reason adolescents act crazy. Their gray matter differs from children's and adults'. *Newsweek, 13519.*

Bell, A., Weinberg, M., and Hammersmith, S. (1981). *Sexual preference. Its development in men and women*. Bloomington: Indiana University Press.

Bellah, R., et al. (1985). *Habits of the heart: Individualism and commitment in American life*. Berkeley: University of California Press.

Belsky, J., Gilstrap, B., and Rovine, M. (1984). The Pennsylvanian infant and family development project, I. Stability and change in mother-infant and father-infant interaction in a family setting at one, three, and nine months. *Child Development, 55,* 692-705.

Belsky, J., Lerner, R., and Spanier, G. (1984). *The child in the family*. Reading, MA: Addison-Wesley.

Bengtson, V. L., and Black, K. D. (1973). Intergenerational relations and continuities in socialization. In P. Baltes and K. W. Schaie (Eds.), *Life-span development psychology: Personality and socialization* (pp. 207-34). New York: Academic Press.

Bengtson, V. L., and Kuypers, J. A. (1971). Generational differences and the developmental stake. *Aging and Human Development, 2*(1), 249-60.

Benson, P. (1997). *All kids are our kids: What communities must do to raise caring and responsible children and adolescents.* San Francisco: Jossey-Bass.

Benson, P. L., Roehlkepartain, E. C., and Rude, S. P. (2003). Spiritual development in childhood and adolescence: Toward a field of inquiry. *Applied Developmental Sciences, 7*(3), 204-12.

Berger, P., Berger, B., and Kellner, H. (1973). *The homeless mind: Modernization and consciousness.* New York: Random.

Berman, E., and Napier, A. (2000). Aging and the family: Dynamics and therapeutic interventions. In W. Nichols, M. Pace-Nichols, D. Becvar and A. Napier (Eds.), *Handbook of family development and intervention.* New York: John Wiley.

Berndt, J., and Miller, D. (2000). *Politics of the spirit: Portraits.* Los Angeles: Center for Religion and Civic Culture, University of Southern California.

Bianchi, S. M., and Spain, D. (1996). Women, work, and the family in America. *Population Bulletin, 51*(3), 1-48.

Birren, J. (1985). Age, competence, creativity, and wisdom. In R. Butler and H. Gleason (Eds.), *Productive aging: Enhancing vitality in later life* (pp. 29-36). New York: Springer.

Blankenhorn, D. (1995). *Fatherless America: Confronting our most urgent social problem.* New York: Basic Books.

Blasi, A. (1980). Bridging moral cognition and moral action: A critical review of the literature. *Psychological Bulletin, 88,* 1-45.

Blasi, A. (1983). Moral cognition and moral action: A theoretical perspective. *Developmental Review, 3,* 178-210.

Blasi, A. (1984). Moral identity: Its role in moral functioning. In W. Kurtines and J. Gewirtz (Eds.), *Morality, moral behaviour, and moral development.* Brisbane: John Wiley.

Blum, R. W., Beuhring, T., and Rinehart, P. M. (2000). *Protecting teens: Beyond race, income and family structure.* Minneapolis: Division of General Pediatrics and Adolescent Health, University of Minnesota.

Bonhoeffer, D. (1954). *Life together: A discussion of Christian fellowship.* San Francisco: Harper & Row.

Bonhoeffer, D. (1963). *The cost of discipleship* (R. H. Fuller, Trans.). New York: Macmillan.

Bonhoeffer, D. (1964). *The communion of saints: A dogmatic inquiry into the sociology of the church.* New York: Harper & Row.

Borrowdale, A. (1996). Right relations: Forgiveness and family life. In S. Barton (Ed.), *The family in theological perspective* (pp. 203-17). Edinburgh: T & T Ltd.

Boss, P. (1987). Family stress. In M. Sussman and S. Steinmetz (Eds.), *Handbook of marriage and the family* (pp. 695-723). New York: Plenum.

Bowlby, J. (1973). *Attachment and loss: Vol. 2. Separation.* New York: Basic Books.

Bowlby, J. (1980). *Attachment and loss: Vol. 3. Loss: Sadness and depression.* New York: Basic Books.

Boyatzis, C. J., Dollihite, D., and Marks, L. (forthcoming). The family context of children's spiritual and religious development. In G. C. Roehlkepartain, P. E. King, L. M. Wagener and P. L. Benson (Eds.), *The handbook of spiritual development in childhood and adolescence.* Newbury Park, CA: Sage.

Bradbury, T. N., Fincham, F. D., and Beach, S. R. (2000). Research on the nature and determinants of marital S=satisfaction: A decade in review. *Journal of Marriage and the Family, 62*(4), 964-80.

Broderick, C., and Smith, J. (1979). The general systems approach to the family. In W. Burr et al. (Eds.), *Contemporary theories about the family, 2*(pp. 112-29). New York: Free Press.

Bronfenbrenner, U. (1979). *The ecology of human development: Experiments by nature and design.* Cambridge, MA: Harvard University Press.

Brooks-Gunn, J., and Reiter, E. O. (1990). The role of pubertal processes. In S. S. Feldman and G. R. Elliott (Eds.), *At the threshold: The developing adolescent* (pp. 16-53). Cambridge, MA: Harvard University Press.

Brown, B. B. (1990). Peer groups and peer cultures. In S. S. Feldman and G. R. Elliott (Eds.), *At the threshold: The developing adolescent* (pp. 171-96). Cambridge, MA: Harvard University Press.

Brown, C. (1991). Trinity and incarnation: In search of contemporary orthodoxy *Ex Auditu, 7,* 83-100.

Brown, W., Murphy, N., and Malony, H. (Eds.). (1998). *Whatever happened to the soul?* Philadelphia: Fortress.

Browning, D. et al. (1997). *From culture wars to common ground: Religion and the American family debate.* Louisville: Westminster John Knox.

Browning, S. (1994). Treating stepfamilies: Alternatives to traditional family therapy. In K. Pasley and M. Ilhinger-Tallman (Eds.), *Stepparenting: Issues in theory, research, and practice* (pp. 175-98). Westport, CT: Greenwood.

Brubaker, T. (1985). *Later life families.* Newbury Park, CA: Sage.

Buber, M. (1970). *I and Thou.* (W. Kaufmann, Trans.). New York: Charles Scribner's.

Canfield, K. (1996). *The heart of a father: How dads can shape the destiny of America.* Chicago: Northfield.

Carstensen, L., and Charles, S. (2003). Human aging: Why is even good news taken as bad? In L. Aspinwall and U. Staudinger (Eds.), *A psychology of human strengths.* Washington, DC: American Psychological Association.

Carter, B., and McGoldrick, M. (Eds.). (1999). *The expanded family life cycle: Individual, family, and social perspectives* (3rd ed.). Boston: Allyn & Bacon.

Caspi, A., Lynam, D., Moffitt, T. E., and Silva, P. A. (1993). Unraveling girls' delinquency: Biological, dispositional, and contextual contributions to adolescent misbehavior. *Developmental Psychology, 29,* 19-30.

Cassidy, J. (1999). The nature of the child's ties. In J. Cassidy and P. R. Shaver (Eds.), *Handbook of attachment: Theory, research, and clinical application* (pp. 3-20). New York: Guilford.

Chao, R. (1994). Beyond parental control and authoritarian parenting style: Understanding Chinese parenting through the cultural notion of training. *Child Development, 65*(4), 1111-19.

Chartier, M. (1978). Parenting: A theological model. *Journal of Psychology and Theology, 6,* 54-61.

Cherniss, C., and Goleman, D. (2001). *The emotionally intelligent workplace.* San Francisco: Jossey-Bass.

Chodorow, N. (1978). *The reproduction of mothering: Psychoanalysis and the sociology of gender.* Berkeley: University of California Press.

Clapp, R. (1993). *Families at the crossroads: Beyond traditional and modern options.* Downers Grove, IL: InterVarsity Press.

Colby, A., and Damon, W. (1992). *Some do care: Contemporary lives of moral commitment.* New York: Free Press.

Colby, A., and Damon, W. (1995). The development of extraordinary moral commitment. In M. Killen and D. Hart (Eds.), *Morality in everyday life: Developmental perspectives* (pp. 342-70). New York: Cambridge University Press.

Colby, A., Kohlberg, L., Gibbs, J., and Lieberman, M. (1983). A longitudinal study of moral judgment. *Monographs for the Society for Research in Child Development, 48* (1-2 serial no. 200). Chicago: University of Chicago Press.

Collins, W. A. (1990). Parent-child relationships in the transition to adolescence: Continuity and change in interaction, affect, and cognition. In R. Montemayor, G. R. Adams and T. P. Gullotta (Eds.), *From childhood to adolescence: A transitional period.* Beverly Hills, CA: Sage.

Curran, D. (1983). *Traits of a healthy family.* Minneapolis: Winston.

Curtis, B., and Eldredge, J. (1997). *The sacred romance: Drawing closer to the heart of God.* Nashville: Thomas Nelson.

Cushman, P. (1995). *Constructing the self, constructing America.* Menlo Park, CA: Addison Wesley.

D'Aquili, E. G., and Newberg, A. B. (1998). The neuropsychological basis of religions, or why God won't go away. *Zygon: Journal of Religion and Science, 33,* 187-201.

Damasio, A. (1994). *Descartes error: Emotion, reason, and the human brain.* New York: Putnam.

Damasio, A. (2002). A note on the neurobiology of emotions. In S. Post, L. Underwood, J. Schloss, and W. Hurlbut (Eds.), *Altruism and altruistic love: Science, philosophy, and religion in practice* (pp. 264-71). New York: Oxford University Press.

Damasio, H. (2002). Impairment of interpersonal social behavior caused by acquired brain damage. In S. Post, L. Underwood, J. Schloss, and W. Hurlbut (Eds.), *Altruism and altruistic love: Science, philosophy, and religion in practice* (pp. 272-84). New York: Oxford University Press.

Damon, W. (2004). What is positive youth development? *The Annals of the American Academy, 591,* 13-24.

Damon, W. (Ed.). (1983). *Social and Personality Development.* New York: W. W. Norton.

Damon, W., Menon, J., and Bronk, K. (2003). The development of purpose during adolescence. *Applied Developmental Sciences, 7*(3), 119-27.

Davis, F. (1967). Why all of us may be hippies someday. *Transaction, 26,* 10-18.

Deddo, G. (1999). *Karl Barth's theology of relations, trinitarian, christological, and human: Towards an ethic of the family.* New York: Peter Lang.

Derrida, J. (1980). *Writing and difference.* Chicago: University of Chicago Press.

Donahue, M. J., and Benson, P. L. (1995). Religion and the well being of adolescents. *Journal of Social Issues, 51*(2), 145-60.

Dreikurs, R., and Soltz, V. (1964). *Children: The challenge.* Des Moines, IA: Meredith.

Eccles, J. S., and Gootman, J. A. (2002). *Community programs to promote youth development.* Washington DC: National Academy Press.

Ehrensaft, D. (1990). *Parenting together: Men and women sharing the care of their children.* Chicago: University of Illinois Press.

Elkind, D. (1997). The origins of religion in the child. In B. Spilka and D. N. McIntosh (Eds.), *The psychology of religion: Theoretical approaches* (pp. 97–104). Boulder, CO: Westview.

Emmons, R. (1999). *The psychology of ultimate concerns.* New York: Guilford.

Emmons, R. A., and Paloutzian, R. F. (2003). The psychology of religion. *Annual Review of Psychology, 54,* 377-402.

Erikson, E. (1968). *Identity: Youth and crisis.* New York: Norton.

Erikson, E. (1982). *The life cycle completed.* New York: Norton.

Erikson, E. H. (1950). *Childhood and society.* New York: Norton.

Erikson, E. H. (1959). Identity and the life cycle. *Psychological Issues, 1,* 18-164.

Falbo, J. (1981). Relationships between birth category, achievement, and interpersonal orientation. *Journal of Personality and Social Psychology, 41,* 121-31.

Feldman, S. S., and Elliott, R. (Eds.). (1990). *At the threshold.* Cambridge, MA: Harvard University Press.

Fernandez-Ballesteros, R. (2003). Light and dark in the psychology of human strengths: The example of psychogerontology. In L. Aspinwall and U. Staudinger (Eds.), *A psychology of human strengths.* Washington DC: American Psychological Association.

Fetzer, J. (1999). *Multidimensional measurement of religiousness/spirituality for use in health research.* Kalamazoo, MI: John E. Fetzer Institute.

Fisher, H. (1996). The origin of romantic love and human family life. *National Forum, 76,* 31-34.

Flavell, J. (1963). *The developmental psychology of Jean Piaget.* Princeton, NJ: Van Nostrand.

Flavell, J. (1985). *Cognitive development* (2nd ed.). Englewood Cliffs, NJ: Prentice-Hall.

Ford, D., and Lerner, R. (1992). *Developmental systems theory: An integrative approach.* Newbury Park, CA: Sage.

Foucault, M. (1984). *The Foucault reader.* New York: Random House.

Fowler, J. (1995). *Stages of faith: The psychology of human development.* San Francisco: HarperCollins.

Fowler, J. W. (1981). *Stages of faith: The psychology of human development and the quest for meaning.* San Francisco: HarperSanFrancisco.

Francis, J. (1996). Children and childhood in the New Testament. In S. Barton (Ed.), *The family in theological perspective* (pp. 65-85). Edinburgh: T & T Ltd.

Freud, S. (1949). *An outline of psychoanalysis.* New York: Norton.

Freud, S. (1954). *The origins of psychoanalysis: Sigmund Freud's letters.* New York: Basic Books. (Original work published 1895.)

Frishman, R. (1997). The race for Alzheimer's treatments. *Harvard Health Letter, 22*(7), 1-3.

Fromm, E. (1956). *The art of loving.* New York: Bantam Books.

Fromm, E. (1964). *The heart of man: Its genius for good and evil.* New York: Harper & Row.

Fromm, E. (1976). *To have or to be?* New York: Harper & Row.

Furrow, J. L., King, P. E., and White, K. (2004). Religion and positive youth development: Identity, meaning, and prosocial concerns. *Applied Developmental Science, 8,* 17-26.

Gadamer, H. G. (1993). *Truth and method.* New York: Continuum.

Gallup, G. H., and Bezilla, R. (1992). *The religious life of young Americans: A compendium on the spiritual beliefs and practices of teenagers and young adults.* Princeton, NJ: G. H. Gallup International Institute.

Gallup International Association. (1999). Gallup international millennium survey. Available: www.gallup-international.com/surveys1.htm.

Gardner, H. (1983). *Frames of mind.* New York: Basic Books.

Garland, D., Richmond, S., and Garland, D. E. (1986). *Beyond companionship: Christians in marriage.* Philadelphia: Westminster Press.

Gay, C. (1998). *The way of the modern world.* Grand Rapids: Eerdmans.

Gergen, K. (1991). *The saturated self: Dilemmas of identity in contemporary life.* New York: Basic Books.

Gibson, E. (1988). Levels of description and constraints on perceptual development. In A. Yonas (Ed.), *Perceptual development in infancy.* Hillsdale, NJ: Erlbaum.

Gibson, E. (1997). An ecological psychologist's prolegomena for perceptual development: A functional approach. In C. Dent-Read and P. Zukow-Goldring (Eds.), *Evolving explanations of development: Ecological approaches to organism-environment systems*. Washington, DC: American Psychological Association.

Giedd, J. N. et al. (1999). Brain development during childhood and adolescence: a longitudinal MRI study. *Nature Neuroscience, 2*(10), 861-863.

Gilligan, C. (1982). *In a different voice: Psychological theory and women's development*. Cambridge, MA: Harvard University Press.

Goldscheider, F., and Davanzo, J. (1986). Semiautonomy and leaving home during early adulthood. *Social Forces, 65,* 187-201.

Goldscheider, F., and Goldscheider, C. (1994). *Leaving and returning home in the 20th-century America*. Washington DC: Population Reference Bureau.

Goldsworthy, G. (1987). *Gospel and wisdom: Israel's wisdom literature and the Christian life*. Greenwood, SC: Attic Press.

Goode, E. (1999, February 14). Middle age is prime of life. *New York Times*.

Goleman, D. (1995). *Emotional intelligence: Why it can matter more than IQ*. New York: Basic Books.

Gottman, J. (1994). *Why marriages succeed or fail*. New York: Simon & Schuster.

Gould, R. (1978). *Transformations: Growth and change in adult life*. New York: Simon & Schuster.

Gray-Little, B., and Burks, N. (1983). Power and satisfaction in marriage. *Psychological Bulletin, 93,3,* 513-38.

Green, J. (1998). "Bodies—that is, human lives": A re-examination of human nature in the Bible. In W. Brown, N. Murphy and H. Malony (Eds.), *Whatever happened to the soul?* (pp. 149-73). Philadelphia: Fortress.

Grenz, S. J. (2001). *The social God and the relational self: A trinitarian theology of the imago Dei* (Vol. 1). Louisville: Westminster John Knox.

Grolnick, S. A. (1990). *The work and play of Winnicott*. Northvale, NJ: Jason Aronson.

Gunton, C. E. (1993). *The one, the three and the many: God, creation and the culture of modernity*. Cambridge: Cambridge University Press.

Haith, M. (1993). Preparing for the 21st century: Some goals and challenges for studies of infant sensory and perceptual development. *Developmental Review, 13,* 354-71.

Hall, G. S. (1904). *Adolescence: Its psychology and its relations to physiology, anthropology, sociology, sex, crime, religion, and education*. New York: D. Appleton.

Hargrave, T., and Hanna, S. (1997). *The aging family: New visions in theory, practice and reality*. New York: Brunner/Mazel.

Hart, D., Atkins, R., and Ford, D. (1998). Urban America as a context for the development of moral identity in adolescence. *Journal of Social Issues, 54,* 513-30.

Hart, D., and Fegley S. (1995). Prosocial behavior and caring in adolescence: Relations to self-understanding and social judgment. *Child Development, 66,* 1346-59.

Harter, S. (1999). *The construction of the self: A developmental perspective*. New York: Guilford.

Hass, L. (1992). *Equal parenthood and social policy*. New York: State University of New York Press.

Hauerwas, S. (1981). *A community of character: Toward a constructive Christian social ethic*. Notre Dame, Ind.: University of Notre Dame Press.

Hayne, H. (2002). Thoughts from the crib: Meltzoff and Moore alter our views of mental representation during infancy. *Infant Behavior and Development, 25*(1), 62-64.

Hays, R. B. (1996). *The moral vision of the New Testament: A contemporary introduction to New Testament ethics*. San Francisco: HarperSanFrancisco.

Heckhausen, J., Dixon, R. A., and Baltes, P. B. (1989). Gains and losses in development throughout adulthood as perceived by different adult age groups. *Developmental Psychology, 25,* 109-21.

Heine, S. J. (2001). Self as a product of culture: An examination of East Asian and North American selves. *Journal of Personality, 69,* 881-906.

Heinemann, G., and Evans, P. (1990). Widowhood: Loss, change, and adaptation. In T. Brubaker (Ed.), *Family relationships in later life* (pp. 142-68). Newbury Park, CA: Sage.

Hetherington, E. (1972). Effects of father absence on personality development in adolescent daughters. *Developmental Psychology, 7,* 313-26.

Hetherington, E. (1993). An overview of the Virginia Longitudinal Study of Divorce and Remarriage with a focus on the early adolescent. *Journal of Family Psychology, 7,* 39-56.

Hetherington, E., Camara, K., and Feathermore, D. (1983). Achievement and intellectual functioning of children in one-parent households. In J. Spence (Ed.), *Achievement and achievement motives* (pp. 205-84). San Francisco: Freeman.

Hetherington, E., Cox, M., and Cox, R. (1982). Effects of divorce on parents and children. In M. Lanab (Ed.), *Nontraditional families: Parenting and child development by M. Lamb* (pp. 233-88). Hillsdale, NJ: P. Erlbaum.

Hetherington, E., and Kelly, J. (2003). *For better or worse: Divorce reconsidered*. New York: Norton.

Hiebert, Paul (1978). Conversion, culture and cognitive categories. *Gospel in Context, 1*(4), 24-29.

Hodgson, L. (1995). Adult grandchildren and their grandparents: The enduring bond. In J. Hendricks (Ed.), *The ties of later life*. Amityville, NY: Baywood.

Hoekena, A. (1986). *Created in God's image*. Grand Rapids: Eerdmans.

Holman, T. B., Larson, J. H., and Harmer, S. L. (1994). The development and predictive validity of a new premarital assessment instrument: The preparation for marriage questionnaire. *Family Relations, 43,* 46-52.

Horn, J. (1982). The aging of human abilities. In Benjamin B. Wolman (Ed.), *Hand-*

book of developmental psychology. New York: Wiley.

Jahoda, M. (1958). *Current concepts of positive mental health*. Oxford: Basic Books.

James, W. (1902). *The varieties of religious experience*. New York: Modern Library.

James, W. (1929). The varieties of religious experience: A study in human nature. *Being the Gifford lectures on natural religion delivered in Edinburgh in 1901-1902*. New York: Modern Library.

Jeeves, M. (1998). Brain, mind, and behavior. In W. Brown, N. Murphy, and H. Malony (Eds.), *Whatever happened to the soul?* Philadelphia: Fortress.

Jewett, P. K. (1991). *God, creation and revelation*. Grand Rapids: Eerdmans.

Johnson, C. (1988). Post-divorce reorganization of relationships between divorcing children and their parents. *Journal of Marriage and the Family, 50*, 221-31.

Jonsson, C., et al. (2001). How do mothers signal shared feeling-states to their infants? An investigation of affect attunement and imitation during the first year of life. *Scandinavian Journal of Psychology, 42*, 377-81.

Jusczyk, P. (1995). Language acquisition: Speech sounds and the beginnings of phonology. In J. Miller and P. Eimas (Eds.), *Speech, language, and communication*. New York: Academic Press.

Keating, D. P. (1990). Adolescent thinking. In S. S. Feldman and G. R. Elliott (Eds.), *At the threshold: The developing adolescent* (pp. 54-89). Cambridge, MA: Harvard University Press.

Kegan, R. (1982). *The evolving self: Problem and process in human development*. Cambridge, MA: Harvard University Press.

Keltner, D., and Haidt, J. (2003). Approaching awe, a moral, spiritual, and aesthetic emotion. *Cognition and Emotion, 17*(2), 297–314.

Kerestes, M., and Youniss, J. (2002). Rediscovering the importance of religion in adolescent development. In R. M. Lerner, F. Jacobs, and D. Wertlieb (Eds.), *Handbook of applied developmental science: Promoting positive child, adolescent, and family development through research, policies, and programs: Vol. 1. Applying developmental science for youth and families: Historical and theoretical foundations* (pp. 165-84). Thousand Oaks, CA: Sage.

King, P. E. (2003). Religion and identity: The role of ideological, social, and spiritual contexts. *Applied Developmental Sciences, 7*(3), 196-203.

King, P. E., and Furrow, J. L. (2004). Religion as a resource for positive youth development: Religion, social capital, and moral outcomes. *Developmental Psychology, 40*(5), 703-13.

King, P. E., Furrow, J. L., and Roth, N. H. (2002). The influence of family and peers on adolescent religiousness. *The Journal for Psychology and Christianity, 21*(2), 109-20.

King, P. E., and Mueller, R. A. (2004). Parents' influence on adolescent religiousness: Spiritual modeling and spiritual capital. *Marriage and family: A Christian journal, 6*(3), 413-25.

Kirkpatrick, L. (1999). *Attachment and religious representations and behavior.* In J. Cassidy and P. R. Shaver (Eds.), *Handbook of attachment: Theory, research and clinical applications* (pp. 803-22). New York: Guilford.

Kivnick, J. (1982). *The meaning of grandparenthood.* Ann Arbor: University of Michigan Press.

Klein, M. (1932). *The psychoanalysis of children.* London: Hogarth.

Koenig, H. G., McCullough, M. E., and Larson, D. B. (2001). *Handbook of religion and health.* London: Oxford University Press.

Kohlberg, L. (1963). Moral development and identification. In H. Stevenson (Ed.), *Child psychology: Sixty-second yearbook of the National Society for the Study of Education* (pp. 277-332). Chicago: University of Chicago Press.

Kohlberg, L. (1984). *Essays on moral development: Vol. 2. The psychology of moral development.* San Francisco: Harper & Row.

Kohlberg, L., and Diessner, F. (1991). A cognitive-developmental approach to moral attachment. In J. Gewirtz and W. Kurtines (Eds.), *Intersections with attachment* (pp. 229-46). Hillsdale, NJ: Erlbaum.

Kornhaber, A. (1996). *Contemporary grandparenting.* Thousand Oaks, CA: Sage.

Kübler-Ross, E. (1970). *On death and dying.* New York: Macmillan.

Kuhn, M., and McPartland, T. (1954). An empirical investigation of self-attitudes. *American Sociological Review, 19,* 68-75.

Langer, N. (1990). Grandparents and adult grandchildren: What do they do for one another? *International Journal of Aging and Human Development, 31,* 101-10.

Larson, R. W., and Verma, S. (1999). How children and adolescents spend time across the world: Work, play, and developmental opportunities. *Psychological Bulletin, 125*(6), 701-36.

Lee, C., and Balswick, J. (1989). *Life in a glass house: The minister's family in its unique social context.* Grand Rapids: Zondervan.

Lemme, B. (1999). *Development in adulthood* (2nd ed.). Needham Heights, MA: Allyn & Bacon.

Lerner, R. M. (2002). *Concepts and theories of human development* (3rd ed.). Mahwah, NJ: Lawrence Erlbaum.

Lerner, R. M. (2004). *Liberty: Thriving and civic engagement among America's youth.* Thousand Oaks, CA: Sage.

Lerner, R. M., Alberts, A. E., Anderson, P. M., and Dowling, E. M. (forthcoming). On making humans human: Spirituality and the promotion of positive youth development. In G. C. Roehlkepartain, P. E. King, L. M. Wagener and P. L. Benson (Eds.), *The handbook of spiritual development in childhood and adolescence.* Newbury Park, CA: Sage.

Lerner, R. M., Dowling, E. M., and Anderson, P. M. (2003). Positive youth development: Thriving as the basis of personhood and civil society. *Applied Developmental Sciences,* 7(3), 171-79.

Levinson, D. (1978). *The seasons of a man's life.* New York: Knopf.

Levinson, D. (1996). *The seasons of a woman's life.* New York: Knopf.

Lewis, M., and Brooks-Gunn, J. (1978). *Social cognition and the acquisition of self.* New York: Plenum.

Loder, J. E. (1989). *The transforming moment* (2nd ed.). Colorado Springs: Helmers & Howard.

Loder, J. E. (1998). *The logic of the Spirit: Human development in a theological perspective.* San Francisco: Jossey-Bass.

Long. J. K., and Mancini, J. A. (1990). Aging couples and the family system. In T. Brubaker (Ed.), *Family relationships in later life* (2nd ed.) (pp. 29-47). Newbury Park, CA: Sage.

Lyon, K. B. (1985). *Toward a practical theology of aging.* Philadelphia: Fortress.

Lyotard, J. F. (1985). *The postmodern condition.* Minneapolis: University of Minnesota Press.

MacFarlane, J. (1975). *The psychology of childbirth.* Cambridge, MA: Harvard University Press.

MacKay, D. (1974). *The clockwork image.* Downers Grove, IL: InterVarsity Press.

Macmurray, J. (1961). *Persons in relation.* London: Faber & Faber.

Magnusson, D. (1988). *Individual development from an international perspective.* Hillsdale, NJ: Lawrence Erlbaum.

Marler, P. L., and Hadaway, C. K. (2002). "Being religious" or "being spiritual" in America: A zero-sum proposition? *Journal for the Scientific Study of Religion, 41*(2), 289-300.

Mannheim, K. (1952). The problem of generations. In D. Kecskemeti (Ed.), *Essays on the sociology of knowledge.* London: Routledge & Kegan Paul.

Marcia, J. (1980). Ego identity development. In J. Adelson (Ed.), *Handbook of adolescent psychology.* New York: Wiley.

Markstrom, C. A. (1999). Religious involvement and adolescent psychosocial development. *Journal of Adolescence, 22,* 205-21.

Markstrom, C. A., and Kalmanir, H. M. (2001). Linkages between the psychosocial stages of identity and intimacy and the ego strengths of fidelity and love. *Identity: An International Journal of Theory and Research, 1*(2), 179-96.

Markstrom, C. A., Sabino, V., Turner, B., and Berman, R. (1997). The psychosocial inventory of ego strengths: Development and validation of a new Eriksonian measure. *Journal of Youth and Adolescence, 26,* 705-32.

Marler, P. L., and Hadaway, C. K. (2002). "Being religious" or "being spiritual" in America: A zero-sum proposition? *Journal for the Scientific Study of Religion, 41*(2), 289-300.

Masten A., and Coatsworth, D. (1995). Competence, resilience, and psychopathology. In D. Cicchetti and D. Cohen (Eds.), *Developmental psychopathology: Volume 2. Risk, disorder, and adaptation* (pp. 715-52). New York: John Wiley.

Matson, F. (1966). *The broken image: Man, science and society.* Garden City, NY: Anchor.

Mattis, J. S., Ahluwalia, M. K., and Cowie, S.-A. E. (forthcoming). Ethnicity, culture and spiritual development. In E. C. Roehlkepartain, P. E. King, L. M. Wagener and P. L. Benson (Eds.), *The handbook of spiritual development in childhood and adolescence.* Newbury Park, CA: Sage.

May, R. (1969). *Love and will.* New York: Norton.

Mayer, J., and Salovey, P. (1997). What is emotional intelligence? In P. Salovey and D. J. Sluyter (Eds.), *Emotional development and emotional intelligence: Educational implications* (pp. 68-84). New York: Basic Books.

McAdams, D. (1993). *The stories we live by.* New York: Guilford.

McCullough, P., and Rutenberg, S. (1989). Launching children and moving on. In E. Carter and M. McGoldrick (Eds.), *The changing family life cycle: A framework for family therapy* (pp. 285-309). Needham Heights, MA: Allyn & Bacon.

McDonald, G. (1980). Family power: The assessment of a decade of theory and research, 1970-1979. *Journal of Marriage and the Family, 42,* 841-54.

McGoldrick, M., and Carter, B. (1980). Forming a remarried family. In B. Carter and M. McGoldrick (Eds.), *The family life cycle* (pp. 265-94). New York: Gardner.

McLean, S. (1984). *The language of covenant and a theology of the family.* Paper presented at the Consultation on a Theology of the Family, Fuller Theological Seminary, Pasadena, CA.

Mead, G. H. (1934). *Mind, self and society.* Chicago: University of Chicago Press.

Mead, M. (1928). *Coming of age in Samoa.* New York: Mentor.

Meltzoff, A. N., and Borton, R. W. (1979). Intermodal matching by human neonates. *Nature, 282*(5737), 403-4.

Michael, R. T., Gagnon, J. H., Laumann, E. O., and Kolata, G. (1995). *Sex in America: A definitive survey.* New York: Warner Books.

Miller, W. R., and Thoresen, C. E. (2003). Spirituality, religion, and health: An emerging research field. *American Psychologist, 58,* 24-35.

Mogelonsky, M. (1996). The rocky road to adulthood. *American Demographics, 18*(5), 26-35, 56.

Moltmann, J., (1996). *The coming of God: Christian eschatology.* Minneapolis: Fortress.

Mortimer, J. T., and Larson, R. W. (Eds.). (2002). *The changing adolescent experience: Societal trends and the transition to adulthood.* New York: Cambridge University Press.

Mowrer, O. H. (1961). *The crisis in psychiatry and religion.* Princeton, NJ: Van Nostrand.

Murphy, C., and Messer, D. (1977). Mothers, infants, and pointing: A study of gesture. In H. Schaffer (Ed.), *Studies in mother-infant interaction*. London: Academic Press.

Neal, C. (1995). The power of Vygotsky. In J. Wilhoit and J. Dettoni (Eds.), *Nurture that is Christian: Developmental perspectives in Christian education* (pp. 123-38). Wheaton, IL: Victor.

Nietzsche, F. W. (1989). *Beyond good and evil: Prelude to a philosophy of the future* (Walter Kaufman, Trans.), New York: Vintage.

Neufeld, G. (2004). The relationship between God image and attachment in a large university sample. Unpublished master's thesis, Mennonite Brethren Biblical Seminary, Fresno, CA.

Neugarten, B., and Weinstein, K. (1964). The changing American grandparent. *Journal of Marriage and the Family, 26,* 199-204.

Neuhaus, R. J. (2000). *Death on a Friday afternoon: Meditations on the last words of Jesus from the cross.* New York: Basic Books.

O'Connor, K., and Ammen, S. (1997). *Play therapy treatment planning and interventions.* New York: Academic Press.

Olson, D., Sprenkle, D., and Russell, E. (1979). Circumplex model of marital and family systems: Cohesion and adaptability dimensions, family types, and clinical applications. *Family Process, 18,* 3-28.

Orr, J. B., Miller, D. E., Roof, W. C., and Melton, J. G. (1995). *Politics of the Spirit: Religion and multiethnicity in Los Angeles.* Los Angeles: University of Southern California.

Paikoff, R., and Brooks-Gunn, J. (1991). Do parent-child relationships change during puberty? *Psychological Bulletin, 110,* 47-66.

Patios, M. (1984). *The church and the healing of families.* A paper read at the Consultation on a Theology of the Family Seminar, Fuller Theological Seminary, Pasadena, CA.

Pattison, E. M. (1977). *The experience of dying.* Englewood Cliffs, NJ: Prentice-Hall.

Pattison, M. (1984). *Intimate, personal, and social networks.* Paper presented at the Consultation on a Theology of the Family. Fuller Theological Seminary, Pasadena, CA.

Peters, T. (1994). *Sin: Radical evil in soul and society.* Grand Rapids: Eerdmans.

Peters, T. (1996). *For the love of children: Genetic technology and the future of the family.* Louisville: Westminster John Knox.

Peterson, G., and Rollins, B. (1987). Parent-child socialization. In M. Sussman and S. Steinmetz (Eds.), *Handbook of marriage and the family* (pp. 471-507). New York: Plenum.

Pettingell, J. (1959, May). Junior at Rich High School has outstanding record. *Park Forest Star,* Park Forest, IL.

Piaget, J. (1965). *The moral judgment of the child* (M. Gabain, Trans.). New York: Free Press. (Originally published in 1932.)

Pinker, S. (1994). *The language instinct*. New York: Norton.

Piper, B., and Balswick, J. K. (1997). *Then they leave home: Parenting after the kids grow up*. Downers Grove, IL: InterVarsity Press.

Pipher, M. (1994). *Reviving Ophelia*. New York: Ballantine.

Plantinga, C. (1989). Social Trinity and tritheism. In R. J. Feenstra and C. Plantinga (Eds.), *Trinity, Incarnation and Atonement: Philosophical and Theological Essays* (pp. 21-47). Notre Dame, IN: University of Notre Dame Press.

Ponzetti, J., and Folkrod, A. (1989). Grandchildren's perceptions of their relationships with their grandparents. *Child Study Journal, 19,* 41-50.

Post, S. G. (1994). *Spheres of love: Toward a new ethics of the family*. Dallas: Southern Methodist University Press.

Post, S. G. (2002). The tradition of agape. In S. Post, L. Underwood, J. Schloss and W. Hurlbut (Eds.), *Altruism and altruistic love: Science, philosophy, and religion in dialogue* (pp. 89-105). Oxford: Oxford University Press.

Presbyterian Church (U.S.A.) (2002). *Book of confessions*. Louisville, KY: Office of the General Assembly.

Pruyser, P. (1975). Aging: Downward, upward or forward? *Toward a theology of aging: A special issue of Pastoral Psychology, 24*(229), 102-18.

Putman, D. D. (2000). *Bowling alone: The collapse and revival of American community*. New York: Simon & Schuster.

Reimer, K. (2003). Committed to caring: Transformation in adolescent moral identity. *Applied Developmental Science, 7,* 129-37.

Reimer, K., and Wade-Stein, D. (2004). Moral identity in adolescence: Self and other in semantic space. *Identity, 3,* 349-66.

Reimer, K., and Walker, L. J. (2004). *Altruistic love and spirituality in L'Arche assistants for the developmentally disabled*. Paper presentation, Society for Research on Adolescence (SRA) bi-annual conference, Baltimore, MD, March 11-14.

Reimer, K. S., and Furrow, J. L. (2001). A qualitative exploration of relational consciousness in Christian children. *International Journal of Christian's Spirituality, 6*(1), 7-23.

Reiss, I. (1980). *Family systems in America* (3rd ed). New York: Holt, Rinehart & Winston.

Resnick, M. D., et al. (1997). Protecting adolescents from harm: Findings from the National Longitudinal Study on Adolescent Health. *Journal of the American Medical Association, 278*(10), 823-32.

Rest, J. (1983). Morality. In P. Mussen, J. Flavell and E. Markman (Eds.), *Handbook of child psychology, volume 3: Cognitive development* (4th ed.). New York: Wiley.

Riegel, K. (1973). Dialectical operations: The final period of cognitive development. *Human Development, 16,* 346-70.

Rochlkcpartain, E. C. (forthcoming). Congregations: Unexamined crucibles for spiritual development. In G. C. Roehlkepartain, P. E. King, L. M. Wagener and P. L. Benson (Eds.), *The handbook of spiritual development in childhood and adolescence.* Newbury Park, CA: Sage.

Roehlkepartain, E. C., King, P. E., Wagener, L. M., and Benson, P. L. (2005). *The handbook for spiritual development in childhood and adolescence.* Newbury Park, CA: Sage.

Rogerson, J. (1996). The family and structures of grace in the Old Testament. In S. Barton (Ed.), *The family in theological perspective* (pp. 25-42). Edinburgh: T & T Ltd.

Rogoff, Barbara. (1990). Apprenticeship in thinking: Cognitive development in social context. New York: Oxford University Press.

Rollins, B. C., and Thomas, D. L. (1979). Parental support, power, and control techniques in the socialization of children. In W. R. Burr, R. Hill, F. I. Nye and I. L. Reiss (Eds.), *Contemporary Theories about the Family: Vol. I* (pp. 317-64). New York: Free Press.

Rowe, J , and Kahn, R. (1997). Human aging: Usual and successful. *Science, 237,* 143-49.

Ruben, K. H., Bukowski, W., and Parker, J. G. (1998). Peer interactions, relationships, and groups. In W. Damon and N. Eisenberg (Eds.), *Handbook of child psychology* (pp. 619-700). New York: Wiley.

Ruth, J., and Vilkko, A. (1996). Emotion in the construction of autobiography. In C. Magai and S. McFadden (Eds.), *Handbook of emotion, adult development, and aging.* San Diego: Academic Press.

Safilios-Rothchild, C. (1970). The study of family power structure: A review, 1960-1969. *Journal of Marriage and the Family, 32,* 539-52.

Salovey, J., and Mayer, J. D. (1990). Notes from emotional intelligence. *Imagination, Cognition, and Personality, 9,* 185-211.

Salthouse, T. A. (1991). *Theoretical perspectives on cognitive aging.* Hillsdale, NJ: Lawrence Erlbaum.

Scales, P. C., et al. (2003). *Other people's kids: Social expectations and American adults' involvement with children and adolescents.* New York: Kluwer/Plenum.

Scales, P., Benson, P., Leffert, N., and Blyth, D. A. (2000). The contribution of developmental assets to the prediction of thriving among adolescents. *Applied Developmental Science, 4,* 27-46.

Scanzoni, J. (1979). Social processes and power in families. In W. Burr (Ed.), *Contemporary theories about the family* (pp. 295-316). New York: Free Press.

Schaie, K. W. (1994). The course of adult intellectual development. *American Psychologist, 49*(4), 304-13.

Schore, A. (1994). *Affect regulation and the origin of the self: The neurobiology of emotional development*. Hillsdale, NJ: Erlbaum.

Selby, P. (1996). Is the church a family? In S. Barton (Ed.), *The family in theological perspective* (pp. 151-68). Edinburgh: T & T Ltd.

Shapiro, P. (1996). *My turn: Women's search for self after children leave*. Princeton, NJ: Petersons's Guides.

Shaver, P., Hazan, C., and Bradshaw, D. (1988). Love as attachment: The integration of three behavioral systems. In R. Sternberg and M. Barnes (Eds.), *The psychology of love* (pp. 68-99). New Haven, CT: Yale University Press.

Sheehy, G. (1978). *Passages*. New York: Bantam.

Sheehy, G. (1991). *The silent passage*. New York: Random House.

Shucksmith J., Hendry, L. B., and Glendinning, A. (1995). Models of parenting: implications for adolescent well being within different types of family contexts. *Journal of Adolescence 18*, 253-70.

Shulman, S., et al. (1995). Peer group and family relationships in early adolescence. *International Journal of Psychology, 30*, 573-90.

Shults, F. L. (2003). *Reforming theological anthropology: After the philosophical turn to relationality*. Grand Rapids: Eerdmans.

Shweder, R., Mahapatra, M., and Miller, J. (1987). Culture and moral development. In J. Kagan and S. Lamb (Eds.), *The emergence of morality in young children* (pp. 1-83). Chicago: University of Chicago Press.

Siqueland, E., and Delucia, C. (1969). Visual reinforcement of non-nutritive sucking in human infants. *Science, 165*, 1144-46.

Skinner, B., F. (1953). *Science and human behavior*. New York: Macmillan.

Small, S., and Riley, D. (1990, February). Assessment of work spillover into family life. *Journal of Marriage and the Family, 52*, 31-38.

Smetana, J. G. (1995). Parenting styles and conceptions of parental authority during adolescence. *Child Development, 66*(2), 299-316.

Smetana, J. G., Yau, J., and Hanson, S. (1991). Conflict resolution in families with adolescents. *Journal of Research on Adolescence, 1*(2), 189-206.

Smith, C. (2003). Theorizing religious effects among American adolescents. *Journal for the Scientific Study of Religion, 42*(1), 17-30.

Smith, C., and Denton, M. L. (2005). *Soul searching: The religious and spiritual lives of American teenagers*. New York: Oxford University Press.

Smith, D. M. (1995). *The theology of John*. New York: Cambridge University Press

Smith, L. (2001, August 12). Betwixt and bewildered: Scholars are intrigued by angst of emerging adults. *Los Angeles Times,* pp. E1, E4.

Stackhouse, M. (1997). *Covenant and commitments: Faith, family and economic life*. Louisville, KY: Westminster John Knox.

Stattin, H., and Magnusson, D. (1990). *Pubertial maturation in female development*. Hillsdale, NJ: Lawrence Erlbaum.

Stern, D. (2000). *The interpersonal world of the infant: A view from psychoanalysis and developmental psychology* (Rev. ed). New York: Basic Books.

Sternberg, R. (1986a). *Intelligence applied.* San Diego: Harcourt Brace Jovanovich.

Sternberg. R. (1986b). A triangular theory of love. *Psychological Review, 93,* 119-135.

Sternberg, R. (1999). Intelligence. In M. Runco and S. Pritzker (Eds.), *Encyclopedia of creativity.* San Diego: Academic Press.

Strassberg, Z., Dodge, K., Pettit, G., and Bates, J. (1994). Spanking in the home and children's subsequent aggression toward kindergarten peers. *Development and Psychopathology, 6,* 445-62.

Strauss, W., and Howe, N. (1991). *Generations: The history of America's future, 1584-2069.* New York: Morrow.

Suggate, A. M. (1996). Ideology, power and the family. In S. Barton (Ed.), *The family in theological perspective* (pp. 237-52). Edinburgh: T & T Ltd.

Swensen, C. (1994). Older individuals in the family. In L. L'Abate (Ed.), *Handbook of developmental family psychology and psychopathology.* New York: John Wiley.

Szinovacz, M. (1987). Family power. In M. Sussman and S. Steinmetz (Eds.), *Handbook of marriage and the family* (pp. 651-93). New York: Plenum.

Tarnas, R. (1991). *The passion of the Western mind: Understand the ideas that have shaped our worldview.* New York: Ballantine.

Torrance, J. (1975). *Reformed theology: A critique of the covenant concept.* A paper read at a colloquium at Fuller Theological Seminary, Pasadena, CA.

Torrance, J. B. (1989). The doctrine of the Trinity in our contemporary situation. In A. I. C. Heron, (Ed.), *The forgotten Trinity: Study Commission on Trinitarian Doctrine Today.* London: British Council of Churches, 1989.

Torrance, J. B. (1997). *Worship, community and the triune God of grace.* Downers Grove, IL: InterVarsity Press.

Torrance, Thomas F. (1992). *The mediation of Christ.* Colorado Springs, CO: Helmers & Howard.

Trevarthen, C., and Aitken, K. (2001). Infant intersubjectivity: Research theory and clinical applications. *Journal of Child Psychology and Psychiatry and Allied Disciplines, 42,* 3-48.

Turiel, E. (1983). *The development of social knowledge: Morality and convention.* Cambridge: Cambridge University Press.

U. S. Bureau of the Census (1997). *Statistical abstracts of the United States: 1997.* Washington DC: U. S. Bureau of the Census.

Vaillant, G. (1977). *Adaptation to life.* Boston: Little, Brown.

Vanier, J. (1999). *Becoming human.* New York: Paulist.

Van Leeuwen, M. (1990). *Gender and grace: Love, work and parenting in a changing world.* Downers Grove, IL: InterVarsity Press.

Van Leeuwen, M., et al. (1993). *After Eden: Facing the challenge of gender reconciliation*. Grand Rapids: Eerdmans.

Vasey, M. (1996). The family and the liturgy. In S. Barton (Ed.), *The family in theological perspective* (pp. 169-85). Edinburgh: T & T Ltd.

Viorst, J. (1986). *Necessary losses*. New York: Ballantine.

Visher, E. B., and Visher, S. J. (1988). *Old loyalties, new ties: Therapeutic strategies with stepfamilies*. New York: Brunner/Mazel.

Volf, M. (1998). *After our likeness: The church and the image of community*. Grand Rapids: Eerdmans

Vygotsky, L. (1978). *Mind in society: The development of higher psychological process* (M. Cole, Ed.). Cambridge, MA: MIT Press.

Vygotsky, L. (1986). *Thought and language* (E. Hanfmann and G. Vakar, Ed. and Trans.). Cambridge, MA: MIT Press. (Originally published in 1937.)

Wagener, L. M., et al. (2003). Religion and developmental resources. *Review of Religious Research, 44*(3), 271-84.

Walker, K. A, Pratt, C., and Eddy, L. (1995). Informal caregiving to aging family members. *Family Relations, 44*, 402-11.

Walker, L. J., and Hennig, K. H. (2004). Differing conceptions of moral exemplarity: Just, brave, and caring. *Journal of Personality and Social Psychology, 86*, 629-47.

Walker, L. J., and Pitts, R. C. (1998). Naturalistic conceptions of moral maturity. *Developmental Psychology, 34*(3), 403-19.

Walker, L., and Reimer, K. S. (forthcoming). The relationship between moral and spiritual development. In E. C. Roehlkepartain, P. E. King, L. M. Wagener and P. L. Benson (Eds.), *The handbook of spiritual development in childhood and adolescence*. Newbury Park, CA: Sage.

Waterman, A. L. (1982). Identity development from adolescence to adulthood: An extension of theory and a review of research. *Developmental Psychology, 18*, 341-58.

Wenar, C., and Kerig, P. (1999). *Developmental psychopathology: From infancy through adolescence*. New York: McGraw Hill.

Werner, E., and Smith, R. (2001). *Journeys from childhood to midlife: Risk, resilience, and recovery*. Ithaca, NY: Cornell University Press.

Whitbourne, S. (1996). *The aging individual: Physical and psychological perspectives*. New York: Springer.

Wigfield, A., et al. (1991). Transitions during early adolescence: Changes in children's domain-specific self-perceptions and general self-esteem across the transition to junior high school. *Developmental Psychology, 27*(4), 552-565.

Wilder, J. E. (1993). *Life passages for men*. Ann Arbor, MI: Servant.

Willis, S. (1989). Adult intelligence. In S. Hunter and M. Sundel (Eds.), *Midlife myths: Issues, findings, and practice implications* (pp. 97-112). Newbury Park, CA: Sage.

Winnicott, D. (1971). *Playing and reality.* London: Tavistock.

Witte, J. (1997). *From sacrament to contract: Marriage, religion, and law in the Western tradition.* Louisville: Westminster John Knox.

Youniss, J., McLellan, J. A., and Yates, M. (1999). Religion, community service, and identity in American youth. *Journal of Adolescence, 22*(2), 243-53.

Youniss, J., and Yates, M. (1997). *Community service and social responsibility in youth.* Chicago: University of Chicago Press.

Zizioulas, J. (1985). *Being as communion: Studies in personhood and the church.* Crestwood, NY: St. Vladimir's Seminary Press.

Names Index